AF270344

Children in War

Children in War

Elon Perry

Pen & Sword

MILITARY

AN IMPRINT OF PEN & SWORD BOOKS LTD.
YORKSHIRE – PHILADELPHIA

First published in Great Britain in 2024 by
Pen & Sword Military
An imprint of
Pen & Sword Books Ltd
Yorkshire - Philadelphia

Copyright © Elon Perry, 2024

ISBN 978 1 03610 848 9

A CIP catalogue record for this book is available from the British Library.

Typeset in INDIA by IMPEC eSolutions
Printed and bound in England by CPI (UK) Ltd.

Pen & Sword Books Ltd. incorporates the Imprints of Pen & Sword Archaeology, Atlas, Aviation, Battleground, Discovery, Family History, History, Maritime, Military, Naval, Politics, Railways, Select, Transport, True Crime, Fiction, Frontline Books, Leo Cooper, Praetorian Press, Seaforth Publishing, Wharncliffe and White Owl.

For a complete list of Pen & Sword titles please contact

PEN & SWORD BOOKS LIMITED
47 Church Street, Barnsley, South Yorkshire, S70 2AS, England
E-mail: enquiries@pen-and-sword.co.uk
Website: www.pen-and-sword.co.uk

or

PEN AND SWORD BOOKS
1950 Lawrence Rd, Havertown, PA 19083, USA
E-mail: uspen-and-sword@casematepublishers.com
Website: www.penandswordbooks.com

Contents

Prologue

This is the story of millions of children around the world who live out their childhoods under the terrifying threat of war, finding themselves spending days and nights in shelters, living in constant anxiety, unable to play freely in their own yard for fear of sirens and shells. Vulnerable, helpless children at the mercy of their bloodthirsty and arrogant leaders. Children in war are the most endangered species in the world. They are trapped in war zones instead of enjoying their days in parks and schools. They suffer from severe emotional and psychological trauma and constantly witness images and situations that will remain in their memory forever.

I was one of them. A child who was trapped in relentless conflicts in the Middle East over the Holy Land and religion - nonsense that serious people labelled politicians took very seriously.

The following story is based on real events. It is about courage and survival against apparently overwhelming odds; a childhood in the shadow of constant war, severe poverty, relentless danger, and fear. An oppressive childhood caused by continuous days of hunger and lack of clothing, footwear, toys, pocket money, gifts, or even birthday celebrations. This is in addition to being one of nine children huddled in two rooms with no privacy and minimal furniture.

It is about a little boy who could not comprehend the link between war and the lack of food, toys, and chocolate. An innocent boy living in a poor and neglected small town where living conditions were extremely harsh, with no running water, electricity, or indoor sanitation. A town that had unbearable existential deprivation, despair, hopelessness, and violence, but on the other hand, housed a plethora of colourful characters.

I was born and raised under an ongoing war between two stubborn nations, each of which claims ownership of a tiny land whose rivers overflow with blood due to their belief. The Arabs felt dispossessed of their land, and the Jews felt a strong need for a refuge where they would be safe from pogroms, persecution, and another Holocaust. But as a child, I couldn't understand this grown-up business. All I wanted was to play football in the yard and dream about finding myself locked inside a chocolate factory. I wanted to play games, swing on a swing, bump up and down on a see-saw, listen to music from an old tape recorder, and if lucky, enjoy a first kiss with a girl. I just wished wanted to live a normal life. However, the politicians decided otherwise and created a prolonged and bloody war, forcing me to spend my entire childhood in bomb shelters, living in perpetual anxiety and seeing a world only beyond the heavy metal door of the shelter.

Because of the personal ambitions of these politicians, thousands of children, both Palestinians and Israelis, were condemned to spend their childhood and youth under never-ending war. A long bloody conflict that ruined the lives of millions of Muslims and Jews who share the same biblical ancestor. Ordinary people whose wish was to live side by side in peace, but who are in reality smacked in the face by the behaviour of their leaders. Pompous men, described as leaders, smartly dressed in suits and ties and speaking nicely in front of a microphone or camera, experts in lying without batting an eyelid. Condemning their citizens to a life of fear and hardship, spending most of their life in severe poverty and deprivation, due to a situation of incessant war, which sucks up a nation's budget to the point of starvation.

My miserable and worrisome childhood only ended when I enlisted in the Israeli army at the age of eighteen. Happy to seek revenge on the enemy that had ruined my childhood I joined a commando unit. I discovered that fighting in a commando unit allowed for incredibly close contact with the enemy, sometimes even face-to-face. That was exactly what I wanted to achieve - to hit with absolute accuracy when I met the enemy. However, although I sought revenge, I avoided harming Palestinian civilians and even risked my life many times to do so. In some particularly intense encounters, I saved many of them from being harmed by cruel terrorists who showed no concern for the safety of their own brothers.

The special military service I was privileged to take part in changed my life and my perspective. These significant changes were to accompany me for the rest of my independent adult life.

I discovered traits about myself that I did not even know existed within me. Characteristics and attributes I had not been able to realise, simply because I had not had the opportunity to apply them during my childhood and youth. Suddenly I found out that I had extraordinary courage. I learnt that I possessed abilities to rapidly solve problems and complex issues, to improvise, to think outside the box, and to see ten steps ahead, sometimes well ahead of most of those around me. It was a comforting feeling for a young man who was fearful, insecure, and an inferior boy.

Most importantly, I was not scared anymore. I became a fearless commando. I became part of a dangerous, exciting, and challenging world.

During my service, I did the impossible, things the average person would never get to do. This includes dangerous activities and operations that are usually only seen in James Bond movies.

I describe dangerous activities and operations I took part in. Bold operations, some of which were banned from being made public by the Israeli censor and only now, 40 years later, are allowed to be disclosed. These include some carried out in cooperation with the Mossad and other Israeli intelligence services; operations and raids on well-fortified terrorist strongholds to which we were sent, despite their slim chances of succeeding, and where the intolerable conditions gave justifiable feelings of fear and uncertainty. Some of them involved face-to-face and short-range combat, where the individual's qualities and skills were the key to success.

I also detail some of the exhaustingly tough unit training regime, which has been described by many as 'Mission Impossible' and is considered one of the most difficult in the Israel Defense Forces (IDF).

However, the message I convey in my book is this: in war, there is only grief.

'There are no winners in war!' I once shouted with tearful eyes at the Minister of Defence who had come to deliver a eulogy at the funeral of a soldier from my platoon, as he announced his promise to continue fighting the enemy until there was total victory.

I hated war. I hated its victories too. I realised that war is a senseless invention of mankind. War is an old-fashioned and primitive act. A failure of the use of human brainpower.

These wars tore me to pieces during my childhood and youth, the years when children and teenagers are supposed to learn, grow, develop, dance, party, dream, and weave plans for the future. Instead, I was doomed to experience those critical years in the harshest possible way.

I describe how I witnessed horrific scenes that will never leave my memory. I saw burnt bodies and watched the agony of my fellow soldiers who were writhing in flames. As I got older, I came to hate everything to do with politics and war.

In the book, I explain my derision of the idea of creating a Jewish state in the Holy Land (Palestine) and blame the Israeli leaders and the 600 members of the Zionist movement who rejected outright other options that were proposed by the British government. By insisting the Jewish state could only be located in Palestine, I was condemned to a life of misery, stress, and anxiety due to constant wars with neighbouring Arab countries.

After I had completed three years of combat service, I became a peace activist protesting against war. I spent 24 hours in a prison cell after setting alight a used tyre in front of the parliament building while holding a hand-written sign stating, 'The faith of mankind is in the hands of fools'.

I continued to encourage peace talks and remained a peace activist, in spite of the heavy price I paid when I received threats on my life from extremists and was fired from my job.

As a journalist, I risked my life travelling to Gaza and the West Bank to spend time with Palestinians in order to hear their views. This led me to a firm conclusion that Palestinians wish to live alongside Israel which provided them with work and business opportunities but the extremist terrorist organisations who controlled Gaza will not allow it.

This story can be an inspiration to people who find themselves in desperate situations. They can learn how against all odds one can survive difficulties in any situation as long as one has the will, perseverance, and belief that anything is possible. The difficulties I experienced in my childhood have followed me throughout the rest of my life and taught me how to make do with little, to appreciate everything, and to live modestly. I learned that I could survive any bleak times and any conditions. This was severely put to the test during my army service in the commando unit.

My willpower forged me and gave me hope, and the possibility to dream and plan a promising and successful future instead of sinking into depression and giving up. Despite the inferno I went through, I did not choose the easy way out by turning to drugs and alcohol, but succeeded in graduating from university with two degrees, working as a journalist and lecturer, and receiving commendations and appreciation for inspiring thousands of others.

As a poor hungry child shrouded in anxiety, I never dreamed that I would have a future. I was sure I would be a bum, a criminal, or a drug user, due to the daily danger of getting caught up in the web of a criminal gang that I hung around with and used to commit petty thefts with, and the constant temptations that were too much for my empty pockets. I never dreamt I would be a brave commando fighter in the best army in the world and perform the impossible.

Chapter 1

In the shadow of poverty and danger

Amidst the darkness, in a small neglected town, nestled within a war-torn region, childhood had taken on a bittersweet hue. The air was heavy with uncertainty, and the sounds of conflict echoed through the streets. There were nights when the sky itself seemed to weep, mirroring the sorrow that had befallen the lives of vulnerable children who did not know how to navigate the bloody storm caused by the decisions of adults.

When I look back on my childhood, I wonder how I survived at all. The oppressive hunger and the unbearable poverty. No pocket money, no birthday celebration, no chocolate, and no bedtime story. No sweet dreams and no laughter. Above all, the fear of the wail of the siren and the incessant war that forced me to spend long days and nights in damp and malodorous shelters.

To ease the constant anxieties and nightmares, our grandmother would put salt under our pillow and assure us that God was watching over us and would protect us if we prayed three times a day and believed in Him wholeheartedly. At school, which was nothing more than three long brown wooden huts, the atmosphere was melancholic and murky. The violent and bullying teachers were convinced that beating a child who dared to ask a lot of questions was the perfect way to turn him into a smart academic. One of them, the flame-haired Mr Meir, beat me for naively correcting him when he got the date wrong of the storming of the Bastille. Another bullying teacher was Sophia the Fat, the elderly spinster who used to take out her frustration and bitterness on us for not being able to get herself a husband.

Out on the streets, there was the daily danger of getting caught in the net of the criminal gang that I hung around with and used to commit petty thefts with. The leader, who was much older than us, noticed my creative mindset and started enticing me with pocket money here and there to lure me into the gang. He even surprised me with a brand-new pair of sneakers so that I would feel indebted to him and the gang and immerse myself in their criminal activities.

My troubles began the night I was born. Instead of joy and celebration, my frightened and trembling mother, who still hadn't recovered from the terrible pain in her bleeding groin, had to carry me all the way to the shelter because that very night the Egyptian army decided to bomb us. As if they couldn't postpone their shelling for a few days, at least until I had taken nutrition from my mother's breasts, or at least until I had opened my eyes to see where they were taking me in such a panic. By the time I was three years old, I had become an expert at running to the shelter.

On a fiercely stormy night in the winter of 1962, with successive bursts of thunder and flashes of lightning getting ever closer, my mother came to the room where each night my two brothers and I would be huddled in the large double bed shared by the three of us. My mother wished to make sure that the window in our room was tightly closed, and that none of us would be alarmed by the deafening noise of the thunder. As she entered the room, she was horrified to discover that our bed was empty. She was overcome by panic and immediately woke up my father who was fast asleep. 'The children are gone!' she screamed and started wailing in fear. My father jumped from the bed and searched the entire house while reassuring my mother, who continued to cry and whimper. Only after many minutes of panic, did they find out what had happened to their small children. It turned out that their usually disciplined children, who had been woken up by the thunder, had jumped out of their beds, and without waiting for instruction, raced down to the bomb shelter just a few metres down the road, believing the thunderous noise was yet another bombardment from Gaza. To us as children, our run down to the bomb shelter was no more than our daily routine, and we were sure our reaction was a necessary and normal act.

To the adults around us, it was a disturbing incident that symbolized the horrific reality we were living in, the madness of growing up under the shadow of war.

Sitting in an underground ditch or shelter became part of our lives. I became accustomed to spending so much time in shelters that each time we ran towards one, I found myself worrying more about the discomfort of sitting for several hours in the damp bunker than about the shelling outside. I was worried about inhaling the breath of others, especially those who had been eating garlic that day, or the smell of baby vomit tinged with the odor of piss wafting in from outside. This in addition to a constant and unbearably strong stench of sweat from those who hadn't showered in days due to the lack of hot water. The only times I enjoyed sitting in a crowded shelter was if I was crammed next to a sweetly perfumed woman or one of the prettiest girls in town.

But sometimes the run to the shelter was fun for us, a kind of competition to see who would get there first. However, for the adults, it was a burden. My mother, heavy with the next child in her belly, would heave herself from the bed, struggling to make her way to the shelter while panting and muttering indistinct words. My mother was always pregnant, every year. I don't remember a day without seeing her body bloated. My parents, like most of the respected townspeople, were pious souls, devoutly loyal to God and tradition, obedient to the divine imperative to breed as many children as possible. In return, God, who was just around the corner, would grant them a life of peace and tranquillity as a reward for their faithfulness. In the meantime, until they were redeemed, they were required to continue showing their loyalty and faith in the almighty God, even if it was laced with great suffering.

Yearning for fresh and pleasant air caused bitter arguments between the adults in the shelter, about whether to leave the door and the steel windows open or not. The fear of hearing the bombs landing outside caused some people to panic and insist on closing them, despite the difficulties in breathing. But fresh air was not the only problem. The whole damn shelter was dilapidated to the point where it seemed about to collapse at any moment. The cracked outside walls were colourful with promising graffitied messages but on the inside, these walls were damp and dingy, never seeing the sun's rays even though the sunlight was gleaming brightly outside. In the winter, lines of leaking water would be seen careering down the walls from the ceiling. None of the adults could do anything about the lurking danger from the damp walls that created a cacophony of hacking coughs and bronchial rattles among us all. They all seemed to be busy surviving hour by hour, helpless, torn apart by their nightmares and constant existential anxieties, and above all, the feeling of personal failure in not being able to provide for their families.

I was born under an ongoing war between two stubborn nations: the Arabs who felt dispossessed of their land, and the Jews who felt a strong need for a refuge where they would be safe from pogroms, persecution, and another Holocaust. Each of them claims ownership of a holy land, a land whose rivers are filled with blood due to their leaders' fanatical belief that they are fulfilling God's wishes. An imaginary god who doesn't bother to intervene simply because he doesn't exist.

As a result, I, as well as other children, both Palestinians and Israelis, did not get to experience a calm and normal childhood, nor a fun-filled youth spent at parties and with the enjoyment of the first kiss, as a happy-go-lucky Swiss boy would. I did not know what a bathtub looked like, and our lavatorial needs were serviced by an improvised WC situated behind the house. Once a week, a truck with a large black container and suction pipes would arrive and pump out everything that had accumulated in the pit below the makeshift toilet. My birthday was never celebrated, and a weekly visit to a cinema was nothing but a wishful illusion. I only got to know what the world looked like outside Israel through a small black and white TV my father had bought with what he had saved by making a little extra income from doing small repairs in the homes of the local people.

I felt exposed and vulnerable, helpless, facing a mighty force called war that was stronger than me. An existential threat that as a child,

I did not have the strength to deal with. Instead of playing football in the schoolyard, or fooling around in the local playground with other children, I was forced to seek refuge inside oppressive bomb shelters from the wars imposed on us by our leaders.

My life was miserable only because of religion and God, the mystical nonsense that causes only bloodshed and grief. The wars over Jerusalem and the Holy Land have all revolved around one idea – religion. Empires throughout history conquered the Holy Land in bloody and brutal battles, convinced that God Himself lived there, hidden in the seams of the cracking walls of Jerusalem. The conflict between the Palestinians and the Israelis is not over valuable oil or diamond mines, but simply over the Holy Land and Jerusalem. And in the midst of it all, children are the victims. Children who did not choose to be born. Children who pay a heavy price for the madness of the adults. I was one of those. I felt like a victim of those rotten and nonsensical wars over the holy land and religion that serious people called politicians took very seriously. Wars, decreed by men dressed in suits and ties, are those who speak nicely in front of a microphone or camera and can lie without batting an eyelid. Those with bloated egos and morbid motivation are driven around in black armoured cars. Accompanied by guards and helpers and advisors who are constantly by their side, straightening their ties, and whispering in their ear, maintaining a serious look as if they are telling them something crucial, but in fact, reminding them of the name of the person whose hand they are about to shake. I was condemned to spend my childhood and youth under never-ending war just because of their personal ambitions; a long bloody conflict that ruined the lives of millions of Israelis and Palestinians, Muslims and Jews, who share the same biblical ancestor.

Chapter 2

My first love, Sima

I was raised in a small town called Netivot, in southern Israel, not far from the border of the Gaza Strip. In those days Gaza was under Egyptian rule, a country which, in coalition with other Arab states, had declared an eternal war on Israel until the day of its destruction.

To strangers entering its perimeter, Netivot had the appearance of a temporary military camp, a kind of wretched and wilting human orchard. The two main streets were long, narrow paths of compacted dirt, from which protruding stones would sometimes injure pedestrians, or would cause cyclists to lose their balance while on their way to work in the industrial area. A car, or any type of vehicle, was rarely seen. The small residential streets, extending out like octopus tentacles on either side of the two main thoroughfares, were narrow, dim alleys with no house names or numbers. The small houses were built in pairs, of uniform shape and size, and in straight measured rows that extended the length and breadth of the town. Outside each house was stretched a grey metal wire used as a laundry line, most of the time densely packed with drying laundry due to the large number of babies and children in each household. In front of our own house was a large garbage can that had a mysterious tendency to disappear for a few days at a time. Only after my father's investigation did it become clear that the disappearance of our garbage can was down to one of our neighbours, who kept borrowing it because of the amount of garbage generated from the makeshift factory behind his house where he would produce mattresses and pillows. At least he was honest enough to return the can clean every time he borrowed it. Once we had solved the mystery, we always forgave him.

From a bird's eye view, Netivot was surrounded by wheat fields to the south and east, and to the west near the border with Gaza. A wide ravine just outside Netivot stretched for several miles from north to south. Around its edge grew seasonal flora that as children we loved to use for games, hiding places, and exploring. The ravine was my school where I developed a love of the natural world. Lizards and snakes in a variety of sizes and colours were seen skipping or slithering between crevices, and from the days spent at the ravine I discovered that I had no fear of snakes, but instead, a great fascination for them. The male residents of Netivot, mainly immigrants from North Africa, were forced to engage in menial work to support their families. Towards nightfall, they used to lock themselves inside their homes and escape to sleep, even though it was only seven or eight in the evening. It was as if they were impatiently waiting for the night to come, as sleep was a momentary balm for them, an escape from the black reality in which they lived. When they walked home through the murky streets, their gait was stooped, slow, hesitant, their lips usually pursed and their eyes bitter, suspicious, tormented, as if they were angry at the whole world. Among these exhausted and tormented residents, hot-tempered boys were competing with each other in amateur boxing matches, consuming each other's anger and frustration, hitting one another vigorously without any pre-agreed rules of the game. Most times the winner would be the dumbest guy in the neighbourhood. On Saturdays, groups of bored children would run after a worn-out piece of cloth wrapped with rags, kicking it around violently and dribbling it between their legs, passing it between each other with great precision until they could successfully direct the mushy cloth towards the space between the scoring markers.

There was Eliyahu Dehan, a particularly edgy boy consumed by the teeth of rage, who would expunge his anger by loudly drumming on four large empty olive tubs that he would arrange in a semi-circle around him, whilst screaming out a horrifying rendition of one or other of Elvis's current hits. Also, there was the ill-tempered but kind-hearted Marco, a talented musician, who back in Morocco used to fill the streets with melodies that seemed to touch the very essence of the human spirit. He was even invited by the King himself to play and sing at court. Marco had foolishly agreed to emigrate to Israel, putting his trust in the empty promises of the Zionist emissaries who assured him that he would scale great heights there, but reality slapped him in the face when he couldn't realise his talent. Instead, he had reluctantly found work in a textile factory. When Marco's wife, Rachel, would ask him to take the woollen blankets outside to air them, he would grab a large wooden pole and hit them with excessively violent blows to take out his anger and frustration. He would beat the blankets for an hour or two, stopping occasionally for a moment to take a deep drag of the cigarette in his left hand, then take a deep breath and resume charging at the blankets as if he were engaged in a life-or-death battle with a ravenous lion. Rachel was a hot-tempered woman. If she heard her children making any noise in an impromptu game of hide-and-seek, she would shout and scold them to stop and be quiet, because good children were children who stayed quiet. When evening came, she would scream out the names of some of her children who were still playing in the dirty backyard, ordering them to come inside because it was already dark. As if in the cover of that darkness, all the evil spirits would descend from the sky.

And then there was the beautiful Sima Malul. I was in love with her. She was my only hope, the subject of my dreams. I discovered that amidst the challenges of surviving the bloody war and its consequences, an extraordinary connection was blossoming. You can survive anything if you have something to live for. Sima was the one worth living for, the only one I wanted to marry and escape that desolate town with. I believed that together, we could chase our dreams in the bustling city of Tel Aviv, where possibilities abounded.

Sima, with her fiery spirit and rebellious nature, even though she appeared outwardly shy and obedient, injected me with what it takes to survive, to hope, to believe in a better future. The problem was her father, Mr. Malul, who did not allow her to leave the house except to go to school or to get a packet of flour or semolina from Mr. Revivo's grocery store, just two minutes' walk from Bar Ilan Street where Sima lived. During the summer, as we all splashed around in the makeshift pool the men of Netivot had voluntarily built with their own hands, Sima was not able to join us. Her father forbade her from wearing a bathing suit, even if it provided ample coverage.

On the few occasions when Mr Malul allowed her to leave the house, he would insist she swathed her face in a tattered scarf, or wore one of the dresses of her mother Sulika - a thick-fleshed woman of short stature, whose clothes, in addition to being regularly stained with deep red paprika and other Moroccan cooking spices, were ragged and larger than they needed to be. If Sima also wore a dress that was larger than her size, Mr Malul decided, she wouldn't attract the attention of Netivot's lusty boys, who regularly sat on the railings by the roadside and whistled at every girl who passed by. Because her father didn't allow her to leave the house most of the time, I started thinking of ideas to make contact with her by the grocery store or near the school she attended, not far from my own school. Some of the serious and respectable people of the local education board had decided to separate the boys and girls into single-sex schools. They believed that such a separation would deepen our faith in God and help us to excel in our studies.

Sima was blessed with a natural beauty. Her melting brown eyes blended perfectly with her facial features and dark hair, and when she laughed, she bared perfectly straight snow-white teeth. Her hair was childishly gathered up by dozens of small black hairpins, and her forehead was covered by a smooth, shiny fringe, cut with painstaking precision above her eyes. Her olive-toned skin was taut on her sexy-looking figure. Despite her small body, she had large ripe breasts and thighs, ready to accommodate the pregnancies she was planning to have. She saw motherhood as the most important task of humanity. To be honest, her small body didn't bother me despite the shame I would bring upon myself if I married her. In Netivot, a thin girl was considered to be from a destitute home where the food was sparse.

What's more, a girl with a thin body would not be able to sustain the copious pregnancies required of her.

Bar Ilan Street in Netivot did not particularly stand out in the landscape of that gloomy and neglected town, where even abandoned dogs and cats had stopped showing interest in the menial contents of its rickety garbage bins. Apart from a large oleander tree under which we would find refuge from the terrible heat of July and August, it was a dull and tired-looking street with rundown houses densely packed together as if seeking to comfort each other in each other's grief. However, when Sima Malul appeared, the aura of the dead street would suddenly brighten and fill with hope. The street lights were no longer murky, the fear of the sirens evaporated, the prolonged hours of sitting in the shelters did not seem so exhausting, and the possibility to dream was suddenly within reach.

Sima and I had first crossed paths one fateful Friday afternoon during a bleak winter. I was just fourteen. She was about my age, or maybe a year younger. This particular afternoon resembled every one of the other Fridays that were characterised by preparations for the holy Shabbat, including scrubbing the entire house, as well as doing the laundry, stewing, frying, baking, and all kinds of tiring tasks for God's coming to spend the Sabbath with his believers. People who hardly ate during the week would spend all their wages on religion and faith and God and all that nonsense. However, this time, apart from the spice-laden smells of food cooking, and the anxious final arrangements and setting out of the Shabbat candlesticks, there was a fire blazing in the sky. Clouds seemingly in an advanced state of pregnancy billowed in abundance over the roofs of the houses transporting the sacred act of my falling in love, and a pure white-feathered dove cooed teasingly from the top of a poplar tree that grew in front of Sima's house. I just happened to be walking by her house that afternoon when she opened the door and grabbed a garlic bulb from the large cluster that permanently hung on the front wall of the house. When I caught sight of her, my heart fluttered and my body started to tremble, until it resembled that of a cornered cat, whose nervous vibrations ploughed through its body whenever it found itself confronting a formidable dog. I felt as if all the streets of Netivot had been emptied of people and all the houses had firmly shuttered their windows to allow me sole communion with Sima.

The courtyards of the houses, usually crowded with garrulous women with an amazing talent for finding a new subject to gossip about, emptied and fell silent at once. Sima was perfectly beautiful. Her eyes held a hint of mystery and a depth of wisdom far beyond her young age. She wore a voluminous skirt which covered her legs until her ankles and above that a long white shirt, in a size larger than was needed. One of its sleeves was carelessly rolled up above her elbow, and the other had flopped down to cover her left hand. Her hair was childishly gathered up in dozens of small black hairpins, and her forehead was shielded by a smooth, shiny fringe of hair, cut with painstaking precision above her dark eyes. Her face was free of any make-up, and her lips were pressed together and pursed outwards, as if she was slightly angry, or struggling with the effort of reaching for the bulb of garlic. As she stretched her body towards the garlic, my eyes were torn from her face and for a brief moment focused on the lower part of her body, which I saw was covered by a sloppy garment that both supported and protected her body, as if she had known about my invasion beforehand and wanted to hide from me the outline of her hips. I didn't talk to her, nor try to show her any hint of my presence.

The whole spectacle on that momentous Friday afternoon lasted only a few seconds. Once she had grasped the garlic, she immediately re-entered the house and closed the door behind her. I wished she could have stayed longer, at least to ensure that the garlic she selected was fresh enough, or to throw a quick glance towards the flock of chickens in the front yard to check if there was enough water in their bowls. I continued to stand motionless in front of the house. My feet were pinned to the ground and my eyes were fixed on the firmly closed door, praying she would reappear, if only for a few seconds. I hoped that the garlic bulb she plucked in one sharp tug would not be enough and her sour-faced mother Sulika, would order her to go back outside to get some more. She had an annoying voice that mother of hers and her yelling was quite a common occurrence in Netivot. She always seemed to be berating her family in loud decibels, as if they were her wayward troops at some important battle of attrition. She was continually looking for a reason to yell at someone as if it was a kind of therapy for her.

In the meantime, the pregnant clouds began to amass above the poplar tree, blocking the sun's rays, and creating a series of cartoon figures that were completely dependent on the movement of the wind, overshadowing the houses and trees. One ray, which managed to pierce through the clouds, cast its light directly on Sima's front door as if instructing me to continue standing in front of her house until she came out again. But she didn't. Instead, it was her mother who came out. I panicked and immediately headed off. Not only was I scared to death of her, but I was also afraid she would accuse me of trying to steal one of her filthy chickens.

That night, I couldn't sleep. Thoughts of Sima gave me no rest.

Chapter 3

Stealing food to survive

I grew up in the 1950s in a large family of nine children, crammed together in a modest three-bedroom house. Throughout my childhood years I was accompanied by the feeling that my parents would have gladly given me up. I was yet another burden to them. I was one in a long succession of newborn siblings that grew over the years. I don't remember receiving hugs and proper attention from my mother from the day the next baby after me arrived. I stopped existing. All the attention would be focused on the new baby and then on the one that came after him. Out of desperation, I often toyed with the idea of an extended stay in hospital. I hoped that I would get seriously injured and would be rushed to the local hospital, where I would be placed in a private bed that would be mine alone. Kindly nurses would take care of me and shower me with love and attention and chocolate, constantly running around and fussing over me, and serving me with plenty of healthy food of all kinds, not just bread and jam mixed with margarine. I guessed there would always be plenty of food in hospitals, after all, no one died of starvation in a hospital.

As a child, I remember continuous days of hunger due to the incessant damn war which sucked up the state budget. I had to adopt a variety of creative solutions to get additional food. For example, if I had a craving for a sweet spread, and we had run out of plum jam in the refrigerator (a product that had a tendency to disappear within minutes), I would simply spread a thin layer of margarine on a thick slice of bread and sprinkle white sugar over it. I was never asked what I fancied for breakfast, as I never had a choice between a hardboiled egg or an omelette. I ate anything and everything my mother put on the table. Consequently, I have never been fussy about what I eat, and have had no problem choosing what to eat when perusing a restaurant menu. When I recently heard my granddaughter objecting to her mother at breakfast that the egg she had been served was not 'runny enough', I felt a sharp pang in my chest. In my childhood there were no problems expressed about the egg put in front of us, whether it was soft, runny, or hard-boiled. In my childhood, there was a problem with the presence of the egg.

Because we never received any pocket money, my friend Asher and I would take ourselves off to Mr Revivo's grocery store and without asking him, we would pick up a broom and sweep the floor of the entire store for him. In return, we were given his permission to choose an ice cream from the freezer. After gaining the trust of Mr Revivo, I came up with a great idea to get myself pocket money on a regular basis; selling empty glass bottles. This would involve my friend and I collecting empty bottles from street garbage bins and the front yards of houses and then selling them to any store that sold drinks. Because it was such an important source of income, we started to think of ways and ideas to increase our income from this source. One of those ideas was the following: during the hours when there was the greatest traffic in Mr Revivo's grocery store and he was focused on serving his customers, we would sneak into the yard behind his store where dozens of wooden crates were strewn with empty bottles of all shapes and sizes. We then furtively placed ten or twenty of them into a box and made our way round to the front entrance of the store. We would wait patiently until Mr Revivo had finished serving his customers, and then we would place the heavy box on the floor and offer to sell him our empty bottles. Mr Revivo would count the number of bottles, sort them by their size and shape and thus determine the price he was willing to give us. We of course never negotiated the price and agreed to anything he offered us. Funnily enough, when he handed us the money, he would often compliment us for our efforts in earning our own pocket money during those hard times of war.

To sate our hunger, we carried out small thefts, especially on Tuesdays, the day of the weekly *souk*, the open-air marketplace in Netivot. While the adults would do their shopping, we, the children, would look for ways to pinch some bakery delights or juicy fruits to appease our hunger and carry us through to our meagre supper, usually consisting of a sliver of omelette, a few slices of cucumber and tomato, made somewhat more sustaining by several slices of bread. We, a gang of five kids, would all arrive in the *souk* at the same time; Me, lazy Moshiko, whining Manny, cold-hearted Asher, and little Sonny.

As we stepped into the bustling *souk*, immersing ourselves in a visual symphony of colours and shapes, a spectacular array of seasonal fruits with their sweet fragrance filled the air. A kaleidoscope of colours greeted us, drawing us towards the wooden stalls that showcased the freshest produce nature has to offer; a selection of vegetables and fruits of all kinds, as well as tempting baked goods. At a cursory glance, one could get the impression that once a week, miserable Netivot had somehow forgotten her poverty. We aimed to filch only the kind of fruits and pastries that could instantly fill our empty stomachs. Large fresh bread rolls or fruits like bananas that could offer a quick and convenient source of energy and a comforting feeling of temporary gratification. To be honest, we didn't think we were about to commit the heinous crime of theft. As helpless children, all we craved on those Tuesdays was to silence the distressing and compelling need for food constantly raging in our empty stomachs. We were all on the verge of collapsing from hunger as we had had nothing to eat at lunchtime.

In addition to shiny black aubergines stacked one on top of the other, there were plump red tomatoes, dwarf green cucumbers and verdant bouquets of parsley, with heaps of onions and potatoes stacked together like two solid mountains bordering the glistening goods. Bunches of bananas, ranging from those with a greenish tinge to those already ripened and vibrant yellow, and small heart-shaped strawberries that boasted the reddest of red, with tiny seeds embedded on their surface. Also, dark purple blueberries rich in antioxidants, massive green watermelons sliced open to tempt customers (including flies and mosquitoes) with their refreshing and juicy bright red interior, exotic golden pineapples, clusters of grapes, green, red, and black, hanging in huge bunches in a tantalising display; their small, spherical forms a treat for both the eye and the taste buds. While most peddlers displayed a selection of produce on their stalls, the last stall, hardly noticeable at first, contained only oranges. However, as you got closer, their vivid, joyful colour became a spectacular sight that exuded positivity. Their juicy segmented interiors were both visually appealing and a source of refreshing tanginess.

On the west side of the market, as if the separation was purposely created so as not to mix the different, yet equally intoxicating, smells, was the bakery. Compared to the fruit stalls, these had shelves, a fact that made it difficult for us to steal without being caught. However, we found ourselves spending more time in the bakery area due to our oppressive hunger often making us feel light-headed and faint. The shelves were adorned with an array of delightful baked treats, each with its own texture, flavour, and visual appeal. We were hoping to indulge ourselves with some of the enticing baked Moroccan delights that were showcased on the warm wooden surfaces: the circular-shaped bread encrusted with sesame seeds, or perhaps the *pideu*, a pastry similar to pizza that was bubbling away on a hot rounded metal base, sending out intoxicating smells of melted cheese, cooked tomatoes and olives, seasoned with oregano and rich green olive oil. Just behind, there would be piles of delicious fluffy bread rolls, brushed with an egg wash before baking to give them a shiny and golden appearance. On the back shelves, more than a dozen wooden trays of *künefe*, a thin shredded dough layered with cheese and baked until crisp. Or *samina*, a sweet semolina cake soaked in syrup, flavoured with lemon and topped with shredded nuts or coconut. And the irresistible *baklava*, layers of wafer-thin pastry filled with chopped nuts and sweetened with honey, begging to be eaten.

In the pedestrian space between the produce stalls sat old Abraham, who sold steaming black Turkish coffee. To add value to his coffee and gain appreciation from his potential buyers, he would employ the traditional method of preparing and serving the coffee. This involved slowly boiling finely ground coffee beans with water and generous spoonfuls of sugar in a medium-sized filterless pot. This was done over a portable stove called a 'Primus', often used for outdoor cooking. Old Abraham could not afford to rent a stall, but everyone, including the Municipal Inspector, always forgave him for placing his makeshift coffee stand in a public passage. Probably because the steamy aroma of his coffee gave people a feeling of home and created an inviting and warm atmosphere. There were those who were willing to swear that the aroma was so strong and overpowering that it managed to invade the territory of the bakery department.

We navigated through the weathered wooden stalls, many of which looked as if they were about to buckle under the weight of the items piled onto them. As we were sniffing around and debating which pastry to lift, a blue-uniformed policeman appeared. It was Yoel Luzon, the sheriff of the town. He also sometimes served as a mediator between brawlers who would beat each other until they bled, and God, there were a lot of those to be found in every corner of the town. The policeman started moving towards our direction. Moshiko's face drained of colour as he looked over at me, seeming about to burst into hysterical tears.

'Don't run,' I quietly instructed him.

Asher, who towered over us all, looked ahead and whispered, 'He's coming towards us. Yes, he is coming for us.'

I turned to face all my co-conspirators. A decision needed to be made whether to run away or stay and pretend to be genuine customers.

I had a remarkable knack for getting out of trouble. It wasn't that I intentionally sought out trouble, but somehow trouble always seemed to find its way to me. However, I had an uncanny ability to keep a level head, even in the direst of situations, using my over-creative imagination to conjure up ingenious solutions when things went awry. Moshiko often joked that I had a guardian angel who looked after poor children and was watching over me to guide me. However, I believed it was simply my resourcefulness and positive attitude that got me through difficult situations and tough times. I discovered that, on occasion, avoiding difficulties was preferable to confronting them head-on, even with bold confidence and creativity. I have always believed that with a positive mindset and a touch of inventiveness, anyone can navigate their way out of trouble, no matter how complex or challenging it may seem. These traits not only helped me to overcome an awful childhood but also proved invaluable when I underwent the rigorous tests required for my recruitment into a commando unit.

I reached out and hugged Moshiko who was still all pale and trembling. 'We are here to buy sweets,' I said in a quiet, authoritative and reassuring tone.

'But we have no money,' little Sonny said.

'Pretend, you fool, pretend!' Asher hissed in his ear.

'I suggest we all calm down,' I said with a quick forced smile. 'Maybe he's here to do the shopping for his family, that's all.'

Meanwhile, Manny the Whiny was clinging tightly to me. He was shaking all over and his eyes were eerily wide like a corpse in the morgue. I put my hand on his shoulder and squeezed it.

'Don't be afraid Manny. No one suspects us.'

As I said it, a pungent smell of urine rose in the air. I glanced at his lower body and noticed to my astonishment that his trousers were wet.

'I'm out of here,' said the shaken Moshiko.

'Don't run, remain still, and keep looking at the products on the stall,' I whispered to him while debating whether to continue comforting Manny or to keep well away from him due to the foul smell that came from him.

But Moshiko was already gone before I had finished the sentence. He had started running in panic between the stalls towards the exit of the souk.

One of the sellers started chasing him shouting 'Thief!'

We didn't understand why, since Moshiko hadn't stolen anything from him. Only after the seller managed to catch Moshiko, strip-searched him, and discovered that he didn't have any items on him, did we realize that someone else had stolen the goods with such impressive sophistication that it had made the seller suspect a totally blameless person. I liked the idea of this and started thinking about the possibility of adopting and even improving it.

Moshiko began to cry, and when the seller eventually let him go, he disappeared from the market.

While we were trying to pull ourselves together after the drama and continue with our scheme to eat something for free, we were caught by surprise. We had spotted one of our teachers, the flame-haired Mr Meir. My heart began to beat so loudly that it felt like it was about to be torn from my body, and my lips began to dry up. He was accompanied by his kind looking wife Abigail, who always showed us understanding and forgiveness. This was in stark contrast to Mr Meir, the monster, who never showed tenderness or compassion towards us, even though he knew our backgrounds. On one rainy day, as I was walking into the school building, I slipped on the muddy and broken path. Instead of comforting me, he scolded me, telling me I fell because I wasn't paying enough attention.

Mr Meir and his wife were moving through the stalls, stopping here and there to handle the goods and consult one another. Mr Meir tried to bargain but the sellers showed no desire to cooperate with him. Perhaps if he had occasionally toned down his angry expression, one of them may have paid more attention to him and agreed to offer a discount.

Manny the Whiny, who was still clinging to me firmly and smelling foul, asked, 'What are they doing here?'

Asher responded mockingly, 'They came looking for you.'

'What a stupid question,' scoffed tiny Sonny and gave Manny a whack on the head.

'What else could they be doing in a market, you jerk?'

I chuckled, 'Stealing.'

'Yes, but why both of them?' Manny persisted in pestering us with his pointless questions.

Asher responded in a strong voice, 'That's because he's the one who controls the money. Now shut up and let us think.'

Mr Meir was of the opinion that only males should control the finances. He never let his wife carry cash, and he had complete control over all aspects of the household budget.

We all froze. We waited to see their movements. It appeared that we were not as fortunate on that particular Tuesday as we had been on the other Tuesdays when we had been successful in swiping something from the bakery, and frequently some dessert as well. In order to sate our hunger until we could see how things would turn out, we had to decide whether to retreat or keep trying to snatch something, even if it was just one piece of fruit. But making that choice while you are extremely hungry is upsetting as well as uncomfortable.

'We have to cancel our plan,' I told myself. I wasn't so much worried about the presence of the policeman. What worried me was Abigail's reaction, the person to whom I had made a promise not to steal anymore after she had caught us taking oranges from her garden. Surprisingly, she hadn't reported us. Instead, she taught us about morals in an informal and congenial way, and I swear we listened to her words with a much greater thirst than we did with her nasty husband.

The entire episode seemed to have gone insane all of a sudden. I discovered that I was more terrified of a woman who had values to teach me than I was of a policeman who could lock me up in a stench-filled holding cell. It was a conundrum. I had to decide quickly whether to stay at the market and satisfy my hunger or to flee in order to avoid being discovered. After all, I had sworn to Abigail and felt I could not let her down. And what about my personal code of conduct? The importance of treating people fairly, respectfully, and with honesty, integrity, and trustworthiness. And the potential financial harm to others, which could weigh heavily on my conscience? Not to mention the humiliation and shame I and my entire family would experience in a small town where everyone knew each other. Despite the seeming chaos, there was an underlying sense of community, where regular customers were recognised and greeted warmly, and vendors often had their loyal following.

And in the midst of the hustle and bustle, where commerce, culture, and human connections intersected in a mesmerising dance, I was the tiny thief debating whether to spoil the perfect microcosm of this great economic activity and social engagement. The social hub where families went shopping together, friends would share stories, and strangers would start up conversations over shared interests. I argued with myself, 'But wait, I'm a poor kid, I'm starving, can you ask a hungry child who can't feed himself to hold on to the values and principles of the adults?'

Anyway, while I was planning my next steps, without my having noticed it, whiny Manny, little Sonny and cold-hearted Asher had all disappeared. I was left alone, standing close to a particularly noisy trader who was plying his wares with deafening shouts, trying desperately to catch the attention of passing shoppers. My vision was becoming increasingly hazy due to my worsening vertigo. I could still see the policeman perfectly despite my failing eyesight because he remained in my field of vision. Mr Meir and his lovely wife had vanished from view. I made the decision to not take any chances. I bowed my head, and proceeded to the market's exit, squeezing between the bodies of honest buyers.

The hunger and the other difficulties I experienced in my childhood followed me throughout the rest of my life and taught me how to make do with little, to appreciate everything, and live modestly. I learned that I could survive any bleak times and any conditions. This was severely put to the test during my army service, and notably on one occasion during the arduous survival course undertaken in the early stages of my service in the commando unit. We were tasked to live for three days in the Sinai Desert on water only. We were left to feed ourselves on what could be found in the area, including any indigenous moving entity. I would not want to bore you with the details of the things I ate during those unbearably difficult days, but I just to tell you that I succeeded. I survived that unpleasant experience not because I was stronger than the others. I survived only because I had previous experience of being desperately hungry.

Chapter 4

Children in war

Children in war are the most endangered species in the world. They are trapped in war zones instead of in parks and schools. They suffer from severe emotional and psychological trauma. They may have fewer resources and support systems to help them cope with the trauma, making their recovery even more challenging. Children in war remain in misery as rising death tolls exceed their parents' wildest nightmares. These children are constantly witnessing images and situations that will remain in their memory forever. I am 66 years old now and not able to erase the horrifying experiences I had as a child in war. Countries like Syria, Yemen, Iran, Afghanistan, Palestine, Libya, Turkey, Sudan, Iraq, and Pakistan have already seen the alarming damage to children, and yet, not a single framework has been adopted by the United Nations that prohibits and protects children from being subjected to war. They are well equipped with budgets and slogans and announcements, but in practice, they do not intervene directly and do not take significant steps against countries where children are trapped in a war decided by adults. They came up with an impressive-sounding initiative, 'The United Nations Convention on the Rights of the Child', which promised that all children are protected by law to be able to live and play in safe and secure environments, and given all the fundamental human rights from early childhood to adult life. Yet, reality shows a gloomy outlook as children are surrounded by perpetual war, on the streets, in their homes and schools, and on the battlefield. Children's rights in every country, with the intervention of the UN, must be enforced to defend children from internal and external aggression that has created a horrific reality – Children in War. While a child needs stability for the development of his self-confidence, war forces families to flee their homes, and poor children are more likely to become internally displaced or refugees. This displacement can lead to further impoverishment and disruption of their lives. The world has failed to adopt a unified strategy that would combat this epidemic and blood is being spilt every day. The safety and security of children worldwide seem to be at stake, as there are more weapons of war being generated than food and shelter for the oppressed segments of society.

When I was twelve years old, the fear of the sirens and bombs began to be replaced by sarcasm and black humour. I would write poems about death and describe my funeral in them. I would tell jokes about orphans and bereavement, and I would make fun of frightened children, whether it was during the run to the shelter or when the bombs were heard. Once I noticed a ten-year-old boy walking very close to a wall, even though no siren sounded and no sound of shelling echoed. I approached him with a smirk on my lips and had the following dialogue with him:

'Why are you walking so close to the wall?' I asked him.
'Because I have to be careful.'
'Careful of what?'
'Of the bombings from Gaza.'
'But there's no bombs now.'
'There will be any minute.'
'There isn't a siren either. That means there aren't any bombs.'
'I have to be ready at any moment,' the kid replied, looking from side to side apprehensively.
'Every day?'
'Yes. This is my life now. We, the kids can't think about playing in the yard or on the swings.'
'Do you want to play football?'
'Are you mad?'
'I think it's quiet now. There won't be any bombs. Let's play.'

'Don't want to take a risk. I don't want what happened to my friend Jacob to happen to me.'

'What happened to him?' I asked sarcastically as if I didn't know about that tragic incident that had been big news in our small town of Netivot.

'His leg was crushed by a bomb,' the kid replied. 'He didn't walk close enough to the wall. Now he has a prosthesis and is in a wheelchair. His sister was also injured.'

'Is she okay now?' At this point, I decided to stop my cynicism and sarcasm. His sister symbolised the tragedy in our delusional reality as she had never fully recovered. The wound in her body was healed but the damage to her soul continued.

'Yeah, she's okay now,' he replied. 'But she has constant stomach pains and is often vomiting. Most of the time she hides under the table and doesn't come out for hours.'

'Why does she hide under a table?'

'Because that's where she feels safe. That's what the teachers told us too.'

'Did your teachers tell you to hide under the table?'

'Only if we hear a siren, but some children are afraid, so they stay under the table the whole of break time. Some are even afraid to go to the toilet because there are no tables there.'

'And what about your mother and father?'

'They're also afraid. My mother cries a lot and takes pills and doesn't sleep at night.'

'And your father?'

'He doesn't cry. But he's very nervous and shouts a lot.'

'Is it difficult for you to live here in Netivot?'

"It's hard but I've nowhere else to go.'

'If you had somewhere to go, would you go?'

'I don't think so.'

'But it's hard for you here. You can't play in the yard like the kids in Tel Aviv.'

'I was born here. My friends are all here.'

'And what if you will make new friends in Tel Aviv? Would you move?'

'Don't know. I am just a kid. Can't answer that for you. Ask my parents.'

'So will you continue to suffer?'

'I guess so. Until the government does something."

"Is it really up to the government?'

'So who is it up to? Us, the kids?'

'I think it's the army, don't you?'

'But the army can't do anything without the government telling it to. That's what my father said.'

'What do you think they should do?'

'Wipe out Gaza.'

'What? Completely?'

'Yeah, destroy it totally,' the kid said and disappeared.

Children in conflict-affected areas are often disproportionately affected by the interruption of their education, as schools may be destroyed or closed and teachers may flee. This can limit their future earning potential. This lack of education can also perpetuate the cycle of poverty.

Perpetual war is a leading cause of intense emotional crises in children which affects their future. It can have long-lasting negative effects on their physical and psychological well-being. In desperate circumstances, some poor children may be forced into child labour or recruited as child soldiers to support their families or due to coercion by armed groups. They are often at a higher risk of being victims of violence or abuse. They are more vulnerable to exploitation, including sexual exploitation and child trafficking.

Since conflict disrupts food supply chains and leads to food shortages and malnutrition, children become the major sufferers as this can have severe consequences for their growth and development.

The effects of war on poor children can have long-term consequences, impacting their physical and mental health, education, and future prospects. Poverty can be a source of grievance that actually fuels conflict. Poverty and war are interconnected because wars force people to flee their homes, leaving behind their livelihoods and sources of income. Refugees and internally displaced persons often end up in overcrowded camps with limited access to basic necessities, leading to a further erosion of economic stability. War often leads to the destruction of infrastructure, businesses, and agricultural assets, causing a severe economic downturn. This destruction can push people who were already living in poverty deeper into destitution. Access to healthcare often diminishes during wartime. Poorer families are more vulnerable to health crises because they may not have the means to access medical care or purchase essential medicines.

The effects of war can linger long after the conflict ends. Rebuilding a shattered economy and infrastructure takes time, and the neediest members of society often experience the slowest recovery. The combination of poverty and war can result in humanitarian crises, with millions of people in need of emergency assistance, including food, clean water, and shelter. Therefore, efforts to break the cycle of poverty and war require addressing both the immediate humanitarian needs of affected populations and the root causes of conflict. Addressing these issues requires not only immediate humanitarian assistance but also long-term efforts to rebuild communities and provide opportunities for these children. Efforts by international organisations, NGOs, and governments are crucial to providing aid and support to poor children in conflict-affected areas and guarantee a stable and secure future for them. Children in war often face unimaginable hardships, and their experiences can be particularly devastating when they come from impoverished backgrounds, and God, I know, I was one.

Stories about impoverished children in war are often heart-wrenching and serve as powerful reminders of the immense challenges they face. While these stories can be difficult to read, they shed light on the resilience and strength of children living in conflict zones. They emphasise the need for international efforts to protect and support children affected by war, ensuring their access to education, healthcare, and psychological support. However, some of them were inspirational.

Amina, a ten-year-old girl from Syria, where a protracted conflict devastated the entire country, lived with her three siblings in a makeshift refugee camp. They had lost their home and possessions due to the ongoing conflict. Her family was among the millions struggling to find enough food to survive. Despite the harsh conditions and limited access to education, Amina showed incredible resilience. She managed to teach herself to read and write using scraps of paper and whatever books she could find in deserted homes. She dreamt of becoming a nurse. Her determination to learn offered a glimmer of hope amid the chaos of war. Her brother, Ahmed, who was just two years older, took on the task of feeding the four little ones after both of his parents were killed during a shootout between the army and the rebels. Ahmed became the primary breadwinner for his family, working odd jobs and scavenging for recyclables to sell. He missed out on schooling but remained committed to ensuring his younger siblings had something to eat each day. Two years later, when an organisation helped build a camp with permanent barracks, including a clinic and a school, Amina attended the makeshift school and volunteered at the local clinic. Despite the challenging circumstances, Amina's determination to pursue her dream and help her community showcased the potential and resilience of children affected by war.

Vladimir, a fifteen-year-old boy from Mariupol, Ukraine, had been separated from his family during their journey to escape the conflict. Some were forced to travel to Moscow to join their Russian family, and some were dispersed in South Ukraine. Mariupol was bombed at the beginning of the war and was almost completely destroyed. Alone and afraid, he joined a group of teenagers and children living on the streets of Mariupol where food and supplies were scarce. With no access to proper meals and shelter in the bombed-out streets, they all faced daily hardships. However, they all had a passion for soccer. Despite his family's displacement due to the conflict, Vladimir continued to practice and play with his friends in makeshift fields. His dream was to become a professional soccer player, and he found hope and solace in the sport, even amid the chaos of war. But what really motivated him to stay alive was to reunite with his beloved family when the war was over. Indeed, seven months after they were forced to separate, a window of opportunity opened and paved the way for the reunification of the entire family.

Between 1991 and 1995, during the bloody war between Croatia and Serbia, un unnecessary fanatical war based on religion, a group of children clung to their innocence, creating a world of their own amidst the turmoil. In a makeshift shelter, Lena, Alexei, Elena, Goran, Natalia, and Nadia huddled together, their faces etched with a mixture of fear and determination. Despite the harsh reality they faced, they managed to find moments of joy in the simplest of things. One of them was a tattered kite that became a source of endless entertainment as they took turns flying it above the rubble-strewn streets.

Lena, the oldest of the group at twelve, took on the role of storyteller. With each passing evening, she would weave tales of fantastical lands where peace reigned and harmony prevailed. Her stories transported her friends to a realm untouched by conflict, if only for a short while.

Alexei, a quiet and introspective boy of ten, had a keen eye for detail. He would scavenge for discarded items and repurpose them into ingenious contraptions. His most prized creation was a small windmill fashioned from bits of metal and cloth, which he placed on the roof of their shelter. It became a symbol of resistance, spinning defiantly in the face of adversity.

Nadia, the youngest of the group at eight, possessed an unwavering spirit. She could often be found tending to the few remaining flowers that managed to bloom amid the destruction. Her gentle touch seemed to coax life from the earth itself, a testament to the power of nurturing, even in the harshest of environments. As the war's grip tightened, the children faced hardships that tested their bonds. Food became scarce, and the laughter that once echoed through their hideout was replaced by sombre conversations. Yet, they refused to surrender to despair. Instead, they channelled their collective strength into a daring plan. With Lena's storytelling as their guide, Alexei's resourcefulness, and Nadia's determination, the children embarked on a mission to bring a sense of normalcy back to their lives. They organised a 'Children's Festival', a day filled with games, laughter, and a makeshift stage for Lena's stories. The village, weary from the weight of conflict, embraced the festival with open arms. For a brief moment, the air was filled with the joyful shrieks of children playing, the sweet aroma of simple treats, and the enchanting tales spun by Lena. In that fleeting oasis of happiness, the scars of war seemed to fade.

As the sun set on the festival, casting a warm golden hue over the village, the children stood hand in hand, gazing at the windmill atop their shelter. It spun faster than ever before, a symbol of their resilience and a reminder that even in the face of adversity, the human spirit could soar.

In the years that followed, the war finally ended, leaving behind a landscape scarred by the past.

However, the children, now grown, carried the lessons of their childhood with them:

Lena became a storyteller who shared tales of hope, Alexei an inventor who transformed discarded materials into art, and Nadia a gardener who nurtured life wherever she went. Their innocence had endured, a beacon of light in the midst of darkness. And though the war had forever changed their world, the memory of that Children's Festival and the unbreakable bond they shared remained a testament to the enduring power of friendship, creativity, and the strength of the human spirit. In the aftermath of war, a sense of fragile peace settled over the land. The scars of the conflict ran deep, but amidst the ruins, a remarkable tale of resilience emerged—one that would inspire generations to come.

As the village worked to rebuild, a group of determined individuals emerged as pillars of strength. Among them were Elena, Goran, and Natalia, once children who had forged an unbreakable bond during the darkest days of the war. Elena, now a young woman with a heart full of compassion, became a teacher. She established a school where children could learn not only the essentials of education but also the values of empathy, understanding and unity. Her classroom was a haven where stories of the past were shared, ensuring that the lessons of war were never forgotten. Goran's inventive spirit had blossomed, and he had become a respected engineer. He dedicated himself to rebuilding the village's infrastructure, transforming it into a thriving community where innovation and progress were celebrated. His windmills, once a symbol of defiance, now dotted the landscape, harnessing the power of the wind to provide energy and hope.

Natalia, now a skilled botanist, turned the village into a lush oasis. The flowers that had once bravely bloomed amid chaos now flourished under her nurturing care. Her gardens were a testament to the enduring beauty of life and the resilience of nature itself.

The trio's efforts didn't go unnoticed. The village began to attract attention from neighbouring communities, drawn by the stories of hope and transformation.

As the years passed, the village's revival became a symbol of what was possible when humanity came together in the face of adversity. The lessons learned from the past were passed down through generations, ensuring that the horrors of war were never repeated.

Elena, Goran, and Natalia continued to inspire those around them, their stories echoing through time like a melody of hope. Their friendship, forged amidst the trials of childhood under war, had become a beacon that guided others toward a future built on understanding, cooperation, and the unwavering belief in the power of the human spirit. And so, the village that had once been a casualty of war emerged as a testament to the enduring strength of the human heart. It stood as a living tribute to the resilience of those who had dared to dream of a better world, transforming a landscape of destruction into a haven of growth, progress, and above all, love.

Children in war lose the language of love, the tranquillity of the mind, the inner state of constant growth, and above all the sense of order. Poor children are especially vulnerable in conflict zones due to their lack of access to basic necessities, such as clean water, nutritious food, healthcare, and education. Poverty exacerbates the challenges they face during wartime. I know how it feels.

I was one of those.

The trauma of being a child under constant war left me with an invisible, non-bleeding, wound. There is a deep scar in my soul, a delicate soul, that belongs more to the world of nature, art, and creativity, and less to the world of weapons and bloody battles. The fear of the siren completely paralyzed me and caused me constant anxiety. Even today, as a mature man, I become panicked by the sound of a siren, even if it's just an ambulance transporting a pregnant woman to hospital. The seeds for the growth of my anxiety were already sown back then and couldn't be treated. Unlike today, there was no awareness in those years of mental scarring. And therefore, no adequate treatment was given to reduce, or cure, anxiety. As a result, my anxiety has evolved over the years to the rhythm of the siren and been watered by the deafening sound of fighter jets and bombshells. I had been a frightened, confused and helpless child living in constant fear day and night. In order to overcome my terrors, I would venture into the caves and dark crevasses in the ravine hoping to encounter a poisonous snake or any other kind of dangerous animal. I would climb to the top of a tree, while the other kids would look up at me and call out to a nearby adult to come and order me down before I fell. My fearlessness honed as a child came in handy when I grew up to become a commando fighter, and when, as an exercise in strengthening courage, we were required to jump from a plane at night in full combat gear, dropping in total darkness into a stormy sea.

Chapter 5

Enrolment into a commando unit

My miserable childhood only ended when I enlisted in the Israeli army at the age of eighteen.

I joined the army thankful for the opportunity to confront those who had ruined my childhood by their acts of terror. I felt this was the only legitimate opportunity to find revenge, as well as a degree of compensation. I wanted to kill those people with my own hands. The question now remained as to which corps to join. Should I join the Armoured Corps or the Navy? The Tank Corps or maybe the Air Force? But then, when I was seventeen, just a year before my enlistment, a letter arrived and spared me from the dilemma I was in. The letter included an invitation to come for tests and exams. I was being summoned for tests and examinations to determine if I was suitable material for a commando unit. Unknown to me at the time, the army had been checking the records of teenagers in every high school to identify suitable candidates to serve in elite commando units, based on their intelligence and personal skills. I had been blessed with a high IQ, perfect physical and mental health, no known allergies to anything, sharpened senses and excellent vision, and most importantly, tons of motivation. It looked like my choice had been made for me.

My military service made significant changes to my life and perspective that would accompany me for the rest of my independent adult life. I have stepped onto the top of the mountain and fallen to the bottom, but both have benefited me. I discovered traits about myself that I did not even know existed within me. Characteristics and attributes I had not been able to recognise, simply because I had not had the opportunity to apply them during my childhood and youth. I found out that I had extraordinary courage, and that I possessed the ability to improvise, to think outside the box, and to see ten steps ahead, sometimes ahead of most of those around me. It was a comforting feeling after many years of lack of self-confidence and feelings of inferiority. Most importantly, I was not afraid anymore. I became a fearless commando doing things I had previously only seen in movies.

I was mentally and physically ready to encounter the enemy.

But if I thought it was going to be easy, I was mistaken. I learned firsthand that war and combat are known for the immense emotional and personal toll they take on individuals. Every operation I took part in, no matter how successful, was always accompanied by the grief, sorrow, and pain of the loss of a company member or the loss of innocent civilians caught in a state of war against their will. Among those losses, one individual stood out for his exceptional leadership and charisma. His name was Dan Dekel.

In the spring of 1976, almost a year into my combat service, my company was tasked to infiltrate a small village in Lebanon and blow up a two-storey house that served as the headquarters and training base of the Palestinian PLO terrorist organisation. As we approached the target, the terrorists inside the house started firing at us from the windows. My entire company, with its three platoons, immediately split into three teams. One began attacking the house from its west side, the second flanked the back of the house from its east side, while my team fought in front of the house, targeting the bunker and its long winding trench from where several other terrorists were also firing at us. Our intention was to get inside the trench, clear it, and then take over the bunker situated behind. Meanwhile, the two other platoons would take over the house. As we approached the trench, the terrorists inside intensified their fire. The bullets whistled by and threatened anything in their path, whether it was a human body or a concrete wall. Grenades were flying through the air. We lay on the ground and waited for the terrorists to use up all their supply of grenades. When that did not happen, Dan Dekel, our commander, shouted an order, and we all, around fourteen fighters, jumped down into the trench, spraying it with our automatic rifles. Once inside, we moved between its narrow sides in one column, with only the fighter at the head of the column being able to shoot forward. If he ran out of ammunition or got hit, he would sit down and cling to the side of the trench to allow the next in line to move forward and continue the shooting, and so on, until the clearance and takeover of the trench were completed.

Despite the intense and stubborn battle that took place inside that trench, we managed to get to the bunker. When we entered it, we realized it was much larger than it had seemed to us from the outside. It appeared to contain several rooms, something that could complicate the purging and taking over of the entire bunker. We threw grenades into each room and started clearing them one by one. Even though their bare light bulbs were still switched on, there was a thick haze filling each room due to the discharge from our grenades. This made it very hard to see what was going on around us. We had to find our way by patting the walls with our hands and making sure there were no surprise doors or exits from the room. Within minutes, we had taken over the bunker, and the trench was totally cleared. The battle was over.

After a final thorough search, we started making our way out of the bunker towards the helicopter waiting to take us back to our base. On the way, I paused for a moment at the point where the wounded were concentrated. I approached three stretchers on the ground. On the first two lay two of our wounded fighters, but on the third, lay a fighter whose face was covered by a blanket.

This is the most frightening moment in any raid or operation, even more than the fear experienced inside a trench when being shot at and seeing your own certain death. This is the moment you are about to find out which of your friends has been killed, as the faces of those who have been injured are not obscured by a blanket. With a trembling hand, I lifted the blanket from the dead soldier's face, and immediately a shiver shot down my spine. My knees buckled. It was our revered force commander, Dan. A special commander, not only very smart, brave and charismatic, but a person with remarkable abilities, a superman who inspired us all.

'How can this be? How can he be dead?' I shouted. I could not tear my eyes away from the motionless face of my beloved commander who had taught me how to overcome fear, how to prevail in the most dangerous situations, and had planted the idea in my head that nothing is impossible to achieve.

'How can such an experienced and brilliant fighter be killed?' I kept muttering and fell to my knees.

One of the fighters came over and gently placed the blanket back over the face of our dead commander. He helped me to my feet and whispered that I must proceed to the helicopter as quickly as possible because we needed to vacate the area before more terrorists arrived. I headed towards the helicopter without looking back. I did not want to say goodbye to my commander. I wanted to cry but my eyes were dry. I could not even force myself to take a sip of water, much-needed after our intense battle. I continued walking like a zombie. When I climbed on to the helicopter, I sat down on the floor, huddled in the corner, my rifle between my legs, my head bowed, not saying a word nor looking at anyone. As the helicopter lifted to the sky, the smell of burnt oil and gasoline rose in my nose. An hour later, at the post-battle debriefing, I finally awoke from my shock, as I was required to answer questions coherently and provide clear operational details.

It was only during this debriefing session, when everyone involved began to describe the course of the battle and its stages, did we learn that our commander had sacrificed his life to save ours in an extraordinary act of heroism. It happened when we were still dealing with the trench. Due to the heavy billowing smoke that blurred and restricted our vision, we had not seen that at the top of the trench, a terrorist was hiding behind a machine gun, waiting until we got closer. The only one of us who had spotted the danger was our commander, who immediately ran totally exposed towards the terrorist, firing at him and paralyzing his actions. By doing so, he not only saved some of us from certain death, but he also made it easier for us to move on towards the bunker.

This act of heroism greatly influenced me throughout my military combat service, which was replete with dangerous shooting incidents, where courage and heroism were much needed.

Dan Dekel was not just a skilled officer; he was a mentor, a friend, and a source of inspiration for all of us. His unwavering dedication to the mission and his genuine care for his soldiers left an indelible mark on my memory.

When we hear or read about an act of heroism, our natural human tendency is to admire, cherish and appreciate it. But when digesting the heavy price paid, we may reconsider these values. This is the conundrum I went through with the heroic death of my revered commander. I sometimes felt schizophrenic. One side of me concentrated on sharpening my fighting abilities, while the other side of me loathed the war, and did not want to hear about acts of heroism during battle. Both these conflicting sides of me were trapped. Neither of them could choose a getaway option because I was in the midst of my compulsory military service. The foundation of heroism is not only courage. It is more the readiness to sacrifice oneself to save others, a willingness that is the definition of the protagonist. Heroism may be manifested in different contexts, both in unique situations and in everyday ones, and is witnessed in many different forms: physical and spiritual, military, civil, national, or social heroism. At its core, heroism is a deep empathy with others. An act of heroism is a value choice, one in which the enactor overcomes his own immediate needs or interests and performs an action for the benefit of one other or the whole. It is a concept that can be traced back to the mythology and folklore of peoples since ancient times, notably in ancient Greece. In human society, the term usually defines a person who is considered altruistic in his actions, an extremely courageous, noble, and resourceful person endowed with chivalrous qualities. But there is another kind of heroism; one which is performed in situations where we are forced into acting heroically.

When I shot a terrorist at such close range that I could see the nicotine stains on his teeth, I was able to save two of my company soldiers, but I did not think I acted heroically. Compared to my commander's act of heroism, during which he saved others, I did not feel I was carrying out this act to save others. I was actually saving myself first. I wanted to survive the situation that was forced on me. I was not happy to kill. Killing is wrong and inhuman. But there are situations where you are compelled to kill, or you will be killed. And sometimes such situations give rise to an act that in the eyes of others is considered heroic.

It became more difficult over the years when I realised that the war was not against the millions of Arabs around us, but against a limited minority of fanatical terrorists. I learned that most Muslims were decent people, not eager for war, and did not entertain the messianic idea of exterminating the Jews. This insight has caused me many dilemmas on the battlefield, or in the pursuit of wanted terrorists who were Muslims, the bad ones.

From the point of view of leaders, war is an opportunity to prove their strength. To them, the goal will forever be victory even if it involves turning green fields into blood-red killing fields. To me, war is the all-time dumbest invention of mankind. War is an old-fashioned and primitive act. It is an act of violence and brute force, the opposite principle of social norms of the progressive enlightened world. It is a failure of the use of brainpower, bringing a sense of uncertainty and helplessness, and shaking the fundamental trust of the victims in themselves, in their leaders, and in the world.

The phenomenon of war has been known since the beginning of mankind and has been conducted from the moment humans chose to live in tribes and ethnic and religious groups while marking and determining territories. Although war between armies and soldiers takes place on the battlefield, the impact on civilians back at home, away from the front, is inevitable. The conflict on the battlefield permeates the civilian population, who find themselves exposed and sometimes more vulnerable than the combat corps. The economic damage, the evacuation of the population, and the inability to maintain a routine life. And worse of all, the psychological damage of traumatized children, who inarguably are the most vulnerable in times of war. Children who had no hand in the decision to go to war. I was one of them.

Chapter 6

Recruitment process

The recruitment process for the commando units in the Israel Defense Forces begins long before the candidate first puts on an army uniform. In all Israeli high schools, teachers are asked to provide the IDF with information about the character traits and skills of any students they find distinctive, particularly those who showed a colourful streak and 'out of the box' thinking.

After the first selection, and only after ensuring they were in excellent health, the commando units' recruitment team would invite the chosen boys to come for a one-day assessment in which the candidate would demonstrate their character and skills through various tests. Emphasis on perfect health is so high that even wearing glasses, or suffering from a minor allergy, can invalidate a candidate. The assessment day, which for some of the boys is a welcome opportunity to have a day off school, is held at one of the army bases, where we would be taken by bus from Tel Aviv. The atmosphere during the day is usually calm, friendly and free of any tough military discipline. In our case, we were even treated to a delicious lunch followed by ice cream for dessert.

At the beginning of the day the tests presented to us are relatively easy and non-threatening, but gradually they become more difficult and challenging. The recruitment team at this stage is not interested in the candidate's courage or his military knowledge, and not even in his level of achievement in the school curriculum, even if he was considered a genius in math and physics. What they want to know is about his character. Does he have analytical skills and how does he react in different situations? Is he a fixated person or is he flexible and open to other ways of thinking and doing? The recruiters at that stage would be looking for those pupils who have creative, imaginative minds, with the ability to improvize and utilize what is available in order to solve a seemingly intractable problem. The candidates are also asked to calculate speeds and distances correctly in a split second, and to find the fastest route out of a labyrinthine puzzle. The second half of the day is when the young candidates are assessed for their physical as well as mental abilities. They are introduced to a physical fitness instructor and asked to follow the strenuous exercises he demonstrates to them. We all thought, quite naturally, that the purpose of these exercises was to test our bodily fitness and ability. But it was only after more than a year, when we had already been admitted to the commando unit and started our service, that we were told that the real purpose of those exercises was to test our ability to withstand pressure, our determination and our perseverance.

A month later, after going through that long day of rigorous initial assessments, I was informed that I was among those who had passed the tests and examinations, and had demonstrated the abnormal required skills (this is usually only about fifty percent of the applicants). I was also informed that I was suitable material for an infantry commando unit. But which one would I be headed for? This I would only learn on the day of my enlistment.

After completing the requirements of the Absorption Sorting Base, which is the starting point of every IDF recruit including the Chief of Staff himself, we boarded a truck to be transported to a remote base, close to the city of Jenin in the West Bank. The surroundings we were met with lacked any spectacular views or green fields. The base was in a rocky area, encircled by hills. The inhabitants' living quarters were tents, huts, and anything else that did not resemble a normal residential structure. My twelve months' period of arduous training to qualify to serve as a member of the hallowed Golani unit had begun.

It started with the three-month basic training period, during which we learned how to use weapons that are commonly used by infantry fighters, such as M16 automatic rifles, hand grenades, bazookas and shoulder missiles such as RPGs, rocket propelled grenades. But mostly the training involved lots of strenuous and gruelling physical exercises. During these initial training sessions, fighters are given the chance to experiment with a variety of simulators for combat in built up and complex terrain; use special means of camouflage; and many other types of combat tools and equipment that contribute to enhancing the unit's capability. Throughout this period, in addition to the tasks and training to test the fighter's personal skills, not a single day goes by without arduous exercises to test both the physical and mental strength of the combatant. It includes walking tens of miles a day over harsh ground conditions, through cloying mud in winter and in stifling temperatures of extreme desert heat in the summer. The aim of these training exercises is to bring the nominated combatant to total physical and mental exhaustion so that his level of endurance can be assessed, and to determine whether he is able to continue his service in the unit. At the end of the three months of basic training, we would all be granted a very welcome three days' rest to spend with family and friends and enjoy the feeling of home again. While we were away, a screening process would be going on to remove those who failed to pass the basic training. Those who didn't meet the required standard for a commando unit would then be transferred to serve in other corps, or as part of the maintenance forces of the Golani Brigade.

Those who did manage to survive the gruelling three months successfully would move on to the next step, a further period of three months during in which they will be shedding gallons of sweat, breaking limbs, and passing out from the unbearable heat during the exhausting exercises.

Three months sounds like a short period of time, but they can still be unbearably difficult. The training was hard and sometimes inhuman, the hours of sleep were few, no more than three hours each night, but the motivation was immense. We went through dozens of uncomfortable situations in which I knew my level of alertness was being assessed. We were forced to get out of a warm, deep sleep, and sent out into the freezing cold of the Golan Heights in mid-February, only to discover it was just an exercise to strengthen our alertness, and train us to be ready in a minute to perform our role as a commando fighter. It did not take me long for such miserable feelings to subside, due to the atmosphere of seriousness, maturity and responsibility pervading among us the fighters. The resentment of being woken in the middle of the night would usually pass once we were standing erect, dressed and in gear, ready for the command to get moving. What guided our thoughts was that sense of first-rate national responsibility, the feeling of being on a sacred and supreme mission.

We were shown how to navigate by using the stars and the moon while walking long distances at night with combat gear on our backs, sometimes weighing nearly eighty per cent of our body weight. We also learned how to use bombs and explosives for blasting through walls and doors, and were trained in how to operate effectively under pressure. We were put in situations where we had to improve our ability to quickly analyse data, and make life-saving decisions instantaneously. Also included was a short parachuting course in which we would perform jumps from a plane, and once this was mastered, we had to undergo a dangerous exercise of parachuting in the depth of night towards an unlit and unmarked destination, while emitting constant and accurate gunfire from our weapon. This exercise was banned later due to an unacceptable number of casualties.

After successfully completing these six months of rigorous training, we were sent to carry out a three-month defensive operational activity. This was primarily on the borders with Syria and Lebanon to combat terrorists who infiltrated Israel from southern Lebanon, but some of us would be sent to carry out this activity in the densely populated areas of the Gaza Strip and the West Bank. Despite being a less dangerous activity than on the border with Lebanon, it was an activity I was not happy to do because of the dilemmas fighters encounter when they come in contact with civilian populations. During this period, our commanders would monitor the soldier's behaviour, his attitude, discipline, and other qualities that indicate his ability to command and lead. In addition, they assess his operational abilities during combat when encountering terrorist insurgencies from Lebanon, or when pursuing a wanted terrorist on a crowded street of innocent civilians in Gaza or Jenin. We the soldiers, of course, did not know that we were being intensely scrutinised. We behaved naturally and this is probably what the commanders wanted to happen. Only when we had finished this three-month operational period, were we told about this by those who had gone before us.

My personal experience of this obligatory defensive operational activity took place on the blazing northern border of Israel, where we were tasked with maintaining calm. This was because all the terrorist activity at that time was based in Lebanon, especially in the southern part of that country, from where terrorists would constantly infiltrate into northern Israel to carry out attacks. These terrorists were particularly cruel as they directed their murderous activities against civilians, and this included children. They refrained wherever they could from encountering us soldiers so they could inflict harm on the soft underbelly of society, the elderly and helpless children.

At first, I was a little disappointed that I was not being sent to Gaza, where I could have exacted my revenge on those who attacked me and my family and ruined my childhood, but it later became clear that terrorism is the same terrorism, whether it is perpetrated from Gaza or from Lebanon.

My platoon was sent to a lookout post called *Motzav Har-Dov*, close to the Golan Heights and Mount Hermon. The outpost comprised a main bunker connected to trenches in which we would have to sleep. Above the outpost were three further observation posts. These were the eyes of the outpost, through which we could overlook and easily observe the whole area of southern Lebanon, and act, if necessary, on almost every movement coming from it.

Each morning we were sent on a seven-kilometre foot patrol along the Lebanese border. An armoured vehicle would follow close behind us, manned by fighters with their fingers gripped tightly to the triggers of their heavy machine guns, ready to paralyse any terrorists found in the area.

Our tasks were divided each day as such: some would be sent to man the lookouts, observing and examining every inch of southern Lebanon through large binoculars, others would be assigned to the patrols along the border fence. Around midnight, some of us, normally ten men, would be sent to the northern side of the border, inside Lebanese territory, to lay in ambush awaiting any terrorists who would try to sneak into Israel during the night or early morning.

After midday, we would rotate our duties. Those who were on patrol in the morning would be sent to one of the lookout posts for a four-hour shift, and those who had spent the morning in the observation lookouts would join the patrol. Those who spent all night in ambush would be privileged to go and get some sleep and be off duty until the evening.

The patrol that took place each morning was not a regular one. It was referred to as the 'fire patrol', as we would be firing our rifles into the bushes and rocks behind the fence every few metres of progress along the seven-kilometre route. This was to root out any terrorists who might have been lurking in the bushes and rocks waiting for an opportune moment to penetrate Israel. Above us hovered a helicopter that would report to us any suspicious movements they picked up. In the event of a report of any terrorists in the field, we would be asked to give chase, sometimes entering a cave or ravine and tackling them head-on. There were some who had to be eliminated in the field at very close range, often in face-to-face battle, and there were others who surrendered. Those who chose to surrender were brought back in handcuffs to Israeli territory and handed over to the GSS, our General Security Services investigators. This type of dangerous patrol was banned after the introduction of electronic means, by which the presence of any terrorists could be picked up by the team in the bunker, ensuring the area was safe before the soldiers started the patrol.

One of those later-banned patrols was unforgettable. It was in December 1975, when a phosphorus grenade was thrown at us by one of the two terrorists we had encountered along the fence, hitting the paramedic who was walking right next to me. When he fell to the ground, I leaned over him and quickly tore off his clothes and combat vest that were starting to burn, while the rest of our fighters stormed the two terrorists and eliminated them in a close-range face-to-face battle. Compared to a regular hand grenade whose shrapnel hits the body, a phosphorus grenade is designed so that when it explodes, flames and white smoke burst out of it. The fire engulfs the body of the attacked soldier and begins to burn the flesh while it gnaws at the muscle and consumes it. The immediate treatment in such a case is to strip the victim of all his clothes and spray water over his body. This type of grenade is often used to trap an enemy or cut off their escape routes. It can also be useful in creating distance between yourself and your attacker, since once it is set to explode in a certain place, it will cover it in flames, thus forcing the attacker to retreat or choose an alternative route. At the end of this gruelling and challenging year, I was delighted to be promoted to the rank of sergeant and was proud to be given the chance to take a modest part in commanding a platoon, under the direction of the platoon's commanding officer. I did not have time to celebrate this due to a series of terrorist incidents that were being orchestrated both by terrorist organisations on the northern border with Syria and in the south by small individual groups of terrorists in Gaza. Immediately after we had completed the full year's training period (in which to my mother's delight I had not been killed or severely injured), we were sent to Gaza to deal with a nasty terrorist incident. As from that point, my combat journey in the ranks of the army began. An intense, challenging and dangerous journey in which I did what I had dreamed of doing, that is to confront the enemy that terrorized my country and sabotaged my childhood.

Chapter 7

Methods of training and operating

There were dozens of uncomfortable situations in which our level of alertness was being assessed. Cold nights when we would be woken from our beauty sleep, ordered to get dressed in full combat gear within sixty seconds, and await our orders, being ready and of the mindset to storm any target. Adherence to this concept of constant alertness was uncompromising among all commanders and fighters. It was embedded within us. The level of individual and company readiness was so high that sometimes in training we felt we were in a real battle, performing with such perfect precision that it gave the feeling of authenticity.

The base where I had spent my training period, close to the city of Jenin in the West Bank, was extensive. It was surrounded by hills and dirt tracks that were used by local villagers for their transportation, which was always by donkey. These paths also served us on our arduous training expeditions, during which we not only learned how to walk long distances with combat gear on our backs but also how to navigate accurately both by day and night. The training ground at the base contained most of the natural obstacles that fighters could encounter on a battlefield, including tangled bushes, rocks, dense woods, steep-sided pits, winter mud, steep hills, and exposed open areas. Also, within the training base was a compound I had not seen during the first three months of basic training. Perhaps in this initial period, I was not yet prepared for what using this compound entailed, or maybe it had only recently been built, either way, the compound contained several elements that simulated various combat modes within a built-up area.

Some of it was designed to replicate a house or just a room, some to replicate a row of small houses, and one that towered above all the rest replicated a three-storey building, mainly to be used for practicing an operation to rescue hostages. In addition, a modular house was built with two rooms and three windows, and a front and rear entrance. This modular structure could cleverly modify its format based on information obtained about a particular terrorist situation and location. Within a few minutes, a house with two rooms and three windows could be transformed into a house with three rooms and five windows. This well-designed training ground allowed commandos to prepare for dangerous and difficult combat, whatever the terrain or weather conditions, any time of day or night, at any distance, and against all odds. Because of this excellent training facility, we were able to practice and become experts in close-range combat, particularly in complicated locations, and in the use of camouflage, as well as in short-range combat where the individual's qualities and skills are the key to success.

Apart from being taught skills such as navigation, climbing, and administering first aid under fire, our physical training exercises included a daunting 190 km trek on foot over dusty and rocky roads, facing steep slopes and areas of ground thick with mud. Just two days after this is completed, we are ordered on a further 110 km trek carrying a stretcher with a 'wounded' soldier on it. Other training exercises involved carrying weapons, ammunition, and personal equipment weighing nearly eighty per cent of our body weight, while climbing a fourteen-kilometre uphill mountain path, scaling a mountain while shooting at marked targets, and parachuting in the darkness towards an unlit and unmarked destination, while maintaining constant and accurate gunfire.

During our navigation course, commanders demanded that we should learn the art of navigation at night in enemy territory, in real time, exposing us to the dangers of a surprise encounter with the enemy. As with parachuting, this was an extreme method of testing courage and giving the soldiers an authentic experience. Although most of us loved the excitement of such a crazy practice, some seniors considered it as unprecedented in training, and it was actually abolished in 1968 due to its high risks.

Another 'highlight' was a week spent enduring hunger, living in a field where we had to forage for our own food each day. This involves eating grass, rhizomes, insects and reptiles, items that you would not find at the supermarket in your daily life. This is a survival course aimed at hardening us to face the harshest of conditions, including persistent hunger, long hours of thirst, very high temperatures in summer and, in winter, unbearable cold. These exercises bring the combatant to total physical and mental exhaustion in order to examine his level of endurance.

In collaboration with an undercover unit, we were sent to a genuinely hostile location, and were shown how, as a solo fighter, we could find way out should we find ourselves trapped in an enemy civilian crowd, or left alone in the field surrounded by enemy soldiers. The principle was to show us how to use our intellect and character skills more than the weapons in our hands.

Techniques we learnt to use within a built-up area were the 'cold entry' and 'hot entry', two different methods of storming and taking over a house, or any structure that has civilians inside and is built in a crowdy build-up area. For a cold entry, we were trained in handling dangerous situations with our bare hands, without firing a single bullet so as to minimize casualties among the hostages or innocent neighbours. This is done after silently heading towards the target and taking it over in the blink of an eye. An example of where this method is used is for breaking into a house to rescue civilians being held hostage by a single-armed terrorist, whether armed with a gun or knife. The decision as to the type of action in this situation would depend to a large extent on the information at our disposal regarding the type of weapon the terrorist possesses. If he is holding a knife, we would choose to first attack without firing and neutralize him by various other means. If he is holding a rifle, we would still first try an assault without firing, or with our bare hands, so as not to injure any hostages. If this fails, then we would have no choice but to shoot the terrorist, but would use the skill of our snipers and our own ability to shoot with great precision.

This cold entry method is also designed for entering a house to capture a wanted terrorist, even if hostages are not involved. Such an operation requires us to have excellent intelligence about the location, usually supplied by the undercover *Mista'arvim* unit, who will have been familiarizing themselves in the area by roaming around the streets and gathering information. To execute this kind of operation, the element of surprise is the key, using deceptions and tricks so as not to be spotted before arriving at the location, as any small mistake could scupper the mission and put a commando's life in danger. The fighters are trained to memorize all details, names, colours and shapes, and be fully aware of any minor change in the area to minimize any chance of being spotted. If our soldiers are attacked, then a stand-by backup unit would arrive quickly on the scene and storm the area, escalating the mission into a larger-scale combat situation, something that commando fighters strive to avoid.

A 'hot entry' involves a noisy assault or takeover of a house, room or any building where terrorists are firing from, using our guns and grenades to fend them off. However, our assault would be totally different if an armed terrorist had barricaded himself inside the property with vulnerable hostages, even if he is directing his shooting at us rather than his captives. In such a case, any shooting from our side would only aggravate the situation and cause the terrorist to panic, and we would need to use our head more than the weapons in our hands. While we assess the situation and plan the right way to paralyze the terrorist, we would send an Arabic speaking special soldier to try to negotiate with him. One of us would count the number of bullets already used by the terrorist and pay attention to the sound of the magazine replacement and gun loading, so we could estimate when he would run out of ammunition. Then, when all options had been tried, we would call on our 'Monkey Team' to break into the premises by climbing up the walls, or abseiling down from rooftops and breaking through a window and paralyzing the terrorist with short bursts of highly accurate shooting. An additional complication may be that the terrorist has children with him, who are being used as human shields. In such a case we would use psychological tools, tricks, and negotiations, and if this did not help, we would simply have to leave and retreat. In addition to the cold and hot entry exercises, we were taught how to deal with incidents of terror activity that involved a hijacked aircraft, train, or bus, when hostages could be held captive by one or many terrorists. To our aid, if needed, we would call on one of these specialist teams:

Snipers Team - These are fighters with an innate skill to hit a target accurately. This has often been revealed to them during sporting activities in their youth. The military, which had been receiving information about their excellent skills since their high school days, will recruit them to be trained to become snipers. During their service, they sharpened their ability in sniper training using various weapons. Their task is to neutralize the enemy by being positioned away from the danger area of their own fighters. While the other fighters are running, jumping, shouting orders, or screaming in pain from having been hit, the sniper will calmly focus all his attention on his target, disengaging himself from the hustle and bustle of the battle.

Burglary Team - In addition to training as commando fighters, these young men learn how to crack all types of locks, iron and steel doors, and heavy metal gates, and break in through reinforced concrete walls. They also train in how to break into a building through a window whilst at the same time firing accurately. This can often be the first force to encounter the enemy, usually terrorists fortified inside a building, and in some cases holding hostages. These fighters come into very close contact with the enemy, sometimes face-to-face, therefore, they are trained to quickly and decisively respond in a short and sharp battle employing 100 per cent shooting accuracy.

Monkey Team - These are nimble fighters who are trained in how to surprise the enemy using unexpected means. You may not believe it, but as part of their training, many visits to the local zoo were mandatory and on an almost daily basis. On their visits, each fighter would carry a personal video camera (this was before the smartphone era), and would huddle around only one cage of all the animal sections housed on the premises. The monkeys. After each trainee warrior sat for hours in front of the 'TV screen' watching and filming the monkeys, he would learn the virtuoso movements of the monkey's feet and hands. Then, during training, he would discover time and time again the resemblance between his agile moves and the monkeys in the film. Through this, the soldier learned how to use his own body's agility in combat situations, whether breaking into a house, while climbing up sheer-faced walls, or abseiling down from rooftops.

Sabotage Team – These are fighters who can be an organic part of their own company or brigade. Alternatively, they can be appropriated as needed from the IDF's Combat Engineering Brigade, which consists of specialized units capable of building a bridge in a short time, or conversely destroying infrastructures in a matter of seconds. They specialize in the use of bombs and explosives for blasting walls and doors, as well as placing explosives in complex situations around enemy targets. Their role is critical in certain situations, and necessary in any operation or battle, even the shortest. They not only help demolish buildings or bunkers where the enemy is hiding, but also help advancing soldiers to clear a field of mines, or roadside explosives.

They are also expert fighters, trained to use all kinds of weapons that are in use among infantry commando units and undergo all the combat training exercises within the unit.

In order to increase and strengthen our courage, it was decided that each one would take a course in parachuting. Those who have experienced jumping out of a plane will understand the paralyzing fear that shoots down your spine, as you stand at the open doorway of the plane, waiting for that dreaded signal to jump, watching from a terrifying height the tiny houses and cars beneath your feet that look just like children's toys. I quite enjoyed these jumps and learned one thing I could pass on. It would be reasonable to think that the first jump would be the most terrifying, but in fact, it is the least scary, and the other jumps that follow are the scariest because in the first jump, you do not know what to expect. From the second onwards, you find yourself preparing for the alarming things you become aware of only after taking the first jump, not before. Things like the harsh blast of wind in your face, the distance and force in which you are kicked sideways away from the plane, and the fear that you will find yourself enmeshed in a tangle of ropes and strings.

The act of parachuting from a plane during the course of a battle, or as a means of arriving at the battlefield, was banned and has not been used by armies since 1956. This was a result of a catastrophe in which thousands of paratroopers were killed as they were dropped over enemy territory to prepare for a surprise attack, but many were jumping to their deaths as they were shot while in the air by the enemy on the ground.

Another exercise was called 'Rescue under fire'. This is an exercise that involves fighters in the field and a helicopter. The principle was to learn how to master our moves and coordinate with the helicopter's pilot during a rescue operation. When seen from afar, it can look easy manoeuvring a helicopter rescue, however, there are many factors that have to be worked against. For example, the wind, the speed and movement of the craft, and the physical condition of those being rescued. We had to simulate a dangerous helicopter rescue to pick up a soldier who could be wounded or dead, or unharmed, but exposed to the risk of falling into enemy hands. This exercise was performed under real fire, with our commanders shooting around us and above our heads to intensify our fear and create the feeling of real combat. The entire exercise of being suspended by rope from a helicopter is normally synchronized between the rescue helicopter pilot and us the fighters, who glide down ropes from the helicopter towards the helpless soldier on the ground.

Our unit operates only on the ground, and specializes in most of the dangerous and complex operations carried out in houses, bunkers, underground tunnels, and enemy ambushes. We were trained to reach anywhere, including deep into enemy territory. Each fighter needs to be well-versed in counterterrorism techniques, and specialize in close-range combat, problematic locations, and using camouflage successfully, as well as close-range combat where the individual's qualities and skills are the keys to success. Even though the IDF possessed the strongest air force, tanks, and artillery, the battle inside trenches, forts, and houses will always be won by commandos who can get into these locations and shoot the enemy with precision, something a jet or tank cannot do. it achieved better results with fewer casualties, and also changed the battle outcome morally and psychologically.

'Planning and memorizing'. We, the fighters, were asked to take part in the planning of an operation, studying and memorizing all its details, so that we could understand what was happening throughout the entire operation, thus increasing our operational capability for a perfect and successful execution. Because of the almost 100 per cent accuracy, we were required to have, we were encouraged to plan an operation, incorporating unpredictable tactics and exceptionally creative actions or responses, sometimes surprising ourselves with our resourcefulness. The logic behind this was simple. If the fighter was involved in the planning, he would be exposed to more details and intelligence that would become embedded in his mind. He could then call on this knowledge during the heat of the battle. This principle, after being proven logical and practical, was immediately implemented and included in the other IDF units' training programmes.

Due to the terrorists' intensified activity, our unit heightened its use of guerilla tactics and trained and worked in close collaboration with the covert Israeli intelligence organizations, the *Mossad* and *Shin Bet.* We were lauded by the Army Chief of Staff for providing a sophisticated response to the new methods of activity of the terrorist organizations, and this has even been acknowledged by the terror organizations themselves.

In later years, we demonstrated impressive ability and managed to successfully handle dozens of terrorist incidents, some of them highly complex and dangerous, under very demanding combat conditions. We learned to be proficient in gathering quality intelligence while deep inside enemy territory and cooperated with other Israeli commando units in some particularly daring operations, which unfortunately the Israeli censor has not revealed to the public, and probably will remain buried inside the IDF archive forever.

In addition, in training and working with *Mossad* and with other intelligence forces, we had the opportunity of working closely with a covert unit of the *Mista'arvim*. These are the counter-terrorism units of the Israel Defense Forces which operate undercover. Their operatives are specifically trained to assimilate with the local Arab population and perform intelligence gathering, law enforcement, hostage rescue, and counter-terrorism. They dress like local Arabs and familiarize themselves with Muslim customs, prayers, and clothing. They have learnt to speak the Arabic language with the appropriate accent for each posting so they can pick up the local gossip in each village. Refining the accent may sound a minor detail but is crucial because the Arabic language has many varying accents and dialects that change from one Arab country to another, or from one neighbourhood to another in those countries. This fascinating unit is involved in various operations to thwart terrorist attacks, capture or eliminate wanted and terrorists, so they must learn to camouflage themselves inside a crowd of Palestinians. They have extraordinary courage and can tackle an armed terrorist with their bare hands.

Compared to medieval battles, where face-to-face combat using a sword was the only option on the battlefield, face-to-face combat now occurs very rarely. This type of confrontation can only take place today in the event of a chance encounter with an enemy, perhaps in a narrow ditch, or in a situation where both have run out of ammunition, or during a malfunction in a weapon that prevents further firing. This kind of combat is as much a mental challenge as it is a physical one. The mental challenge brings the commando soldier to higher self-awareness and an enhancement of his physical readiness. In face-to-face combat, every fighter's ability is put to an extreme test. Through tough training, we, the commandos, developed physical strength that prepares us to deal with the possibility of death or severe injury.

One serious face-to-face encounter with the enemy I was involved in was in Gaza in 1986 when I was serving as a reserve combatant. My platoon was attacked by three armed terrorists while we were on patrol. I started pursuing one of them through a crowded residential neighbourhood in Gaza. He shot at me and I fired back at him. I noticed that he wasn't wearing a combat vest, so I guessed he had only one magazine. When he stopped shooting at me, I knew that he would soon run out of ammunition. I got close to him and shouted 'Surrender!' in Arabic. But instead, he jumped on me and started to physically grapple with me. He was bigger than me in size and weight and managed to knock me to the ground, where we continued to struggle. He tried to snatch the rifle out of my hands while twisting my right leg and trying to break it. I didn't want to shoot him dead, however, when I realized that I had no chance of physically wrestling free, I shot him in the stomach. He continued beating me and then, leaving me with no choice, I repeatedly shot him from zero range. I could smell his sweat. I could see the nicotine stains on his teeth. These kinds of details you don't often get to see in a war.

Chapter 8

I was sent on a mission

Summer of 1973, I was fifteen. The hot weather was blanketing the landscape of Netivot in a stifling embrace. The sun beat down relentlessly, its fiery rays casting long shadows that offered little respite from the intense heat. The streets were nearly deserted, as most residents sought refuge indoors, behind closed shutters and drawn curtains in an attempt to keep out the scorching heat. The few brave souls who venture outside moved slowly, their steps languid and deliberate.

I was on a mission. My mother had asked me to get some ice from Mr Assoulin, the man who sold ice in Netivot. On my way, with the bucket in my hand, I couldn't resist and so I turned left, taking me about a hundred metres out of my way. I arrived in Bar Ilan Street, and stood in front of the house where my love Sima Malul was ensconced, hoping she would come out to get some fresh air so I could 'bump' into her and make contact.

Mr Assoulin did not make the ice himself, nor did he have any ice storage facility. He didn't even have a refrigerated truck, in which the ice was normally transported in those days of the late 1960's. He had a horse tied to a cart on top of which he had built a large cooling box lined with double sheets of aluminium on its inside walls to keep the ice frozen. Mr Assoulin would buy great slabs of ice from a large refrigerated truck that came down south from Tel Aviv every morning. He would ride his cart out to the main road that stretches between Netivot and Tel Aviv, about five hundred metres outside Netivot. At an appointed time, he would meet with the ice merchant from Tel Aviv and buy large slabs of ice from him. After loading the ice onto his cart, he would then break the slabs into smaller chunks to be sold to the people of Netivot. We never knew about the existence of the truck from Tel Aviv because Mr Assoulin hid it from everyone in order to increase his own sales. We only found out about this when his idiot son, Amos, who had the habit of reacting hastily before what he was being told was completed, revealed his father's secret. This had happened after a row between father and son regarding the sale of the ice. Amos, after realizing that his father did not much trust his son's business acumen and was never going to take him in as a partner, sought to exact revenge and divulged his father's trade secret to all and sundry. Such was the interest, one might think that this fool revealed to the people of Netivot the secret of the creation of the universe.

'Is my Sima now toiling in the kitchen?' I wondered while leaning against the rusty metal pillar that supported the fence of the Zagori family's house, directly opposite Sima's house. 'Is she kneading dough, slicing vegetables, learning the nuances of Moroccan seasoning, or is she just peeling heads of garlic and placing them naked from their skins on the counter so that her mother Sulika can concentrate on the act of cooking and the amount of seasoning and will not have to bother herself with a simple job like peeling garlic. And what will she be doing after completing her simple tasks? Does her mother force her to stay in the kitchen until the cooking is done, or sit on the windowsill and gaze at the noisy children in the yard?' Perhaps she was reading an interesting book, or is she just flipping through one of those cheap magazines she got from Michael Biton's salon, the charming hairdresser who was always nice to pretty girls. He gave them out of date magazines for free, or would spray them with an expensive perfume he told them he had brought from Paris.

Mr Malul was well-liked and respected in Netivot. When encountered by the common folks in the market or at the synagogue, they would kiss his hand and mutter blessings that were understood to them only. He would then straighten up and raise his head as if he had just won first prize in a challenging general knowledge quiz. Although he was extremely fanatical about the way to raise and educate girls, he possessed a sharp mind, with a definite street smartness. He had a remarkable ability to relate to the common people of Netivot and make them believe he was their saviour, even though he knew nothing and had never attended a formal educational institution. In the front yard of the house, usually filthy and swarming with flies, he maintained two goats and ten chickens that squawked and made incessant noise. The stench emanating from his house was unbearable, but his neighbours did not dare to complain about it. At most, they gave carefully worded hints to his wife Sulika to convince him to move his smelly safari to the large open space behind the house. But unfortunately, even Sulika seemed to have been afraid of Mr Malul. She appeared unsure of herself, usually sullen, in addition to her perpetually angry countenance. The town's chattering old women claimed her hatred sprang from her childhood as an orphan in a house of strangers who never gave her love. When she cried from longing for her parents who had been murdered by robbers in Morocco, Mr Malul would peel almonds for her, dip them in rose water, and tenderly raise them to her mouth.

The hypocrisy of Mr Malul's neighbours was absurd. They could at least politely ask him to clean up his filthy yard and remove the cans and rusted metal lying all around. Instead, they kissed his hand and showered him with silly blessings as if he were the Messiah himself. But despite this, I had to respect him in order to keep alive my chances of marrying his lovely daughter. I'd say hello to him with a quick nod of the head but never kissed his hand, which must have been filthy from the hundreds of mouths that had already kissed it.

Sima was not seen leaving the house. She probably did not need cool fresh air, and her mother Sulika did not need anything from Revivo's grocery store. 'Why don't I knock on the door and introduce myself?' I pondered. But then I remembered the ice. I panicked, as everyone back at my house would be feverishly waiting for me. I rushed to Mr Assoulin's and filled the bucket with ice. When I returned home, sweating all over from the effort of walking and carrying the heavy bucket, my older brother knocked me to the floor with a vicious punch, 'How long should it take you to get some ice? You idiot!'

With each passing day, my feelings towards Sima and my constant longing to see her only grew more potent, and so I started looking for ways to be around her, or to 'bump' into her.

I thought of going to Bokovza the Irishman, a small-time renovations contractor who was my neighbour and a friend of Mr Malul. But then I remembered Miran, his sister, with her annoying habit of poking her nose into every conversation. The concept of 'private conversation' was not in her lexicon.

Yitzhak Bokovza was not Irish. 'The Irishman' nickname that was given to him, was because he was black-haired and green-eyed, and looked like a footballer from an Irish team whose name has evaporated from my memory. Bokovza was tall and broad-shouldered. His face was freckled, and his small green eyes sank into his face when he laughed. Due to his short fuse, his lips were white like a sheet but his smile was warm and genuine, lighting up his face and the world around him. His clothes were worn and sloppy during weekdays, but on Saturdays, he would be decked out in a three-piece suit with a matching tie, and would anoint his hair with a cheap greasy pomade, giving him the look of Cliff Richard or Elvis. But despite his pleasant smile, Yitzhak Bokovza was a hot-tempered man with a turbulent nature, subject to sudden outbursts of rolling thunderstorms. At the end of each eruption of anger, he would immediately relent, soften his voice, apologize awkwardly, and bow his head as if his outbursts were just a short attack of coughing. He would then imitate comical characters and make jokes about his hot-blooded character. Within minutes, he would reconcile with those around him and laugh at his own jokes and impersonations.

I thought of coming to his house and asking him to somehow help me get in contact with Sima, even just as friends, to study together and do our homework together.

I then heard that Sima liked to read books. Although there was a makeshift public library in Netivot, her father, the pig, did not allow her to visit it after he had gone to the library one time to check who was there and what they really did between reading the books, if they read the books at all. After a thorough investigation, I discovered that Mr Malul would allow his daughter to study and gain knowledge beyond school hours only if she was accompanied by her sister Susan, who had a talent for making up stories and dramatizing facts to draw attention to herself. All this pointed to my options getting slimmer. I had no choice left. I would wait for Sima at the library and would try to be careful with the gossiping Susan.

Chapter 9

At the library

Although it was only a grey building clad with asbestos, with cracked walls decorated with colourful graffiti proclaiming love and infatuation and inscriptions in black that cried out the state of our reality, the municipal library that stood a few metres away from my house was, for me, a ray of light. It was another way of escaping the inferno, a sanctuary of knowledge and tranquillity, a place where the whispers of old books echoed like forgotten memories. This time, however, I was even more excited to visit it so I could see Sima, who would come several times a week, always accompanied by gossiping Susan who had been appointed by Sima's father to protect her from the hormone-filled boys.

I always loved being at the library. I had loved the smell of books from the tender age of three. At the nursery, while other children would be playing happily in the sandbox, I would cling to the hem of my teacher's dress, and urge her to teach me to read using one of the books from which she would tell us stories. To my disappointment, she was no different from the other adults around me who were firm in their beliefs, 'You will only learn to read when you reach first grade!'

'But why?' I cried.

'Because that's what everyone does!'

Sometimes I would beg my mother to teach me to read. That way I wouldn't need to bother her with my tiresome questions, but she couldn't read or write. In Morocco, in the village where she was born, they had never heard of a school. Besides, as a girl, she would not have been allowed to go anyway. The fate of female children was predestined to marry and give birth to ten children, cook, do the washing, and be a servant to the patriarch, her husband. As for the boys, only those who could withstand the effort of travelling two hours each way to the nearest town would be granted permission to pursue an education and perhaps become highly respected professionals such as teachers or rabbis.

I was an infuriatingly inquisitive child but the adults around me did not have the patience to satisfy my curiosity. I wanted to study the wonders of the world, the changes in weather, the flow of electricity, and the mysteries of the human body. I once asked one of the teachers where dreams go after we wake up, and where the geese fly to in the winter, when lakes freeze over and turn into solid ice floors. He looked at me as if I was a raving lunatic and screamed, 'Stop with your stupid questions kid!'

As a child with an insatiable curiosity, I found solace in the library. My love of books led me to spend countless hours engrossed in the worlds between the pages, even though most of the time I was busy finding food in shamefully creative ways. I also had to please my gang buddies by agreeing to go on secret operations in the market, especially Moshiko, who relied heavily on me and saw me as a kind of older brother. Moshiko was orphaned at the age of two and was adopted by his grandmother Maruma.

In the year 1966, the year of great austerity and recession, it was deemed necessary by libraries to set rules and regulations regarding the lending of books. Each child was allowed to borrow only one book and had to return it within five days. Whoever was late in returning the book would be severely punished. And as if that wasn't enough, there was also a great lack of books, and every book that was on the inventory list was considered a priceless asset.

Every time I finished reading my weekly book, I had a feeling of transcendence and spiritual purification. I once got through an entire book in one day and was sure I would be allowed to take another. To my disappointment, Ninet Buchris, the director of the library, scolded me and advised me in her teacherly tone to read more slowly, and not to finish a book in one day. I was only eleven years old, yet I learned from

Mrs. Buchris, who was a highly educated academic, that reading too much could be destructive and cause irreversible damage to the brain of a diligent child. And because I didn't want to upset Mrs. Buchris, I tried to adjust my level of curiosity and my quick learning ability to learn to what she suggested and agreed to borrow only one book a week.

After more than half an hour of nerve-racking waiting, the fear that Sima would not come began to creep into my heart. According to the stories I'd heard about him, her father was unpredictable, unable to control his swinging moods. Perhaps he had barred her from visiting the library because she refused to wear one of her mother's embarrassing dresses, or maybe it was something else. A look of despondency crossed my face. 'At the very least, I can stay in the library and dive into some exciting stories until she comes,' I muttered. After all, I loved the library, only this time, because of the tense anticipation that tore me apart, I couldn't enjoy the stories. I rose from my chair to make my way out. But then she appeared. Sima, my Sima. My heart skipped a beat. 'How beautiful she is,' I thought to myself. She walked into the library, bold and self-assured, and began browsing the shelves. Although my whole body felt paralysed, I dragged myself to the spaces between the shelves, directing my feet to the row where she was standing and rummaging through the books. The gossiping Susan who was glued to Sima's side didn't really show any interest in books. This complicated my plan to make contact with Sima. I started looking for a creative solution and immediately found one. I asked Ronit, one of the girls, whom I had reliably been told was madly in love with me and would go to any length for me, to concoct some juicy gossip and take Susan aside to share it with her. If books didn't interest her, then gossip surely would.

Ronit, through whom I learned that ignoring a girl can actually make her develop stronger feelings for you, readily agreed to carry out the task and smiled as she walked over to Susan with a smile.

The ruse worked. Susan moved away from Sima and together with Ronit sat down at one of the tables. I threw a piercing look at Ronit who understood what I meant and quickly advised Susan that they should leave the library and go somewhere they could be alone, because gossip should be kept private and it is best to be as far away from other people as possible. Susan fell headlong into the trap and left with Ronit.

Ronit was a clever girl with an easy-going nature. The problem was that she wasn't gifted with mind–boggling beauty. She had a long, aquiline nose and eyes that were too large and seemed out of proportion to her small face. Sometimes her eyes were so prominent that they would almost pop out of their sockets. You can't always get what you want in a girl…

I approached Sima. Somehow, I managed to control the shaking that overtook me. As our eyes met, time seemed to stand still, and in that moment, an unspoken connection was forged. The musty smell of the books in front of me began to blend with the sweetness and lustre of her face.

'Can I recommend a book to you?' I asked. My voice had almost choked. She didn't even turn to look at me and just kept leafing through the books.

'Try this one,' I said, reaching for one of the books on the shelf. She stopped her seemingly fruitless search. Then she turned to face me. 'Oh, it's you…' she murmured and smiled. 'You're my aunt Habiba's neighbour,' she said sweetly while continuing the task of browsing through the books.

'What a coincidence,' I said. My self-confidence was beginning to return. Everyone knew everyone else in our little town. It was sometimes beneficial, and sometimes it just caused conflicts. This time I had no idea where it would lead. Perhaps her aunt had told her good things about me, or maybe bad things. Maybe she had spotted me stealing with the gang, or maybe she had seen me spending hours at the library.

And after the boring chat, we stumbled simultaneously upon an old, tattered book. Its pages were worn, but we both had a strange telepathic feeling that the contents of the book might be interesting. That's the nature of faded tattered books. They always smelled of mystery and a potentially fascinating plot. As we read aloud to each other from the pages, the world around us seemed to fade, replaced by the courageous characters painted by the words. In those short moments, the book became our sanctuary, a place where we could escape harsh reality even for a little while. Each page turned was a step away from the horrors of war and a step closer to a world where dreams still flourished. Dreams of a world where the sounds of laughter drowned out the sounds of sirens and gunfire. Where children could play freely without fearing a passing plane, and where the magic of stories could heal our scars and wounds. And even though the scars remained, they were now accompanied by vibrant brushstrokes of hope and resilience.

'Sima, you must hear an interesting story,' Susan's irritating voice was suddenly heard.

I moved away to the other shelves. Sima turned and stood in front of Susan.

'What kind of amazing tale do you have for me this time, Susan?' she asked nonchalantly, pretending to be interested in her sister's nonsense.

I left the place right away. Although a twinge of disappointment lingered within me, I recognized that this was merely the initial stride of a prolonged journey. A huge grin lit up my face.

Chapter 10

The oppressive absurdity of war

I was born under fire and brought up under constant fire. I did not choose to be born into such a reality. I did not choose to be born at all. For a helpless and inexperienced child, I probably witnessed death too many times and in too many situations. From the moment I was born, almost every day I felt that this was the day I could die or be severely injured. During the 1950s, 60s and 70s, we suffered from incessant shelling and attacks by terrorists armed with large knives, who were insurgents from nearby Gaza. As a result, my entire childhood was swathed in fear and anxiety. I felt exposed and vulnerable. Sometimes I would panic and my body would stiffen every time I heard an innocent civilian plane passing overhead. Those constant fears led to incessant anxieties and difficulties in concentrating at school by day, and my bedwetting by night.

The constant war between 1956 and 1973 tore me to pieces during my childhood and youth, the years when children and teenagers are supposed to learn, grow, develop, dance, party, dream and weave plans for the future. I was doomed to experience those critical years in the harshest way. I did not choose to be a pawn in this madness called war between Israel and its neighbouring Arabs. My dreams were about movies and theatre and wild rock concerts. All I really wanted when I was fifteen was to continue playing with the rock band my friends and I had pulled together, and to cover with sweet and innocent amateurishness the songs of legends like Deep Purple, Led Zeppelin, Black Sabbath, and Pink Floyd. If I had been able to choose where to be born, I would have chosen England, from where most of the music legends came from, where people didn't fight over religion and land, and where the futile concept called 'Zionism' did not exist. But sadly, as my childhood and youthful years went by, I realised that my reality was far from what I dreamed. I was doomed to spend my life under an ongoing war over a tiny little piece of land that for some was considered holy and for which crazy people were willing to fight fanatically at any cost.

War is not only the rumble of the tank and the smell of acrid black smoke, but it also inflicts trauma on those directly or indirectly exposed to it. A trauma that causes a fracture in a person's psyche, rending a deep tear in his or her mental tissue. It creates a terrifying situation in the mind that makes a person feel abandoned and helpless, while crying out for help. War is a protracted violent struggle between armed bodies, which can be states, tribes, or different factions within a nation. They all have one thing in common; a bloody and deadly catastrophe committed by the intelligent beings of the human race. War can include not only the threat of death, but also the undermining of a person's perception of their world as a safe place, bringing a sense of uncertainty and helplessness, and shaking the fundamental trust of the victims in themselves, in their leaders and in the world. There has never been a quiet time in history when it comes to human conflict.

Humanity has been engaged in wars since the dawn of its development.

The phenomenon of war has been known since the beginning of mankind and has been conducted from the moment humans chose to live in tribes and ethnic and religious groups, while marking and determining territories. But since the age of wars over territories and food, humanity, encouraged by its leaders, has invented other types of wars with their twisted mindsets. Wars of nationalism, when one country wishes to prove superiority by invasion and violent subjugation. Wars of imperialism, when leaders believe that by conquering other countries, they will bring glory and esteem to their nation. Wars of revolution, when people rise up against corrupt or despotic leadership, such as the French Revolution (1789-1799), and the Portuguese Revolution (1640-1668). Civil wars, such as the American Civil War (1861-1865), Russian Civil War (1917-1923), Spanish Civil War (1936-1939), Korean

War (1950-1953), Yugoslav Wars (1991-1995) and the Lebanese Civil War (1975-1990). But above all, wars are executed over religion.

Religious conflicts often have very deep roots, adding fuel to the fiery battles and being the leading motive. Religion, if misinterpreted, results in brainwashing, extremism and loss of human compassion. Poisoned believers can bring themselves to easily murder in the name of religion, something we have been witnessing over recent decades, when extremist Muslims have blown up office towers, buses, trains, planes, and restaurants, killing secular people or those of religions who, according to their warped view, are carrying out an act of apostasy against Muhammad and Islam. The objects of their hatred also include non-fanatical members of their own Muslim religion.

Religious conflicts can lead to an endless chain of retaliatory wars being set in motion which are very difficult to end. Not only different religions will fight against each other, but conflict over religion can also arise between different branches of religion. Protestant and Catholic Christians in Ireland, Sunni and Shiite Muslims in Lebanon, and so on. One of the most notable conflicts was the Crusades, under the leadership of Pope Urban II, when a long and bloody campaign was instigated to try to regain control over the Holy Land.

In the Middle East, where various religious groups compete for territory and influence, the situation is worsening from year to year, and will do as long as the sects and groups in conflict are motivated by religion. Religion is a powerful tool, so it's not surprising it has resulted in tremendous conflict throughout history.

Since our birth, we, the children, experienced only war and terror that damaged our tender souls. We cried out for help but the wailing of the sirens kept drowning our screams. We could not understand the link between war and the lack of toys and chocolate. All we knew about the wars was the obligation to run as quickly as possible to the nearest shelter. What really interested us were sweets, games, and some assurance that we would have at least two meals a day. I certainly do not remember dessert options during those years, only a large jar of jam from which we all sweetened our tongues. We, the children, paid a heavy price for the actions of the adults. We could not comprehend what the adults knew and understood. While they knew that the shortages were the result of constant war, we could not understand the link between war and the lack of toys and chocolate. All we knew about the wars was the obligation to run fast to the nearest shelter.

The unbearable shortages, the lack of clothing, toys, or basic food items was hard not only on us as children, but greatly affected our parents too, who felt utterly frustrated. The shortages worsened further during 1965 and 1966, the years in which Israel needed to purchase weapons to deal with the threats from all the neighbouring Arab countries who were vowing to wipe our country off the map. In mid-1965, there was a very deep recession that threatened to destroy Israel from within rather than from the outside Arab threat. This was a hopeless situation, forcing my father to swallow his pride and join the long line of people standing outside the town hall, where they would occasionally hand out second-hand clothing, footwear and toys donated by Jews from America who wanted to help us cope with the situation. Some said they were altruistic people, and some argued they were only trying to ease their own consciences about letting us building the Jewish state as a safe refuge, while they lived far away from the battlefield. I did not care who was right. What interested me was getting the biggest suitcase from the tall pile of suitcases.

But not only children are, and forever will be, victims of war, even though they are the most vulnerable and are more likely to develop fears than adults. War causes extensive damage to all. It creates a perfect storm of death, agony, grief, serious injury and disfunction. It raises the levels of psychological distress and the number of those affected by mental illnesses, including trauma, anxiety and depression.

Chapter 11

My parents' fatal mistake

The two-bedroom house where my eight siblings and I shared was exceedingly cold in the winter and oppressively hot in the summer due to the low-grade materials used in its construction. An air conditioner was a luxury we couldn't afford. In the summer, we would drench ourselves with tap water, and in the winter, we would wear several layers of clothing, wrap ourselves in blankets and huddle around a paraffin heater, toasting on its bars slices of bread coated with margarine. Thin streaks of black smoke would billow from the heater. Dad suggested we should open a window because it was dangerous to inhale the toxic black smoke, but then Mum would whine again about her constant sensitivity to the cold.

My father and mother should have stayed in Morocco where they had married and enjoyed a fearless and comfortable life. Instead, they were convinced by Zionist activists to leave everything behind and emigrate to the Holy Land where God awaited them with open arms.

They, like tens of thousands of other North African Jews, fully believed in the Zionist idea of returning to their promised land and in the establishment of a new Jewish state, where they would be protected by God and lead a life of prosperity in the land of milk and honey. However, in reality, this was proven to be a failed idea which precipitated only incessant bloodshed; no safe haven for persecuted Jews around the world, and no sign of God's spirit hovering above the bleeding mountains of Jerusalem. It is true that the idea succeeded in establishing a Jewish state, but in practice, it is not and has never been a safe haven for the persecuted Jews. The Jewish state was born under war and lives by her sword to this day.

Before they married, my parents had only had one date. She was fifteen and he was eighteen. My father had encountered my mother on random occasions, usually when he had gone to consult my grandfather, a respected judge in the community, to ask him to mediate between him and his business partner. My mother had served him steaming mint tea with soft marzipan cookies. He would glance at her as she gently laid the items down on the intricately carved cedar side table, but she would modestly bow her head and quickly disappear into the kitchen. On one such occasion, when my grandfather began his task of mediation, my father suddenly interrupted him and asked for my mother's hand in marriage. My grandfather, who was by all accounts favourably impressed by my father due to both his good looks and his being a savvy businessman at such a young age, gave his consent. The date he suggested would give this ardent teenager adequate time to determine if he was sure of the choice he was making. My mother's opinion was not taken into account. In 1930's Morocco, women's opinions were of no importance. Their role was just to be a hardworking housewife. After all, a woman's brain was nothing but a feeble mass of cells that were incapable of developing far beyond their capacity at infancy, making them entirely dependent on their man for protection and provision.

A week later, my parents went on a date that was chaperoned by my aunt, who was four years older than my mother and thus trusted to supervise the young couple. Only a month later, there was a big wedding feast. The wine flowed like water and glittering platters were filled to the brim with the most sumptuous of Moroccan delicacies.

Over the coming years, my father, at the age of twenty-two, managed to establish a lucrative textile factory. This was in addition to the grocery business he already shared with a partner who had an annoying tendency to argue over minor issues, and worst of all, always disagree with whatever others suggested. This behaviour hindered my father, who was always coming up with creative ideas to expand the business. When my father boldly invested all his savings in the textile factory, he did it as a desperate move to get rid of his annoying partner and start his own independent business.

My parents were living a happy and luxurious life in Morocco, where they owned a thriving business and lived comfortably in a huge villa with servants and all amenities. But then they made a reckless decision that would haunt them for the rest of their lives.

On a cold February night, they had boarded a rented boat that would take them to Palestine, the holy land of the Jews, where they could find the God who had promised them safety in a place brimming with milk and honey. My grandfather, who had been an esteemed judge in Morocco and was well-connected to the King's court, took care of the paperwork and all that was needed for the journey. He then boarded the creaking boat along with my grandmother and their three children. In their innocence, they had all believed the Zionist emissaries, sent by the then Israeli Prime Minister David Ben-Gurion to convince them to follow God's commandment to settle the Holy Land, while promising that God would provide for them and protect them.

Their journey from Morocco was fraught with dangers, both from the stormy seas and from the authorities in Morocco, whose pride and honour were affronted every time a Jew applied to leave their country and emigrate to another. There were moments of fear caused by powerful spotlights from the shore that illuminated the darkness and exposed the boat and its passengers. Some were the spotlights of the Moroccan border guards, and subsequently from some of the other North African countries en route, who were happy to hand back to Morocco Jews who had dared to betray their country by leaving it. On my family's journey, after they had managed to pass the coasts of Algeria, Libya and Egypt without incident, and were approaching the eastern edge of the Mediterranean, from where they could already smell the fragrance of the Holy Land where God was awaiting them, they were attacked by a small boatload of piratical thugs. After a violent and sustained struggle, the pirates succeeded in robbing my family of the gold jewellery they had brought with them to start their first steps in the Promised Land. But God was not there to protect them as they believed, nor was He when they arrived in the Holy Land where they found themselves in a midst of an endless bloody war. And as if that weren't enough, they had to face poverty and humiliating shortages due to the damn war that swallowed the entire already-tight government budget. I was born about a year after they arrived in the land of milk and honey, and on the day I was born, my fate was sealed. I became part of the humiliating struggle throughout my childhood and youth.

My grandmother Aliya was never the same after arriving in the Promised Land. She was considered a princess, endowed with divine beauty and wealth who suddenly found herself facing harsh cultural and geographical changes that wreaked havoc on her tender soul. Although she never graduated from school and barely knew how to read and write, she had an amazing talent for designing expensive colourful carpets, which she managed to sell to wealthy homes throughout North Africa. However, as she settled in the Holy Land the light in her melting eyes began to fade and no laughter was heard from her anymore. Everyone had talked about her stunning beauty back in her young days, even though she would dismiss them with flushed cheeks. Her blue eyes sparkled like the ocean glinting on a sunny day, and her facial features were exquisitely balanced, with her jawline adding a touch of sophistication to her appearance.

As a child, I didn't have enough opportunities to enjoy her warm presence, her endearing smile and tireless generosity. She got old too quickly and hence her visits became very rare. But when she did, she always brought us fine French chocolate; only God knew where she had acquired it from during those hard days of recession. Sometimes she would also bring us the sweetest toffees filled with vanilla syrup, which we devoured with pleasure even though we noticed she had wrapped them in the same handkerchief she used to wipe her nose. When I was thirteen, she could not be present at my Bar Mitzvah, my big day, the day on which it was declared to the whole world that I was no longer a child. By that time, she was enduring great pain. However, she didn't complain nor whine like other women who tended to complain in a petulant and childish way. Certainly not like her whinging neighbour Aliza, who could not let a day pass by without finding something to grumble about. I was once witness to a short conversation between Aliza and her husband in which she asked him in a self-pitying tone:

'Is it that you don't love me anymore, my darling husband? You never say anything nice to me like you did when you were courting me.' 'I love you; I love you,' replied her husband, as if trying to shoo away a troublesome fly, 'but now please just shut up and let me drink my beer in peace.'

When I reached the age of twenty-one, my grandmother was by this time already permanently confined to her bed. Next to her were dozens of different untouched medicines that looked like they were begging to be used.

'Why don't you take your medicine grandma?' I asked, worried.

'My healing will only come from God, not from these wretched chemicals,' she murmured in a weak voice, closing her blue eyes that had once shone and shaken up the hearts of all the men of Morocco. Then she gazed fixedly at the ceiling, and while crossing her hands tightly over her belly, muttered the short prayers she pulled up from her memory. Through her, I saw the unfairness of getting old. The most unjust thing in life is how it ends, if you don't get killed in a freak accident pretty young. Old age is humiliating and full of suffering, the constant reflection on memories is painful and movements are slow. By the time the elderly have finished chewing their main course with the few teeth left in their mouth, the others have already finished their dessert. Besides, old people tend to talk a lot and repeat everything they say at least twice. It drove me nuts, people repeating themselves.

My grandfather, David, was a handsome, charismatic man, an esteemed judge back in Morocco. His confidence and self-assurance were evident in the way he carried himself, making him stand out in any room and leaving a lasting impression on everyone he encountered. His confidence never overshadowed his kindness; instead, they complemented each other. He treated others with respect and consideration, making his attractiveness go far beyond just his looks. He was a born leader. He always put himself forward to mediate between quarrelling couples, in order to make peace between them and prevent divorce at all costs. In the Jewish community that he led, people respected him and tended to heed his advice.

When he landed in the young Jewish country, he was imbued with Zionism and a belief in returning to the land where King Solomon had lived and where God's spirit hovered, caressing and comforting and protecting every Jew in it. However, when he found himself facing the harsh reality of poverty and constant war, he had to bite his lip. The Zionist dream was far from his reach, and God, the mighty saviour, was nowhere to be seen. Instead of working at the academy of law, or at least as an administrative clerk at the local court, he was sent to work in agriculture, a demanding job that his body was not built for. When he sought to protest this, the astonishing reality became clear to him that office jobs, not to mention those in academia, were all given to those from Europe who arrived many years before him. Only after a while did he realise that he had become enmeshed in a type of discrimination based on genetic background, discovering that North African Jews were considered primitive by the Europeans, who by then were controlling most of the establishments in the young Jewish state. After biting on his lip for too long, he felt compelled to look for other ways to generate income. One of them was to mediate in disputes for small sums. One of his regular customers was a gentleman named Betito, who had an annoying tendency to fall out with almost everyone in Netivot. Mr Betito, a less than shrewd amateur merchant, was selling clothes he imported from Turkey. To increase his profits, he would attach a sticker to them stating they were imported from Paris. This deception, in addition to his unpleasant nature, was the main cause of his endless quarrels with people. From his appearance, he seemed to suffer from feelings of inferiority and didn't really like himself much. People who don't like themselves, have a tendency to quarrel with others. Anyway, due to his many arguments with people in the town, he would come to my grandfather on a regular basis to seek his advice.

One evening, he had a bitter argument with my grandfather's neighbour Aliza. A fierce argument that led to violence. Betito had sold Aliza two of his 'expensive Parisian dresses'. After discovering the fraud, the irate Aliza demanded her money back. Mr Betito refused and told her that he had already spent the money. Aliza, accompanied by her husband Hanania, plus two more friends, didn't believe him. This resulted in a verbal battle accompanied by colourful language and juicy curses, until the inevitable explosion when they all started hitting each other in crazed blindness.

Chapter 12

My best friend's death on the battlefield

When I joined a commando unit, I thought I would be able to face the enemy and take revenge, but I did not anticipate the pain of losing my best friend. I believed that commandos were invincible superheroes.

Zvi was the best friend I ever had throughout my entire life, to whom I could divulge my deepest secrets, as well as laughs and gossip. Not only did we find similar character traits in common between us, but even our dates of birth were remarkably close. He was born on 16 May, 1957, and I was born on 18 May, 1957.

Zvi was a member of my company with whom I shared the tent we slept in during training sessions, and with whom I shared my fears before and after every operation, battle or dangerous raid. Although we were punished many times for mischievous or impudent behaviour, we never ceased to continue with it simply because we knew that our commanders saw us as excellent, talented, brave, and most of all, miraculously disciplined soldiers in battlefield operations.

Neither of us liked convention. We laughed at those who performed each everyday task according to all the rules. We considered rules and norms as a recommendation only. However, at the same time, in an emergency, during battle, in the moment of truth, we both proved great combat ability and extraordinary discipline.

Zvi was only twenty when he was hit in the head by a single bullet fired by a terrorist during a raid in southern Lebanon, and died after twenty-three days fighting for his life.

In 1977, as terrorism towards Israeli civilians inflicted by the PLO terror organisation from southern Lebanon intensified, the Israeli Cabinet decided to permanently eradicate the terrorist cells throughout

Lebanon. Our unit was sent to carry out one of the missions, in this instance the destruction of three bunkers in which terrorists were hiding, as well as a large ammunition depot, situated 500 metres away from the bunkers.

The target: a town called Bint Jbeil, located about four kilometres north of the Israeli border and near the Israeli agricultural settlement of Moshav Avivim. The town was chosen for this attack because it was a significant firing base of the PLO, and according to intelligence reports, several PLO headquarters were concentrated there due to the 'Wild West' atmosphere in southern Lebanon at that time. The outbreak of the civil war in Lebanon in 1975 created chaos in most parts of the country and allowed the establishment of Palestinian terrorist organizations in southern Lebanon. The PLO was the most powerful and well-equipped force, numbering thousands of terrorists. Many of the recruits who joined it were not only from among the Palestinians themselves but also from other countries and were handsomely paid by the PLO for their service.

The PLO enjoyed unlimited support from Syria and Iran and this instilled in them a sense of superiority not only in their war against Israel, but also against the Lebanese Christians who, with regard to the Palestinians' conflict with Israel, were considered too moderate by not showing any interest in their jihadi war against the Jews.

Our force was divided into two teams: one would attack the three bunkers from the southern ridges of Bint Jbeil, and the other would destroy the nearby weapons depot. We all believed this was going to be a short-lasting action, the type of which we had performed many times before, and that we would soon be back at base and playing cards. Nevertheless, we prepared for the mission seriously.

But the supposedly 'short action' threw up a nasty surprise. After entering Lebanon and when we were only one kilometre away from the target, we ran into a sophisticated ambush. We found ourselves facing massive fire from machine guns, rifles, and hand grenades.

The battle was ferocious. We fought like lions and were determined to eliminate the terrorists in the ambush no matter what the cost in lives would be, so we could quickly reach the target and accomplish the mission we had been sent for in Bint Jbeil.

My reconnaissance squad, which included Zvi, saw an opportunity to set an example for the eight rookie warriors who were with us. We started advancing discharging massive fire towards the small hill from which the shooting was coming at as. Our commander leading the onslaught found himself face to face with one of the PLO terrorists who suddenly came out from behind the hill and was shooting as he ran towards us. Fortunately, the terrorist could not fire accurately, perhaps through fear, or from panic. Either way, our commander was able to eliminate him with a short round of fire.

We divided into several squads and continued the onslaught on the hill, purging it and all who were hiding behind it. Remarkably, we managed to eliminate all the terrorists in the ambush without any casualties among our forces. However, the action was over yet. During our march onwards to Bint Jbeil, we had to face yet another nasty surprise. It turned out that there was a second ambush lying in wait, as the PLO plan had been to mislead us into feeling confident that we only had one ambush to deal with. More terrorists started firing and throwing hand grenades at us. Even though we were very experienced and trained for the possibility of encountering an ambush and eliminating it quickly and successfully, this time we were caught by complete surprise. This was a strange occurrence, as for every operation we went on, we would always receive the most accurate and reliable intelligence. This time, however, the intelligence we had did not indicate the presence of any ambushes, let alone two. Only after the post-battle debriefing would it become clear that the two ambushes had been set up just minutes before our force arrived. Anyway, despite this unforeseen situation, we fought on.

The problem with this second ambush was the doubling in size of the terrorists' forces fortified behind two hills, not just one hill as in the earlier ambush. Instinctively, without being instructed to do so by our commander, we all split up into several squads and fired as fiercely as we could within our limits of vision. We progressed slowly, crouching down and walking towards the hills with our backs hunched, constantly firing as we proceeded. Within a few minutes we had managed to eliminate some of the terrorists whom we could spot as they raised their heads over the hills to improve their firing. Others of the terrorists got up and fled northwards, heading towards Bint Jbeil.

But the battle was not coming to an end. Although we managed to eliminate some of the enemy, and forced others to flee, there were still at least twenty more terrorists behind those hills heavily firing at us. Suddenly, they changed tactics and started firing shoulder missiles at us. It was difficult for us to run for cover because we were vigorously engaged in the onslaught. In addition to the use of shoulder missiles that sowed fear in us, the amount of gunfire from the terrorists' Kalashnikovs sprayed the entire area and there was not a single inch of ground that was not sprayed with fire. There was a feeling of suffocation and loss of hope amongst us. Five of our fighters fell to the ground covered in blood, and we could not determine if they were killed or wounded. They made no sound or cries of pain, but knowing the nature of our warriors, one can be sure that even if they had been wounded, they would not make any cries of pain. They would remain quiet and in pain as they bled until we had completed the onslaught.

One of them lying there was my best friend, Zvi. I had a hard time watching him bleeding profusely. But there was no time to express my feelings or make room in my heart for any emotion. All I had to focus on at that moment was to keep up the firing on this disturbing and nasty ambush that had disrupted our entire operation plan for the Bint Jbeil bunkers.

As we continued firing at the terrorists, we heard a surprising and sudden order to retreat.

The chief commander of the operation, who was part of the front command squad monitoring the operation back across the border in Moshav Avivim, had sent an order to our commander in the field to retreat to the Israeli border. Only later did we realize that the chief commander had received hot information about additional forces of terrorists who were flocking to the battlefield.

Our field commander ordered us to lie on the ground and find shelter among the rocks, while radioing the operation commander back at Moshav Avivim, asking his permission to remain in the But in the army, you do not express any disagreement with the commander, especially during a battle. The order to retreat must be immediately obeyed.

A strange feeling swept over us. Confusion and inability to digest the order to retreat and abandon our wounded soldiers in this blazing enemy territory and at the mercy of the terrorists. We felt we were being asked to betray the principal value on which we had grown up on not only as solders, but also as teenagers who were exposed to heroic war stories.

'Do those in the front command squad know something that we fighters don't?' we asked ourselves, but we couldn't think of any possible answer to this question.

The fire intensified. The primary concern was being hit by the missiles launched at us. We looked towards our friends lying on the ground, covered in their blood. We couldn't bear the notion of abandoning our wounded comrades in the field.

It was clear to all of us that every second counted. Then, despite the order to retreat, we made the decision to take action. Supported by our other fighters, who managed to silence the terrorists' fire for a few seconds, we raced towards our fallen friends and managed to drag them as far away from the fire zone as we could.

While running back towards the Israeli border, our commander panted to us that a special unit was already on its way to rescue us. Indeed, within minutes, we heard a sound of a helicopter above us. The pilot did not need us to direct him as we normally would do. He found us right away, and the special unit mounted a dangerous rescue and evacuation operation from the helicopter, carried out under constant enemy fire.

When we arrived back at our base, none of us wanted to talk. We were all feeling low, bitter and frustrated. Aside from the obligation to speak up during the debriefing, we were all enveloped in silence throughout the rest of that day. We were hungry, but we had no appetite for food. Two of our friends were dead, and another three were injured, one of them very badly. My friend Zvi.

After we had returned to base, during the debriefing, it became clear what had prompted the commander-in-chief to order us to retreat and even abandon our wounded. He had been alarmed about the number of terrorists that were on their way to the battlefield, and that his decision to order us to retreat was not because of our operational inability to win the battle, but rather a political one. He simply wanted to prevent the incident from flaring up into a long and bloody war.

While in a coma, Zvi fought with the same intensity as he had shown in dozens of daring and dangerous operations. He was bold and courageous and I had no doubt that inside him, he was determined to defeat the slow death that was gnawing at him on that hospital bed. He was a young lion who did not expect to die on a bed with crisp white cotton sheets. He had envisaged his death would come in front of nests of guns or tanks, on burning earth, with his body sweating and tense, not with his body loose, motionless, sterile and dependent on all the instruments that were connected to him. I spent forty-five hours sitting beside his hospital bed, refusing to lose hope and whispering words of encouragement into his ear, totally believing that he could hear me. And despite being a confirmed atheist, I read a few verses of prayer from the little book his mother had placed by his head. I prayed to Moses, to Mohammed, to Jesus, to the Buddha, and to anyone who could help. My combatant's instinct was to save him, to storm, to shoot forward at those who had fired at him, but I felt helpless and unable to do anything to bring him to life again.

I had suggested to Zvi's family that they go home, have some much-needed rest, and let me stay the night by his side. Throughout the night I held onto his hand, squeezing it with a short, steady pressure in the hope of a response from him, a sign of awareness that he was feeling my touch, but no sign was given by any part of his motionless body. After more than ten hours of trying, my eyes were no longer functioning. They drooped downwards and I fell asleep on the hard armchair.

When I woke up after about an hour and heard the voices of the medical staff, I found that Zvi was dead. He had died while I was sleeping, as if he wanted to spare me pain. As if he did not want me to witness his last breaths.

The faces of the medical staff who tried with such devotion to bring him back did not express any hope, knowing that his chances of recovering, or at least opening his eyes, were slim.

I looked at Zvi one last time before they covered his face with the white sheet. He was so peaceful. Still so handsome, the same good-looking wild young man who never hesitated to storm and lead. The same daring warrior who always ran fearlessly into danger was now lying before me motionless. The tough, but yet at the same time hilariously funny, young fighter who was always the first to volunteer for any dangerous mission. He saw the task of eliminating terrorism as the most supreme and sacred task during his combat service, and strove to kill as many terrorists as possible. However, at the same time, he was cautious of shooting if we encountered civilians.

Despite his zeal and his almost uncompromising professional fighting ability, Zvi had always mocked and condemned wars and leaders of countries that go into any war that was not a purely defensive one. The irony of my friend Zvi was that he hated war but loved to take part in it.

I did not want to believe he was dead. I wanted to believe that he was just playing a joke on me. Soon he would open his eyes, wink his left one, burst into his infectious laugh, and say, 'Hey! It worked on you.' After all, he had done this so many times during difficult exercises when he flopped to the ground pretending to have been accidentally shot by one of us. And it was not only during exercises that Zvi would wind us up. He once did this during a real battle, while we were pursuing

My first love Sima Malul

As a child in a shelter during the 1967 war

Inside the shelter in 1967

The gang. Moshiko, Me, Little Sonny, Tall Asher, Manny

In my class at school

The *souk*, our market

My little town Netivot

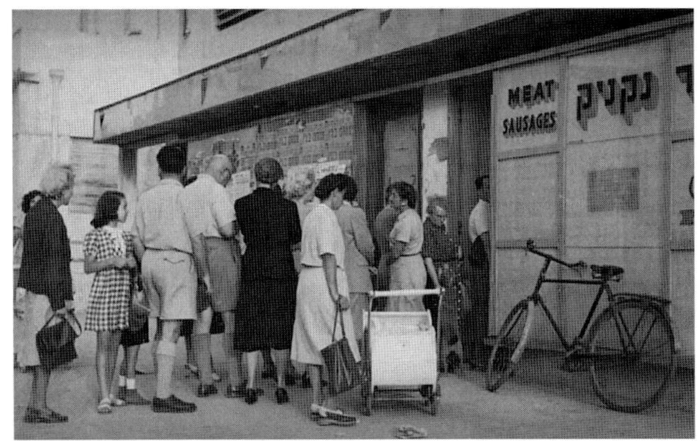

Queueing for meat, 1965

The ice seller, 1962

The cinema, 1970

The milkman, 1960

Shops of Netivot: stationery, Revivo's store, Biton's barber shop and the *souk*

Victor Ben-Atar (standing)

Me 10 years old, 1967

Age 16 happy after winning a Hifi
set in a trivia competition, 1973

During the battle in Ein al-Hilweh refugee camp, 1982 Lebanon War

On the way towards the coast of Beirut, 1982

On a break during the eighty-mile trek for completion of my six-month training course, 1975

Aged eighteen, during my first three months of training, 1975

After completing my twelve-month training, 1976

After completion of the six-month training course, 1975

Completion of the arduous six month training course to determine continuation in the Golani Brigade. (Author inset on the right)

Trenches for hiding behind our school

The wealthy people of Tel Aviv

Our school in Netivot

In the shelter

a wanted terrorist through the streets of Gaza towards the Jabaliya refugee camp. Zvi had spotted a couple of young Palestinians throwing stones at us from the roof above a shop, while we were focused on not losing sight of the wanted terrorist. As we were all running down the narrow alleys of the crumbling refugee camp, he keeled over on the ground, groaning and clutching his chest. When the paramedic approached him, he jumped to his feet and burst out laughing, saying 'I got you.'

When I tackled him about it, hinting that we might not help him if one day he would really be injured, he gave me a mischievous smile and said, 'This is my way of dealing with the fear.'

Whoever fought on the battlefield and yet claims he was not terrified during a battle is lying.

The dryness in the mouth, the sweat all over the body even in very cold winter weather, the white haze over the eyes, and the accelerated heartbeat.

We were all scared, but the practice was not to show it outwardly. We were wrapped in an invisible shell of armour that embedded in our being the feeling that we were tough commando fighters and that showing weakness or fear did not exist in our character. Zvi had found his own solution, and it was one that was not written in the textbooks from which we had learned the fighting methods of the best army in the world. He probably had realised this long before any of us.

My dead friend was special. A young man with rare character traits that the adults had not understood when he was a child, and the commanders did not understand when he was a soldier. That's why he and I bonded. We found ourselves very similar in our character and qualities, and at the same time, looked unusual in the eyes of others. We each felt we had found our soul mate.

The love between us was immense. I once joked that it was a shame he was not a girl so I could marry him. Surprisingly, he answered me the same way. I once even gave up a twenty-four-hour vacation I was planning to spend with my girlfriend Talia, just to be with Zvi at one of his family events. His parents always welcomed and hosted me in their home as if I were their second son.

He and I had been party to so many shared experiences during our days of training together. As well as wild evenings, Zvi and I had shared the contents of our food parcels received from home, and even our supply of ammunition. We were peas from the same pod; wild and rebellious, out-of-the-box thinkers and willing to break the rules. And there were many we broke. There were times we would 'avail ourselves' of (in actual fact steal) a military jeep and crazily take off towards the city of Tiberius and its lively beachside nightlife, conveniently located not far from our base on the Golan Heights. There we would hit the most popular nightclub and would swagger around proudly wearing our combat uniform.

As we sped towards Tiberius with our hormones raging, we felt invincible, but at the same time we could not help feeling a little fearful of the trouble that could await us if we had been caught stealing a military jeep, leaving the base without permission and above all, abandoning our rifles, which we had left behind in our barracks carefully hidden under our mattresses. For this last matter alone, we could face a severe term of imprisonment, as a combat soldier must never let his weapon out of his sight. The phrase instilled into us was, 'You can leave your wife and your mother, but you must never leave your weapon.'

The unit's cedar tree emblem on our sleeve would not only guarantee free entry to the nightclub and a handsome discount on drinks, but we would also be surrounded by a bevy of admiring local girls. It wasn't due to our look as Zvi and I happened to be two rather good-looking and confident young men, but rather because of the locals' admiration. Due to the ongoing terrorism in 1975-1978 against Israel's northern settlements, especially Tiberias and Kiryat Shmona, an atmosphere of appreciation and admiration arose among the locals towards Israeli commando soldiers who served in the area. We were also plied with free meals or drinks in the cafés and restaurants of the area as we were seen as heroes by the community.

As we entered the club, Abba's song 'Ring Ring' was playing, and we headed straight to the dance floor. Even the DJ left his booth to dance wildly around the floor with us, and we were soon surrounded by locals, some of whom went to the bar and got us cold beers. It was a heady atmosphere, with the mixed odours of beer, sweat and cheap perfume and the taste of lipstick as the two girls threw themselves upon us throughout the night.

My best friend Zvi, who was funny, naughty, extremely brave, smart and wild, was dead, but in my heart he would always be alive.

Chapter 13

Saving the life of the enemy

When I joined a commando unit to avenge those who had ruined my childhood, I never dreamed that I would find myself in scenarios when, instead of killing them and exacting my revenge, I would actually save them from certain death.

Saving the life of an enemy under fire is a complex ethical and moral dilemma. It is a challenging situation that requires careful consideration of the circumstances and a commitment to upholding the laws and principles of warfare. Someone deciding to render aid to an enemy under fire must also consider the rescuers and their unit's safety. Attempting to save an enemy's life can put one's own life and the lives of their comrades at risk.

International humanitarian law, as outlined in the Geneva Conventions, requires the humane treatment of wounded or sick enemy combatants. It is generally considered a war crime to intentionally kill or neglect a wounded enemy soldier who poses no threat. The decision to save the life of an enemy under fire can vary widely depending on various factors, individual values, rules of engagement, and the specific circumstances of the situation. However, there are situations during battles when these rules of engagement become blurred, particularly in close-quarters combat. For instance, when we approached an enemy soldier who wished to surrender by giving a hand signal, he tossed a grenade at us, critically injuring one of our team. This gave rise to a dilemma. On the one hand, you want to spare the life of a human being despite him being an enemy, but on the other, you are putting yourself and the other fighters in your team at risk.

As a soldier, you want to act according to the conventions of war, and as a human being, you wish to act according to an unwritten convention, the moral duty to save a human life regardless of his identity. In our eyes, saving his life would allow us to accomplish two objectives: first, we would treat his wound in accordance with the rules of war, and second, we would yield valuable intelligence from him. However, this injured opponent genuinely committed treason by launching the grenade at us. At the conclusion of the combat, our firing response resulted in the death of this opponent, who had a chance to survive but he spoiled it by his own hands.

The following is an instance where the injured adversary I saved raised bewilderment and a silent war between my conscience and my intense desire for revenge. After all, I had joined the commando unit mainly to take revenge on the enemy who ruined my, and dozens of other children's, childhoods. In this rare occurrence that doesn't occur often in combat, I had the upper hand and was legally allowed to kill, but I chose not to instigate the rule that states you have the right to kill anyone who comes to kill you. In addition to trying to shoot me during the gunfire exchange when we first came into contact, he also continued firing at me when I yelled at him in Arabic to lie down. Despite the opportunity I provided him, he made it plain that he intended to shoot me by aiming his weapon in my direction rather than raising his hands and surrendering.

In the hot summer of 1981, my company was assigned a mission to clear a ravine near Sidon, 30 km south of Beirut, from a group of terrorists who were continuously firing at us. I was a reservist; it was just two years after I had completed my three years of mandatory service. (The term 'reservist' is given to those who have completed three compulsory army service, after which they must continue to serve once or twice a year for a period of two or four weeks).

The exchange of fire was intense, as the terrorists were hiding in small caves and niches in the rock and it was difficult for us to accurately identify the source of the shooting. We had to use the M72 LAW, a portable one-shot 66mm anti-tank missile, something we would normally only use for attacking sturdy buildings or tanks or armoured vehicles. But we had no choice. The stubbornness of the terrorists, despite the many losses among them, and their continued firing at us from the ravine, had almost exhausted us. But we were equally stubborn. We knew that these terrorists were planning to establish themselves along the entire ravine, which was an important strategic point in southern Lebanon. We were also aware of the cruel fact that these terrorists used refugees from the Ein al-Hilweh camp as human shields, either in exchange for payments or through threatening to harm them. Our force commander called in combat helicopters to bomb the terrorists dispersed around the ravine, but as we waited for the helicopters and continued firing towards the ravine, some of the terrorists emerged from the top of the ravine and began running away northwards. Two of them lay on the ground and fired missiles towards us, serving as a covering force for their fleeing comrades. The term covering force can refer to soldiers, tanks, artillery, or jets who fire on the enemy to protect friendly troops when they are advancing, retreating, or operating on the battlefield. A short battle ensued in which we fired at the two with precise waist-height shots from the M72 LAW weapons. Only later during the debriefing did it become clear to me that the two had not been neutralized by me or my four assault comrades, but by our unit's snipers who were scattered around the sides of the assault area.

The mission to purge the ravine was nearly completed, even though we had not been able to eliminate all the terrorists. Our consolation was that we had at least taken over the ravine and were now in a position to completely eradicate the terrorists and their activity from it.

We began to make our way down into the ravine while firing single bullets to deter any remaining terrorists. We knew we had to carefully scan every inch and clear the area of weapons and terrorists, including collecting the bodies and treating any wounded we found. As we made our way down, we heard a new command on the radio. It turned out that another force of ours, who happened to be on a separate mission on the northern side of the ravine, had encountered and fired at the terrorists who fell into their hands as they fled over the top of the ravine. The terrorists in their stupidity then turned round and headed back into the direction of the ravine as they fled from our force to its north. We ran towards the returning group of terrorists and started firing.

The party began.

Masses of smoke and the overpowering smell of burning ash. The noise was so deafening from the shooting coming from all sides that we could not hear the orders of our commander. The terrorists, at last, realized they were trapped and there was nowhere for them to go. To this day when I remember it, I still wonder why they had not chosen earlier to simply lie down and surrender. After all, they must by then have read the battle and realized that they had no chance of surviving it. From this encounter, I began to be familiar with the fanatical views of the terrorists, and the way they were trained and brainwashed. These principles were introduced to the world when the phenomenon of suicide bombers began.

Suddenly, there was a huge explosion. The sky was filled with a huge sheet of white light, which shrouded everything. Small rocks that had flown up into the air from the force of the explosion began to slowly fall from the sky. There was a deathly silence. The shooting stopped abruptly. The terrorists thought we had all been killed and we thought they too were all dead. None of us could work out what had caused the horrific explosion. Only in the post-battle briefing did we find out that it was the blast of a large explosive device that had been hidden by the terrorists in the ravine. Apparently, one of the terrorists had still been hiding inside one of the caves down in the ravine. He emerged and activated the explosives to make his mark as a suicide bomber.

Lying flat on the rocky ground, I patted my body several times to check if I was alive, then slowly raised my head to see what was going on. I could not see anything clearly. Nor could I distinguish which of the wounded and dead lying around were from our forces and which were the enemy. I got to my feet, and when I realized that I was not injured, I ran to the wounded man who was closest to me, lifted him onto my back, and started running eastward, towards the main road, away from the brutal scene of carnage. During my heavily-weighted run, I heard the noise of shots and the explosions of grenades behind me. I did not look back, or think about lying on the ground to take cover for myself and for the bleeding man I was carrying. My one thought was to save us both from this horrific killing field. I had neither the time nor wherewithal to think about the identity of the wounded man while the echoes of explosions and shots were following me so closely. One thing I was aware of, and remember to this day, was the drops of the wounded man's blood on my neck. They were warm.

The fire behind me intensified. It turned out that more terrorists, equipped with shoulder-fired missiles and numerous hand grenades, had arrived in the combat area and began firing at us frantically. The shooting at us from the terrorists was almost catastrophic, as the terrorists took advantage of the shock we were in from the explosion, which had caused a temporary debilitating confusion among our forces. Despite the fact that the shooting at us was forceful and continuous, I kept on running with the wounded man on my back. I expected at any second to be hit by a bullet. The belief that the injured person on my back had in me to take him to a safe location, away from this blazing area so he could receive treatment, kept me going and injected the energy I needed to continue with all my might towards the main road. I was hoping there would be a military truck by the main road to transfer him to the closest hospital. But the shots behind me intensified. I started losing hope. My vision was hazy from the beads of perspiration falling from my forehead. I didn't believe in any god, so I didn't have anyone to pray to. Additionally, I had no one to turn to for assistance because everyone was occupied with retaliating against the terrorists' relentless shooting. I was alone. A warrior on the run. Panting heavily and perspiring profusely, not knowing who I was carrying on my back.

After about 700 metres, when I realized I was out of range of the fire, I stopped. I laid the man on the ground facing upwards, took a flask of water from my combat vest, splashed his mouth and face, and tried to communicate with him to see if he was alive. To my concern, he did not respond. After a few minutes, his eyes flickered open and he whispered in Arabic '*Shukran*' (thank you).

I jumped to my feet and aimed my weapon at him.

The shock that this man was in fact my enemy almost caused me to have a heart attack. At that moment, I realised that I was saving the life of an enemy soldier who only minutes earlier had been trying to kill me. It also dawned on me that I had put all this physical effort into saving an enemy soldier whom I doubt would have done the same for me. Instead of risking my life for him, I could have quickly found myself some shelter and avoided being hindered by him in my escaping the fire. This is in addition to the effort involved in carrying him on my back while running, something that slowed my pace to the point where my life was in danger.

He did not try to get up, but looked at me imploringly and said in Arabic, 'Please have mercy on me in the name of Allah. Please, in the name of Allah.'

'Why would I feel sorry for you?' I asked him. 'You just tried to kill me.'

'I have a two-month-old daughter. I got married just a year ago. Please. I beg of you.'

'Why didn't you think about your baby before coming here?' I sniggered.

'I desperately needed money and what they paid me is high.'

'So, you're here for the money?'

'Yes. I don't care about Lebanon. I don't even live in Lebanon.'

'Where are you from?' I asked.

'I'm from Gaza.'

Now I was astonished. I paused for a moment, bent down towards him, and stared into his eyes.

'Whereabouts in Gaza do you live?' I asked, wanting to check if he was lying. I knew the whole Gaza Strip like the back of my hand.

'Beit Hanoun,' he said quietly sighing.

Straight away I believed him. Something in his face and voice indicated he was telling the truth.

Beit Hanoun was a well-known refugee camp in Gaza. But it was not only utilized to lodge destitute refugees. Additionally, it served as a base for extremely vicious terrorists who would use whatever means necessary to kill Jews who resided nearby, just two-three kilometres away. I had visited this camp on numerous occasions, both as a soldier and as a journalist, to speak with locals about the Israeli-Palestinian conflict.

I continued to dab him with water, cleaning his injury as well as I could, but I could not clear the confusion in my head. Should I stop attending to him and shoot him? What if the perpetrators of the terror that engulfed my boyhood just a few years ago were this terrorist's ancestors? He does, after all, stand for the terrorist groups that have attacked and continue to attack Israelis. 'Why don't I shoot him right now and end this rant?' I murmured. The possibility that this person would join the terrorist group again when he recovered and murder some of my people was too disturbing for me to ignore. But then, the resounding voice of conscience emerged and threatened to haunt me for the rest of my life for killing an unarmed, wounded person.

I was facing a serious dilemma.

Suddenly there was the noise of yet another huge explosion, followed by another and another. I lay down on the ground but knew I had to get myself away, as I was within range of the fire.

I noticed a hill about 300 metres to the east, which would be a safe direction to head in, due to the presence of Israeli forces there. I got up, and before I could start running, the man on the ground pulled me by my trousers and begged me to take him with me.

'Please don't let me die here, please,' he cried in Arabic.

I just did not know what to do.

The stress and tension I was experiencing were foreign to me. I had been through many dangerous situations, during some of which I foresaw certain death, however, this time it was different. This time another factor was involved. The resounding conscience that relentlessly weighed on me. I never knew that pangs of conscience could be so heavy and affect one's actions until I experienced it firsthand that day on the battlefield.

I felt helpless, unable to control and manage my thoughts and decisions. I was sweating profusely and the noise of the explosions was deafening. There was no one around me I could talk to. My vision began to blur again. Years later, on a visit to my local clinic due to a persistent headache, the doctor explained to me that there was a link between stress and vision, which can cause a temporary impairment in one's ability to see clearly and distinctly.

The wounded terrorist kept begging me not to leave him there. My thoughts were vague, and in the background were the echoes of the explosions. The noise of war. The smell of war. I had to make a rapid decision whether to run towards the hill where I knew there would be shelter, or stay with the wounded terrorist and take care of him until our rescue forces arrived. I assumed they were probably already on their way to the burning area, after hearing on the radio about the battle in the ravine and the continuing explosions. To take the latter option, I would have to use greater-than-usual mental powers to erase from my mind the identity of the wounded person lying beside me. I owed it to my conscience, to the values I was educated in. But yet, I felt this was beyond my abilities. Pictures of my horrific childhood kept emerging from the depths of my memory. Gloomy scenes of funerals and wounded and crying mothers tore me apart. Memory is an important tool but it also tortures you. But then, I hit on a solution. Imagination.

I began to imagine myself as a doctor who, on the day he qualified, swore that he would treat any person, regardless of his race, beliefs, or heritage. When that imaginary scenario did not help, I tried to imagine myself injured in Gaza and that some of the locals had rushed to help me. I based this on a real event we had encountered during a patrol in Gaza. We were attacked by a hand grenade that was thrown at us by a terrorist who then fled the scene. The locals immediately helped us and even repelled other locals who tried to lynch us.

But then I found myself wrestling with other thoughts. How could I think about saving someone else, when I could hardly save myself in this inferno? What about the burden of having to carry him on my back? He was at least 70kg in weight. It would undoubtedly hinder my running. After all, this wasn't a member of my platoon, whom I would not be hesitant to save from a burning building. The explosions continued unabated, and with each second that passed, they also became closer. This was the craziest situation I had ever encountered and remained so during all my long years of service filled with dangerous situations.

Then something occurred that put an end to all my hesitation and concerns as well as the tense battle between my wailing conscience and myself. Something unconnected to the horrifying bombings. It was a fire that started to move quickly in our direction and that appeared to have been caused by the intense shelling igniting a field of thorn bushes.

At that moment, human instinct prevailed. The same instinct that is inherent in us all from the day we are born; a person's or an animal's natural desire to flee a burning place. In this instance, however, there was another factor, a wounded helpless human who desperately needed help to move his body. This caused another instinct to emerge. The human instinct to save a person or an animal from a burning place.

I picked up the bleeding man, the same enemy who had been trying to kill me, placed him over my right shoulder as we had practised, and, with his arms and legs dangling in front and behind me, I started running wildly eastwards towards the hill and the main road, away from the fire.

The correct way of carrying an injured person is based on a fundamental law of physics. The carrier must stabilize the injured person's body while maintaining a precise balance whereby the limp body is lifted over the carrier's shoulder with exactly half the body behind and the other half in front. The injured person's crotch should therefore be positioned on the carrier's shoulder. This balance makes carrying the person much easier and even reduces the weight being carried. The wonders of physics.

The hill was quite a distance so it took me a while to get there. During my run, with the echoes of the explosions in the background, my convoluted thoughts suddenly came back, as if my mind was determined to make the rescue task even more difficult for me.

'Why should I rescue him under fire and risk my own life to save him?' I was thinking to myself, while panting and slowly being drenched in gallons of sweat. 'Would he have done the same for me? Why don't I just dump him in the field? This man tried to kill me,' I scolded myself. And what about the vengeance I sought when I enlisted in the army? After all, I had fantasized about coming face to face with the adversary who had destroyed my youth at close range, where I could look straight into his eyes and shoot him, all the while beaming with a triumphant smile.

But then I had a baby-related thought about him. 'What sin had she committed that should deny her the right to know her father?' I chided myself. Suddenly, I was able to visualize the heavy price children pay in times of war. The term 'children in war' suddenly took on a realistic meaning. Amid the inferno and confusion, I could see a tangible example of the price children pay for the wars and conflicts of the adults.

'Madness!' I screamed while running. 'How crazy is war! How irrational!' I was screaming loudly so as not to break down. I shouted nonsense; meaningless, illogical sentences, just to keep up my physical, but mainly, my mental strength.

After about ten minutes that felt like an eternity, I arrived heavily panting and sweating at the main road where Israeli forces were positioned waiting to enter the city of Sidon. I was sure there would be a medical team amongst them, or at least a paramedic. I laid the wounded man down on his back and told him in Arabic that he would be fine, and that Israeli soldiers would take care of him. He nodded and again whispered, '*Shukran.*'

I looked at his face and asked him his name.

'My name is Azem Salim… I'm from Beit Hanoun… Gaza,' he whispered.

After a few seconds of silence, he grabbed my hand in an anxious way, 'Will your friends treat me the same way you did?' he asked.

I smiled and placed my hand on his shoulder. 'You can be sure that from here you will be fine, we are the Israeli army.'

I left him and went to find the commander to report a wounded man, but when I got there, I realized that this force was not just waiting there to enter the battle happening in Sidon. It was also a medical concentration point where wounded soldiers were brought for initial treatment and triage, and then evacuation by helicopter to Haifa's Rambam Hospital in Israel.

I felt relieved. I approached the officer in charge, who was a doctor by profession, and drew his attention to the wounded man I had brought. He approached him immediately, and after a quick check, he determined that his condition was not particularly serious, and instructed one of the paramedics to treat him.

While trying to decide whether to stay, or return to my company and the battle going on in the ravine area, I noticed a helicopter with its doors wide open. It looked like the pilot was waiting for permission to take off. I got closer, and then I saw three seriously injured soldiers lying on the helicopter floor. One of them was undergoing an emergency operation performed by another doctor. Also standing nearby was the driver of one of the armoured vehicles who had delivered the injured soldiers. He explained to me that it was necessary to perform this urgent operation to stabilize the man's condition before he was flown for further treatment at Rambam Hospital.

Out of curiosity, I approached the helicopter's open doors to take a closer look at the surgery being performed. The image that appeared before my eyes was terrifying. The seriously injured soldier being operated on was my own friend from my company. A very close friend with whom I had started my service in the unit. A friend with whom I had shared a tent during our training period in the desert sands of Sinai and up on the Golan Heights.

I was speechless. After all, I had been through in the battle by the ravine, followed by the crazy run with a wounded enemy over my shoulder, and now watching my friend dying in front of my eyes, I felt I was about to lose consciousness. I felt a pinch in my heart. I no longer had the strength to bear sorrow or pain. I was physically and mentally exhausted. I looked painfully at my friend who was motionless, covered in tubes and various means of resuscitation.

After spending two months in the hospital, he miraculously made a full recovery. He was then informed that if the doctor's field surgery hadn't been successful, he would not have made it to the hospital alive. Four months later, he was already able to get on his feet and walk. It was a happy moment not only for me as a close friend but for his mother too as he was her only son. His mother had lost her husband in a tragic car accident and had refused to remarry saying she did not have the emotional capacity to replace her first love.

It was only after the emergency surgery on my wounded friend was over and the helicopter had taken off for Haifa, that I approached the paramedic and drew his attention to the minor, albeit still bleeding, injury from the ricocheted rock that had caught me in the stomach while I was carrying the wounded terrorist.

The paramedic laid me out on a stretcher. 'You can stay here now,' he said while rolling up my shirt and disinfecting my bleeding torso. 'I'll give you written permission that will exempt you from going back to the battlefield.'

I smiled, 'No. I must return to my company.'

He looked at me quizzically while bandaging my wounds.

'I'll be fine,' I continued, 'just take care of the wounded man I brought in,' I said while glancing at the blood-soaked terrorist who at that moment had become a human being like me.

'Yes, of course, I will,' he smiled.

From his smile and his facial expression, I felt he knew the identity of the wounded man I had brought for treatment. This is one of those moments where no words are needed. The looks between us conveyed an unequivocal message – lives must be saved regardless of the identity of the wounded. In this case, this particular medic was special in his ability to separate his emotions from his role. He had lost his brother in the 1973 war, and his uncle was seriously injured in a terrorist attack in Jerusalem. A more instructive example cannot be found than that of this remarkable medic.

I patted him on the back in sympathy and began to make my way back to the ravine where the noise of the battle still echoed in the air. My vision was impaired by the dense dust and black smoke but I managed to arrive unharmed and rejoined my comrades who were still engaged in the damned battle.

One afternoon, about two years later, I received a phone call. I was already a journalist and an anti-war peace activist. On the line was a guy who spoke to me in less than perfect Hebrew with a heavy Arabic accent. 'This is Azem Salim, do you remember me?'

It took me a few seconds to recover from the incredible shock. 'Of course, I remember you,' I responded. Foregoing any small talk, he wasted no time in telling me why he had called.

'I want to thank you from the bottom of my heart for saving my life.'

'You don't have to do that,' I replied, but he insisted and suggested we should meet. I agreed and asked when and where. 'I live in Gaza, remember? Maybe you can come down to Beit Hanoun because I can't get a permit to enter Israel.'

My initial thought was that he was planning some kind of ambush to hurt me. It would be easier for him to do that in Gaza surrounded by a group of terrorists who had assigned him the task of handing me over to them on a silver tray.

I hesitated at first, but then being aware of the presence of the many forces from the Israeli army stationed in Gaza, I agreed. He gave me an address in the Beit Hanoun refugee camp, and I set off for Gaza the next day. As a precaution, I asked a friend of mine who owned a pistol to join me. We crossed into the Gaza Strip, dressed in civilian clothes and using my private car. I easily found the road to Beit Hanoun. I had been in Gaza hundreds of times before, not only as a soldier but also as a journalist to interview locals, and as a civilian who liked to shop and have my car repaired there, as goods and services were always much cheaper.

At the checkpoint located just before entering the refugee camp, Israeli soldiers asked me why I wanted to go to Beit Hanoun, as Israeli shoppers normally frequented the main street of Gaza City. I told them I needed to visit someone. The soldiers warned me off, but I was determined to continue.

The road into Beit Hanoun had a threatening feel. Throughout most of the Gaza Strip, I felt protected by the presence of Israeli soldiers, but Beit Hanoun was a different story. Soldiers would venture inside the camp only if there were terrorists they had to apprehend. Nevertheless, we got into Beit Hanoun without incident and managed to find the address I was given by Azem.

My friend waited in the car while I knocked on the door of the house. A young, teenage-looking girl in a long robe with her face covered by a veil opened the door. I introduced myself in Arabic, explaining I had come to visit Azem Salim. She looked at me pleasantly and said, 'I am his wife.' Then from behind her appeared a tall older man, who reached out and warmly shook my hand and invited me inside. We sat down in the living room and I was served coffee and Arabic cookies. Then expressing the deepest sincerity, he said to me in Arabic, 'I wish to thank you for saving my son Azem's life. All of us in this family thank you for what you did.' I smiled awkwardly. Then I asked where Azem was. He bowed his head, as if ashamed and embarrassed, debating how to tell me.

'I am sorry but Azem cannot meet you.'

'But why?' I asked.

'He has received threats from one of the terrorist leaders not to dare to meet with you.'

I looked at him, slightly worried about my own safety in Beit Hanoun.

'They told him not to even consider thanking you,' he added in a tone of sincere sorrow.

I bowed my head and stared at the cup of coffee in my hand. 'How can we make peace between us with such hatred,' I muttered to myself.

'I had to use my connections and offered a compromise,' the man said while pouring more coffee. 'A compromise in which Azem's wife and I would meet with you and thank you on behalf of all of us.'

'Regardless of what the others in Gaza think, you still deserve to be shown our gratitude,' the young wife said.

There was a brief silence in the room. I could feel the sympathy they were both feeling for me at that moment. I found myself genuinely concerned for Azem's welfare as I knew how vicious and brutal these terrorists were in Gaza. During my years of military service, I learned everything I needed about them. I had studied their fighting techniques, their mentality, their Arabic language, and even their holy Koran. But what really concerned me was learning that they would not think twice about killing one of them if they suspected him of being an informant collaborating with Israel.

I once witnessed such an execution while on a patrol on the streets of Gaza. The scene on that day was in a square on the main street of Gaza City when a member of Hamas dragged a young local Palestinian by his hair to the centre of the square and shot him at close range in the head. We chased the perpetrator but could not catch him. Only after two weeks did our undercover *Mista'arvim* unit manage to track him down hiding in a basement in northern Gaza. This was thanks to a local informer who worked for Israel and who was able to provide accurate intelligence about the whereabouts of the wanted fugitive.

Strange as it may sound, I felt enveloped in sympathy and a kind of love. I believed them, and I believed that Azem would have been happy to meet me if he had not been threatened by those terrorists. A group of extremists who were always the ones who thwarted any possible chance of peace between the two hawkish nations. Historically, these Palestinian terrorist organizations adopted a militant approach against Israel in the wake of the surge of radical Islam that plagued the Middle East in the late 1970s and early 1980s. This process, which has been reflected in events such as the Islamic Revolution in Iran and the assassination of Egyptian President Anwar Sadat by the fundamentalist Muslim organisation known as the 'Muslim Brotherhood', has also taken root within Palestinian society. In the 1970s, the number of mosques in the Gaza Strip and the West Bank doubled, and senior members of the Muslim Brotherhood were able to reach positions of power in the religious leadership.

For many years, terrorism against Israel was mostly carried out by the PLO, the Palestine Liberation Organization, led by Yasser Arafat, who was personally involved in planning many of these attacks against Israel. He remains a guiding spirit of revolution to his followers and supporters, even though after his death, following international investigations, over one billion dollars of public funds were found squirrelled away in his private bank account and in corporate investments. Although in 1993 Arafat had signed a peace agreement with Israel, documents found in his office in Ramallah suggested that he had used Palestinian Authority funds to finance terrorist activities, instead of improving infrastructure, building schools, and creating hope for the younger generation of Palestinians. Arafat also managed to deceive the EU and the US who contributed millions of dollars each year to improve the miserable conditions of the Palestinians, but he channelled these funds to arm and improve his organization in order to increase their acts of terrorism against Israel.

I got back to the car where my 'protector' friend was patiently waiting for me and asked him to take the wheel and drive us home. On the way, I described to him what had happened.

'Fanatical bastards,' he uttered. 'I have no doubt that Azem was deeply disappointed by having to forego your meeting.'

The fundamental dilemma in the case I have related was not whether any human life should be saved if at all possible, as I believe that in every human being, the instinct to save a life is pre-programmed and embedded. Therefore, to me, the question of whether we act on the impulse to save a life, or at least to assist in saving a person, is not a weighty issue in which diverse views need to be expressed. But if this is so, to what extent should you increase the risk to yourself to save another life? The dilemma in my case was complicated at least sevenfold. It was not simply about saving the life of an enemy who had already surrendered and was not about to harm me. In such a case the dilemma does not exist, as I am committed to honour the Geneva Convention, as well as the values embedded into me in my military service. The dilemma was not only about saving the life of someone who had just been trying to kill me. But my dilemma was further exacerbated when I saved his life while risking my own, carrying him while I was being fired on for 700 metres, getting wounded, and with my own physical strength slowly ebbing away.

I can state with certainty, despite the many years that have passed since the incident, that the fear of dying from the continuous fire during the rescue, was remarkably less than the confusion and frustration that caused my mental state to unravel during those dreadful moments. Nevertheless, when encountering such a situation, something, be it a mysterious instinct that we did not learn in school or any academic institution, awakens in us, guides us, and even directs us in how to behave or react as an empathetic human being. When that happens, the dilemma disappears. You are scared beyond words but you just keep going because the conscience and values you grew up with command you to do what needs to be done. In a situation like this, if you are a fighter acting on behalf of a moral army, you adhere to the rules and guidelines that most armies of the world are committed to. Apart from these, you find yourself clinging to other principles, ones that have not been dictated by military commanders, nor by conventions and conferences. These rules pulsate inside your own body.

I admit that I had been worried about carrying an enemy who could perhaps decide to strangle me, but from the moment I dragged the wounded man away from the fire zone, I knew I was doing the right thing. Once you are involved in the event, and the adrenaline is coursing throughout your body, you act in automatic mode. Miraculously, in those moments, the fear dissipates as if swallowed up by the earth. Feelings and emotions are also temporarily out of the picture. All that is left is the urge to apply the combat practices you have learned and get safely out of the situation. Evacuating a wounded combatant from the fire zone is part of this. You do not involve emotions and do not waste time checking the identity or rank of the wounded person in need of immediate evacuation.

Here is another situation of saving the life of the enemy;

In the 1982 Lebanon War, a soldier called Daniel Sason from my unit found himself in a similar situation to mine when he was placed in the thick of bloody combat. Our entire company was split up into different forces that headed simultaneously in the direction of Beirut. Daniel was in another team, about a hundred metres away from me, but his story resonated throughout Beirut.

Daniel was a dedicated and compassionate soldier. He had joined the Israeli army not out of a desire to harm others, or to seek revenge, but only to protect his homeland. He often found himself questioning the morality of war, but he believed in his duty to protect his country.

On that particular day, as bullets whizzed past him and artillery shells exploded nearby, Daniel's squad came across a wounded enemy soldier. The young man was lying in a pool of blood, clutching his leg, and moaning in agony. His uniform was tattered, and his face was contorted in pain. For a moment, Daniel hesitated. He knew that saving the enemy soldier would not be an easy task. His own squad members were wary and sceptical. They argued that the wounded soldier might be playing possum, waiting for an opportunity to strike when they got closer. But Daniel couldn't ignore the desperate human being in front of him.

Despite the chaos around them, Daniel made a snap decision. He signalled to his comrades to provide covering fire, allowing him and a medic to rush to the wounded enemy's side. Bullets zipped overhead as they reached the injured soldier and began to administer first aid. As they worked to staunch the bleeding and make the wounded soldier as comfortable as possible, he looked up at Daniel with a mix of surprise and gratitude in his eyes. Ahmed, the wounded man spoke only Arabic, while Daniel spoke only Hebrew. However, even though they couldn't speak each other's language, the universal language of compassion and care needed no translation.

Word quickly spread among both sides of the battlefield that a soldier from the enemy side had been rescued by his adversaries. The fighting seemed to pause for a moment as the news spread. Soldiers on both sides watched in amazement as Daniel and his squad evacuated the wounded man to a nearby medical facility. In the days that followed, the wounded enemy soldier recovered from his injuries. Unlike in my case, in which the wounded man I saved was not given the opportunity to meet me, Daniel was given one. It turned out that the injured man was a member of the famous Jamail family, a noble family that was once compared to the American Kennedy family.

As the years passed, the story of Daniel and Ahmed became a symbol of hope and resilience not only in their own war-torn nation but throughout the world. Their legacy extended far beyond the borders of their homeland, touching the hearts and minds of people from all walks of life.

Over time, their efforts bore fruit, and the wounds of war began to heal. Daniel and Ahmed's story became a symbol of humanity's capacity for compassion even in the darkest of times. Their act of mercy inspired others, and a ceasefire was eventually negotiated. Peace talks began, and the conflict that had torn the land apart for years slowly came to an end when the PLO organization left Lebanon for Tunisia.

The story of Daniel and Ahmed has served as a powerful reminder that compassion and forgiveness had the potential to transform lives and reshape nations. Their extraordinary journey from enemies on the battlefield to ambassadors of peace left an indelible mark on history, demonstrating that it was never too late to choose the path of reconciliation and that the bonds of friendship could bridge even the deepest divides. As they grew older, Daniel and Ahmed remained close friends and mentors to the next generation of peacemakers. They continued to travel together, sharing their story and wisdom with audiences around the world.

Chapter 14

The dilemma of hungry children

For Rosh Hashanah, the Jewish New Year, it was customary to buy fresh new clothes for children.

I don't mean a three-piece suit or any of those costly branded garments that people in Tel Aviv would buy for their spoiled-rotten children. We just hoped to get a new white shirt and a pair of dark-coloured trousers, that's all. If we were lucky, we would get shoes too. But that did not happen every year. Regrettably, there was one painful Rosh Hashanah when we were unable to obtain new clothes or indulge in lavish food. Instead, we had to wear the same clothes as the previous year, and make do with *matbucha*, a Moroccan stew made with lots of tomatoes and red peppers, which we ate with bread. A lot of bread.

This was in 1966, the year in which a severe recession prevailed in the young country of Israel. It wasn't as a result of fluctuations in the stock market but of the damn war that sucked up the entire state budget. Everyone was fighting for survival; their dilemma was not whether to choose some indulgent delicacies such as lamb chops or beef cuts, or settle for chicken only. They couldn't even afford a few of those cheap sausages to cook with vegetables and rice to give the illusion of a meat meal. All to honour the holy festival of Rosh Hashanah which, according to Judaism, God had commanded us to celebrate in his honour.

The wealthy residents of Tel Aviv never faced a dilemma when it came to food. Their tables were perpetually brimming with a plethora of dishes, not only to appease their own hunger but mainly to impress their guests. In contrast, working-class people like my parents had to line up for food.

Long and laborious queues formed in Netivot in the 1960s for basic items such as chicken, sausages, bread, oil, rice, sugar, powdered milk, and tinned meat. These products were distributed in rations to each family based on the number of children they had, using government food vouchers.

One day, my father returned home with a black eye and two loaves of bread in his hands after waiting tensely in line for meat, or at least for some sausages. He had been punched during a skirmish amongst others waiting in line. While my father remained patiently in line, the meat ran out each time he got to the front of the queue because some violent people pushed themselves to the front. As a result, a scuffle broke out in which my father was not a participant but still ended up being punched.

Finally, despite his best efforts, my father was unable to get meat for our Rosh Hashanah dinner. Despite continuing to stand in line, he only brought home two loaves of bread and two tins of meat that the government imported from Britain for its working-class citizens.

Unfortunately, such stressful queues were not just for food. There were several for job hunters as well. My father would get up as early as 4.00 am to be among the first people in line at the employment exchange. He went there every day and waited in line for hours, just to return empty-handed in order to avoid getting involved in any of those nasty conflicts.

The wealthy residents of Tel Aviv did not have to line up in order to obtain meat. They would drive to Moskowitz's farm in the north of the country to buy a whole sheep, which would be slaughtered and cleaned for them. Then they would invite their pampered guests, who would all bring gifts of a significant monetary value, not based on their beauty or practicality, but so they could impress the hosts with their financial prowess.

'Why don't we steal from the rich?' I asked cold-hearted Asher.

'Are you crazy?' Whiny Manny responded in his annoyingly high-pitched voice.

'What can we steal from them that we don't have here?' replied Asher.

'I'm not talking about food, you idiots,' I hissed. 'They've got tons of jewellery hidden under their mattresses or stashed away in drawers.'

'And what will we do with the jewellery? Who'd buy jewellery from ten-year-old children?' ventured Manny, throwing away the gum that he had been chewing since the morning. 'Everyone would suspect that we had stolen it and then we'd get into real trouble.'

Silence fell. The little whiner had finally said something that made sense. Moshiko started scratching his forehead and while doing so his well-worn hat flew off his head. He never took that filthy hat off, even when he slept. Asher stared at me as if he was sure I had an answer. But the truth was that I had none. Maybe we should consider a different kind of theft.

'How about stealing clothes from the washing lines?' I suggested.

'That would be stupid,' said Moshiko, reaching down to pick up his hat from the floor, 'in a small town like Netivot where everybody knows everybody. They'd immediately recognize their crappy clothes on us.'

'Not in Netivot, idiot,' I said and slapped him round the back of the head, 'I meant in Tel Aviv. I'm sure those pampered children get new clothes every year.'

'I don't feel comfortable stealing clothes,' said little Sonny who suddenly broke his silence.

'We're little thieves, Sonny, that's what we are, and it doesn't matter what we steal,' said Asher.

'It does matter,' Sonny responded with the seriousness of a teacher. 'We steal food in order to survive, clothes and jewellery aren't food. We won't die if we don't wear clothes, but we might die if we don't eat.'

We all looked at Sonny in silence. I could not determine whether it was because we didn't like what he said or because his words gave us a slight jolt in our internal struggle – the desire to ease our suffering always jarring against the teachings of right and wrong.

'We'll be caught in the end, so we'd better stop before it's too late,' Little Sonny added decisively before I had finished determining which of the two options.

'We know stealing is wrong,' Moshiko reasoned, 'but for us, little children who depend on the adults to feed and clothe us it's the only way.'

'I agree with you about the food,' replied little Sonny, 'but not about the other things.'

"Stealing is stealing regardless of what you steal, so stop sounding so pious," Manny laughed.

'I'm not! I always agreed to participate in stealing food. Why? Because I was hungry, but guys, jewellery and clothes are a different story.'

'Why, what makes that different, it's the same fucking theft, isn't it? Manny started getting angry.

'If we are caught stealing food,' replied little Sonny, 'we will gain sympathy from those who will catch us and who will show understanding and compassion towards hungry children, but if we steal jewellery, no one will show any mercy towards us.'

Asher threw him an angry look, 'The choices we make when faced with adversity, and especially with hunger, can't be judged because of our age,' he said. 'I know what it's like to go to bed hungry, my days are scarred by struggle and hardship, and for my age, it's hard to bear. Every day is a battle against my damn hunger and misery. I didn't choose to be born, so why do I have to suffer like this? The ones who brought me into this world have the responsibility to feed me, so when they fail, then I steal, just to survive another day. Do you think I enjoy doing this shit? Stealing brings me no good, only fear and a heavy burden of guilt.'

We sat ourselves down on the ground in a tight circle. None of us had anything more to say. Moshiko began scratching his forehead again, this time holding his ragged hat in his left hand. Asher cupped his head between his hands and stared at the faded green grass. We all knew stealing was our only way of enduring another day in the face of adversity. Every day, our stomachs would growl noisily, a cruel reminder of our empty dinner plates. We couldn't resist the aroma of freshly baked bread wafting through the air from the bakery in the *souk*, and we couldn't pass by the colourful fruits without grabbing some. After all, we were only taking what we needed to sate our hunger on that day. At the same time, we all felt guilty. Even as young children, with each theft our guilt increased, casting a shadow over our stolen morsels of happiness. We knew it was wrong, but the gnawing ache of hunger clouded our judgment. When our tiny hands reached out, swiping loaves of bread and juicy fruits, conscience was creeping into our hearts, and the adrenaline coursing through our veins was always mixed with guilt, creating a bittersweet cocktail of emotions.

'I guess we're good kids after all,' I smiled silently. 'Look at how we, ten-year-old children, talk about topics such as conscience and principles of morality as seriously as adults.'

'That's because we're smart kids,' replied Moshiko with a quick laugh.

'Yeah, we all are, except you, clod-head,' Asher grinned, slapping him on the back.

Chapter 15

Boys do not cry

In our school in Netivot, which was made entirely of brown wooden huts and looked more like a concentration of grain warehouses than knowledge repositories, there were good teachers and there were evil teachers. Each one of the evil teachers possessed a set of leather straps and wooden or metal rulers. They used to hit us with the rulers on our shoulders, back, legs, and especially on the palms of our hands when the fingers of the palm were clenched. They could always find a reason to beat us. We, the children, thought that it was our fault and that we had done something naughty. We did not yet think like adults; that these teachers suffered from some kind of personality disorder. Who had time to bother with such minor infringements when the whole country could go up in the flames of the damned war? These so-called education experts would beat us if, say, we made a mistake in spelling some damn word. Or if we whispered something to someone whilst they were talking. They beat us if we were just one minute late coming into class. They even beat those who had managed to enter the classroom on time but were slow in settling themselves into the cold metal chair that was welded to the wooden desk. They beat us if we dared to laugh at another pupil's mistake, or at some fart that was circulating in the air. But the most frequent beating was over religion and God and all the religious nonsense we were forced to believe in. Such as if you couldn't explain with perfect precision how God created the world and you mistakenly said it was done in seven days instead of six. Or if you were asked to read something from the holy books and you couldn't find the correct verse, or you did not pronounce the name of the prophet or the priest correctly, then you would be ordered to turn round to face the blackboard to receive several lashes from the leather straps.

One of them, Mr Ozer, our history teacher, would refrain from beating us if he believed we were mistaken about a historical fact, but he would go on the attack and beat us if we were mistaken about anything related to religion or God. In one of the history classes about the establishment of Israel, I decided to tease him. On that day, the principal of the school was present in the classroom with a guest from the Ministry of Education, who had come to check on the academic attainment level of the underprivileged pupils of Netivot (but not the teachers, God forbid). I assumed such a dignified presence would deter Mr Ozer from hitting us. Sadly, I was wrong.

I raised my hand to ask Mr Ozer's permission to speak. 'We founded a Jewish state to escape pogroms, but instead we entered an unending struggle with our Arab neighbours. So why here, in a never-ending war, rather than, say, America?'

'God, in his goodness, sent us back to the land of our ancestors as he promised to Moses and Abraham, the father of the nation,' said Mr Ozer with a smile, something he had never done before. I laughed, wishing that the honoured guest would visit more frequently.

'If that's the case, why doesn't he defend us against the Arabs?' Moshiko enquired.

Mr Ozer responded solemnly, 'This is God's will. He is testing our faith in Him.'

'Testing us by killing us?' I laughed.

'Yes, and also, God punishes us for our sins.' Mr Ozer said in his usual authoritative tone, trying hard to shut my big mouth up.

'And why does he do nothing to those who kill in his name?' I said aloud, aware of the dignitaries present, who were listening with great interest. They were surprised because they didn't expect eleven-year-old children in a neglected town to be able to express an opinion on a topic that was surely intended for adults.

'He should emerge from the clouds and burn them,' Moshiko chuckled.

"Or maybe there is no God," I ventured confidently. There was silence in the classroom. It seemed like I had just thrown an atomic bomb.

'Don't go talking like that son,' Mr Ozer said and his face turned red.

'Maybe God was invented by humans,' I continued while placing my trust in the presence of the principal and the guest from Tel Aviv. The truth is that I was not interested in whether there was a God or not, what I was interested in was chastising Mr Ozer.

'What makes you say that?' the honoured guest gently enquired.

A wave of encouragement enveloped me. From the expression on his face, I did not sense the threat of being called forward to the front of the class to face the blackboard and receive several lashes from Mr Ozer's leather straps.

'People in the past were ignorant due to the lack of scientific knowledge,' I said with the seriousness of a renowned philosopher. I felt I was on a roll. 'When an earthquake occurred, they interpreted it as God's anger and strengthened their faith in God's existence by attributing earthquakes to his wrath. The proof is that for thousands of years, all mankind believed in the existence of God, and today, with the development of science, most of mankind does not believe in the existence of any God because science can now explain how destructive natural phenomena occur.'

I glanced over at the fair-haired guest. It seemed as though he was somewhat impressed. However, neither he nor the others in the classroom were aware that the words I had just recited were in fact quoted from an article I had read in one of the encyclopaedias at the municipal library.

Silence prevailed. I couldn't determine whether I had pissed off the principal or satisfied the guest, who didn't try to shut me up or scold me. I was only afraid of the possibility that I would be expelled from school for being a bad influence or an apostate, which could have a devastating effect on the rest of the children.

'Do your family at home believe in the existence of God?' the guest asked in a polite and pleasant tone. I couldn't help but wonder why our teachers in Netivot couldn't speak to us with the same kindness as this important guest.

'Yes, sir. Of course,' I said immediately. 'However, my uncle Moises, who chose to emigrate to Madrid instead of coming here, and became very wealthy, is not a believer.'

'It's because he didn't receive the right education,' said Mr Ozer, who was now glaring fiercely at me.

On that particular day, Mr. Ozer's fierce glare didn't scare me as much as it usually did. I sensed that he was trying to restrain himself because of the guest's presence. This made me want to provoke him even more.

'We bring God into our homes when there are problems,' I continued, reciting a quote from something I had once read. 'But throw him out the window when our troubles go away.'

Suddenly, Mr Ozer had had enough. He walked over to me and without warning, raised his hand and delivered a swift slap to my face. 'How dare you talk like that boy?!'

The world seemed to slow down for a while as my cheek stung with pain. I was now frightened. His face was flushed with anger, and his voice grew louder.

'I am only expressing my thoughts,' I said with a broken voice while touching my sore and reddened cheek with my trembling hand. My eyes welled up with tears. Gasping in disbelief at the shocking turn, I looked at the guest. He didn't say a word but the shock on his face said it all.

It turned out that I was mistaken in assuming that Mr Ozer would act differently because of the presence of the school principal and his distinguished guest. And if you thought that this monster was immediately suspended from his job as a children's educator, or at least summoned to a hearing before a Board of Education committee, you were wrong.

Compared to Mr Ozer, the devil, our grammar teacher, Mr. Ezekiel was more open and allowed me to express my beliefs. He was known for his kind heart and gentle spirit and had never been involved in any kind of conflict or argument with people in Netivot. He was content with his peaceful existence and had always believed in the power of kindness and tolerance to resolve any disagreement.

'My God is the sun,' I once said to him during a spontaneous chat about religion we were having with him in the playground. 'It is eternal and can be seen, compared to the invisible, intangible God we Jews believe in.'

'And who created the sun if not God?' Mr Ezekiel asked with calmness and empathy.

'The stars created the world and the sun is one of them,' I said.

'And who created the stars?' he responded with a forgiving smile.

I gave up.

It was only the female teachers who didn't beat us. They treated us as if they were our mothers. At most, they would reprimand us and discipline us with the heavy punishment of having to stay behind at playtime. Even Rebecca Shulman, who taught us arithmetic, never beat us, even though her husband, the formidable Daniel Shulman, was one of the teachers who was equipped with leather straps and rulers of all sizes. He would beat us if we didn't remember the words of the national anthem by heart, or if we didn't know how to subtract 40 from 1080, or if we didn't know how to identify the holy city of Jerusalem on the large map of the country that was stretched across the wall. Sometimes this monster would go to another class to help other teachers who were having trouble dealing with particularly noisy pupils. He would then attack one of them with strong punches as if he were in a boxing ring. We weren't even allowed to cry, even if our hands were swollen blue or red and bleeding. And it's not that the teachers forbade us to cry. This came from the pupils themselves. They would mock the one who dared to cry and would call him 'pussy.' It wouldn't end within the confines of the school; these bastards would run around telling the whole neighbourhood and then your fate would be sealed. You would have turned into a 'weak pussy' overnight and you would receive barrages of humiliation. There were some, especially the boy named Aharon Damari, who was considered the leader of the class, who said that it was better to cry when the teachers beat us because it gave them satisfaction. If you didn't cry, he reasoned, then the teachers would get angrier and increase the intensity of the beating because you had made them look weak. You made them feel frustrated and humiliated and most importantly, you made them feel they had failed in their mission to educate you by way of their damn beatings.

The majority of the kids did not agree with Aaron. Their principle was that if you cried you might pay a heavy price while in school and during after-school hours. After all, you spend time with your classmates not only at school but also at the only grocery store, at the only library, at the only barber shop, and in every corner of the town. What bothered us and angered us more than the beatings themselves, was the reaction of our parents when we complained to them about the violent teachers. 'You deserved it,' they would answer us with contempt. 'You must have done something naughty.' If we complained to the school manager, Hanan, who was as tall as a water tower and whose moustache reminded us of Charlie Chaplin, then he would look at us reproachfully and say, 'Maybe you should start behaving like men and stop whining like babies.'

Compared to our boys' school, which felt like a Spanish torture chamber during the days of the Inquisition, the girls' school was a more pleasant and safe environment. The staff there didn't hit the girls and didn't scare them with threats. From that we learned the first important lesson of life – men are the bad guys and women are the ones imbued with refinement and tenderness.

I must admit that there is some truth in it. In everyday reality, we boys were the ones who beat the girls during games. We the boys committed petty thefts in the market and in Mr Revivo's grocery store, constantly tiptoeing on the edge of the law. It was only the boys who were part of the criminal gang in town, a gang I myself was entangled with, finding myself struggling to resist the allure of the criminal world almost on a daily basis. The leader, who was not a child like us, but an adult of about twenty-two years of age, tried to entice me further into a life of crime after he recognized my creative thinking and labelled me as the smartest member of our group. As a result, I lived under the shadow of the looming danger of being ensnared by the criminal gang I had fallen in with.

As the leader showered me with attention and material possessions, I couldn't help but feel a mix of conflicting emotions. On the one hand, the allure of easy money and the excitement of being part of a close-knit group tempted me, but on the other, a voice deep within me recognized the danger and the potential consequences of continuing down this path.

As time went on, I became increasingly aware of the risks associated with my involvement in the gang. I realised that I was on a dangerous trajectory, one that could have severe repercussions for my future. And so, one morning, on my way to school, I made the pivotal decision to stay well away from the gang. Escaping the clutches of the criminal gang was not an easy task, after all, I had been honoured with the title "The Smart Kid of the Gang", but the weight of the potential consequences, both legal and personal, became too much to bear. I had chosen to break free from the grip of the criminal gang, severing ties with the leader and all his temptations.

This experience taught me valuable lessons about the dangers of associating with the wrong crowd and the importance of making wise choices. By breaking free from the gang, I was able to embark on a new path, one that would lead me towards a brighter and more fulfilling future.

Besides, I had Sima. Her presence in my miserable youth gave me hope and motivation to conquer the challenges of my dismal reality.

I believed our love was radiating like a beacon of hope, like a force that could overcome even the most insurmountable of obstacles. Even though I knew our journey wasn't going to be without challenges, I somehow believed that we would easily navigate life's challenges together. I can only imagine the speed of my heart racing if she realized her feelings mirrored mine.

Chapter 16

The storyteller of a little town

Old Masoud was the 'storyteller' of Netivot who captivated his listeners with the tales he told, regaling whoever would listen with his stories. He was eighty years old but always lied about his age. At his venerable age, he was long past having a regular job, so he would sit every day at the coffee shop, the only coffee shop that served as a spice shop too.

His clothes were sloppy and his shoelaces were regularly undone. Often, he would wear one sock that was a different colour from the other. His body was bent and his tired shoulders drooped below his neck. The teeth that once lived behind his pursed lips were mostly missing, so he had a tendency to cover his mouth with his hand whenever he gave one of his loud laughs.

When he laughed, his tiny eyes would completely disappear into his face, and his wrinkles would gouge into his cheeks making them appear like a ploughed field. Old people like to tell stories, and most of all they love having willing listeners; the problem is that they tend to repeat themselves over and over again, and often have bad breath. Despite his extreme age, Old Masoud rarely displayed the annoying tendency to repeat himself.

Masoud had nine daughters and two sons. He believed in producing a lot of children when he was younger. 'Sustenance comes from God,' he would respond to Dr Berman, who was very aware of the Masouds' precarious financial situation and repeatedly tried to dissuade him from getting his wife pregnant yet again. In Netivot, it wasn't only Old Masoud who practiced this folly, which condemned children to a life of poverty and pain. The concept of 'planning the family structure' was foreign among observant Jews who believed that God commanded them to bring as many children as possible into the world. It is written in the book of books. We, the teenagers, always mocked this 'God's command' and we were sure that men invented this mitzvah only to satisfy their sexual hunger. Their inability to provide for their children in times of war and recession never bothered their conscience.

Although he often smiled and told interesting stories and made people laugh, old Masoud was sad deep in his heart. His son, Haim, had been killed in a motorcycle accident while riding behind his reckless adventurer friend Yehoshua. His wife Jajal had recently died. He loved her very much. He had married her when they were both only nineteen.

Jajal had an unassuming beauty, with sparkling eyes that held a hint of curiosity and a smile that could light up even the gloomiest of days. She had lived a quiet life back in Morocco, looking after her family's colourful spice shop in Beni Mellal, which had been in their family for generations.

One bright spring morning, a young man named Masoud walked into the shop. He was new to Beni Mellal, having recently moved there to escape the hustle and bustle of Casablanca.

As he stepped inside, the bell above the door chimed, and Jajal looked up from arranging the spices in glass jars. Their eyes met, and at that moment, something magical seemed to pass between them. Masoud was captivated by Jajal's warmth and kindness, and she was drawn to his gentle demeanour and the way his eyes held a trace of mystery. He asked for three small jars of paprika, turmeric and cinnamon, and as they conversed, they discovered a shared interest in the simple joys of life.

Over the following weeks, Masoud became a frequent visitor to the spice shop. Each time he visited, he and Jajal would engage in conversation, sharing stories of their childhood and dreams for the future. With each passing day, their connection deepened, and an unspoken bond began to form between them. As summer turned to autumn, their relationship blossomed into something more profound. The air was filled with the fragrance of blooming romance, and it became clear to both of them that they were falling in love.

One crisp autumn evening, as they sat on a park bench beneath a canopy of golden leaves, He took her hand and confessed his feelings. With a nervous smile, he told her that she was the reason he had found solace in the town he had moved to and that her presence had turned the new place into a home. Jajal's heart raced and with tears of joy in her eyes, she admitted that she felt the same way. Their love story unfolded like the pages of a cherished book and their love only grew stronger with time.

They navigated the highs and lows of life together, supporting each other's dreams and weathering challenges as a team for nearly sixty years, until she sadly passed.

His daughter Shoshana, a beautiful young raven-haired and dark-eyed girl, decided to find herself a well-established Ashkenazi husband from Tel Aviv and ventured all the way to the big city, where she cleaned the homes of the wealthy until her dream groom appeared and redeemed her.

But not only Shoshana dreamed of improving her future. There were quite a few gamblers, most of them men, working-class labourers who would fill out Lotto forms that promised large prizes. When they failed to win a penny, they would vent their frustration by beating their wives. And there were those who would thrust their sorrow into the mysteries of religion and its promises, in the hope of receiving help from some imaginary God. My father was not a gambler. He did not drink alcohol or smoke cigarettes. He was a frustrated hard worker who found no opportunity to apply his skills, but nonetheless, he never turned down any type of work, so as to keep us going. He once started work on expanding our small house but then the damn war of 1967 broke out and he had to abort the idea. I saw the pain in his eyes every night when we four boys would sleep huddled together under thick blankets on a long narrow mattress laid on the floor. After rising in the morning, my father would stuff the mattress behind the closet so that it would not take up space or obstruct the movements around the house. The furniture in our house was minimal; a dining table, a few chairs, and one wardrobe. Immediately after supper, which usually consisted of eggs, tomatoes, and lots of bread, obtained cheaply and in large quantities, our kitchenette would be turned into a bathroom. My mother would place a large plastic tub in the centre of the floor, in the space between the table and the sink, and would fill it with cold water from the tap over the sink. Due to the volume of the tub, a short rubber hose was required, one end of which was attached to a tap and the other end my mother would hold over the tub. After checking if the hose was tightly connected, she would turn on the tap and fill the tub with cold water. She would then pour boiling water into it from the kettle that stood on the Primus stove, checking the heat of the water with her elbow. Only when she was comfortable with the temperature, would she call us in turn, to stand inside the tub to be washed. When the bathing ceremony was over, we would curl up on our extra wide mattress, each in his own designated couple of feet of space. After we had finished our bedtime ritual of quarreling, emitting cackles of strange boyish noises, pulling each other's hair, and pinching each other's buttocks, we would close our eyes and be swallowed up into a deep sleep, where our dreams would take us to another place with visions of candy treats in a variety of shapes and colours, and large mountains of chocolate, and the wish that kept recurring – to be left behind inside a chocolate factory.

In the tiny houses of Netivot, there was no internal toilet, only a wooden hut at the back of the yard. Once when I was five years old, I accidentally got my leg stuck inside the fetid hole full of poop, and it was only after my anguished screams had alerted my older brother and his friends playing in the back yard, that I was able to be pulled out. This memory haunts me to this day, despite my efforts to see this shameful occurrence in a humorous light and laugh about it, instead of still feeling horrified. You can bury your past, but you can't make it completely disappear from your life.

Chapter 17

My first baptism of fire

Although it was dangerous and turned out that I almost lost my life, it was exciting and gave me a chance to face the enemy. It is only natural to fear the first baptism of fire even if you are a courageous commando. In my case, though, I was actually anticipating it since it was the chance I had been waiting for to call to account the terrorists who had deprived me of a normal, calm childhood. Everything I had learned and practiced during that almost inhumanly tough twelve-month training period, was now to be applied in the field, in a physical battle against a real enemy. I am not ashamed nor embarrassed to admit that I was scared as hell of what was to come. A crippling fear shot through my body from the top of my head to my toes as we approached the target. My lips turned dry and rivers of sweat covered my forehead, even though the temperature outside was cold. This was the genuine fear of real battle. But I felt I was ready as this would be the kind of combat that I had practiced for and was awaiting.

The target for my first combat experience was to be a well-fortified compound of bunkers in southern Lebanon of the terrorist organisation the PFLP-GC, the Popular Front for the Liberation of Palestine-General Command, led by the notorious mega terrorist Ahmed Jibril.

This form of combat is characterized by an element that does not favour the attacking force, and this concerns the position. For the attacking force, taking on a fortified target is immensely challenging, as the soldiers have to perform their onslaught from an inferior and lower position. They are totally exposed to the enemy, who is firing from above while being well dug into, and thus protected by a concrete bunker. In addition, there will inevitably be some unexpected obstacles discovered when arriving in the area, and when entering the trenches that lead to the bunkers being destroyed. In my first combat operation, there were indeed discoveries that had not been brought to our attention by the intelligence provided to us while preparing for the operation.

Nonetheless, the adrenaline rush in a real encounter with live fire did not diminish, despite the knowledge that fighting inside trenches or fortified targets is fraught with unparalleled dangers.

To our relief, this raid on the PLFP-GC compound was not going to be in an urban area populated by civilians. It would be in an isolated area, far from the civilian population. We have always feared encountering a civilian population during battles and operations. It was a nightmare for us because the terrorists would use them as human shields, with the full knowledge that Israeli soldiers would refrain from firing on children or civilians. In addition, fighting in an area populated by civilians would normally leave us with no flexibility or freedom of manoeuvre that is needed during battles in trenches and fortified compounds. According to the information we received, the battle this time appeared to be against terrorists only, something that made us all very pleased. We all remembered the heart-breaking cries of children cringing in the corner of a room in a house we had entered. How they wept bitterly and their whole body shook was a sight we will never forget. Instead of concentrating on the wanted terrorists who tried to flee the house while shooting at us, some of us had to swing our weapons behind our backs and gently approach the crying children and calm them. In many operations, we had to penetrate not one, but several, locations in southern Lebanon and surprise the terrorists in their fortified bunkers, in civilian locations such as houses and warehouses, and even in mosques and schools. The intelligence equipment in Israel's possession at the time was not as sophisticated as it is today. It was not able to provide us with an accurate picture of the terrorists' bases, their size, the number of terrorists occupying each base, and the type of weapons they possessed. Therefore, we could only find this out by entering the area on foot, covering miles over hard and rocky ground, and climbing the high terraces used by the rural farmers.

I loved my military service, which gave me an opportunity to build my character and the self-confidence that continues to accompany me to this day. But despite this, I hated the shocking scenarios of the wounded innocent civilian populations, especially children.

My entry into real combat was now approaching.

From our practice and preparations, we learned that there could be face-to-face battles against PFLP-GC terrorists who were fortified in underground bunkers on the rocky slopes surrounding the city of Damour, south of Beirut. Although I had already experienced face-to-face combat during a period of operational activity on Mount Dov, this one would be different. Compared to the incident on Mount Dov, which was pretty short and straightforward and against only two or three individuals, this was to be a long and complex battle in trenches and bunkers, where there would be a real feeling of war.

During the civil wars that have taken place in Lebanon in recent centuries, Damour has been a major axis where battles have been fought over and over again. Damour was the silk capital of Lebanon between the seventeenth and twentieth centuries. This was in addition to its being a beautiful resort town that attracted many travellers and tourists. During World War II, Allied forces took over Lebanon, setting Damour as an ideal base from which to fight in the Middle East and southern Europe. Since then, many efforts have been made to rehabilitate the city. Sadly, not only did it not recover its former glory, but it came to be regarded as a perfect place for terrorist organizations to stage their attacks against Israel. Among them was the PFLP, the Popular Front for the Liberation of Palestine.

The well-fortified compound of bunkers we were tasked to raid had already been attacked by our airborne forces several times in the past weeks, but nonetheless, the Air Force attacks had been unsuccessful and the compound was still standing. The bombs dropped by the pilots were accurate but ineffective as they could only scratch the surface. The terrorists sat protected and invulnerable inside the well-built bunkers. They felt confident and encouraged to increase their acts of terrorism. The only solution was to send a commando force that would reach the target from close range, to conduct accurate and individual fire contact with those sitting inside the bunkers. Thus, a force from my commando unit had been selected to carry out the mission. I felt lucky to be one of the chosen ones. However, I had not been chosen just because I was an outstanding soldier or a special warrior. I was chosen for the simple reason of giving me the opportunity to take part in a real combat. This would train me as a commando fighter for the rest of my military career, in which I would engage the enemy as an experienced warrior on a daily basis.

The success of these terrorist organisations in establishing themselves in southern Lebanon would not have been possible without another critical factor beyond the location and conditions of the terrain in the Damour area. That is the anarchy that has ruled Lebanon since the beginning of its civil war in 1975, allowing free rein of activity to terror organizations. Beirut, which was in the 1960s described as 'Paris of the Middle East', began to be destroyed by internal conflicts and gradually its splendour decayed. Syria and Iran supported most of the terror organizations, and the Soviet Union provided them with weapons.

All operational preparations for the raid on the PLFP-GC compound had been completed and each fighter had memorized all the details and the structure of the entire compound. According to the plan, our force would split into two separate teams of fighters upon arriving at the compound. One was tasked to attack the main bunker, which was on the right-hand side of the compound and served as the main headquarters. This bunker was marked on the fighters' map as the highest and the largest of the bunkers. The second force, which I was in, was tasked to attack the three other bunkers on the left. From the intelligence information we received about the structure of the bunkers, their layout, and the ground conditions, it was clear that the task of capturing the main bunker would be more complex than the other three bunkers.

The bunkers we were assigned to take over were smaller and not so high up, and could certainly be climbed very easily. In contrast, the 'top bunker', as we called the main bunker, was not only higher than anything in that area but was also booby-trapped by explosives that endangered anyone who approached it. The team whose task was to attack this bunker was also joined by three fighters from the Engineering-Sabotage Corps, whose job was to defuse the explosives in order to prepare safe access for us to break into the bunker. Their other function was to carry on their backs our explosives which would be used to blow up and destroy the bunkers just moments before we retreated.

The element of surprise matters, and so we reached our destination late at night after an arduous trek over very difficult terrain. The rocks we were walking over were so sharp that they had almost penetrated the thick soles of our sturdy commando boots. As we reached the perimeter of the compound, we cut a narrow opening of half a metre wide in the fence that surrounded it, and continued to move towards the bunkers, a distance of about 200 metres away. We were proceeding quietly, in single file, and holding onto the shoulder of the person in front to minimize our chance of stepping on a mine. This was because of the information passed on to us suggesting that there was a high probability that mines had been placed near the fence we had just come through, as well as in the surrounding area. This type of walking towards the target also helped us ensure we were proceeding in the right direction in the darkness, as we couldn't use any means to light our way, not even a tiny flashlight. This way, we could also be sure that the entire team remained connected, and would be following our commander who was leading us and navigating the way towards the compound.

During the walk, orders were relayed from our commander at the front by way of each fighter whispering it to the fighter immediately behind him. One of the orders was to replace our magazine of red tracer bullets with regular ones. This was so that in the event of a shooting encounter before entering the trenches and bunkers, we could disguise our position as much as possible. Red tracer bullets help to direct night-time shooting as the shooter is able to see the bullets coming out of his rifle and thus improve his aiming according to whether they are finding the target. But on the other hand, if you are the shooter, then the enemy is able to trace the source of the shooting and thus your own position.

We approached the objective.

Usually, when we enter an enemy area, the feeling is of fear, anticipation, and tension, walking into the unknown and the unfamiliar. However, this time, for some reason, a strangely calm feeling flooded us. We felt everything was going smoothly without any glitches. If the terrorists had not discovered us up to this point, then the chances were high that they would not be able to do so at all. That way we could catch them completely unawares.

'This is too good to be real,' one of us whispered,

I, too, was a little worried. I was afraid the terrorists were waiting for us in an ambush where they would slaughter us all. However, our force commander leading us did not seem at all alarmed. This offered us a sense of comfort. We had always put our trust in our commanders. They were more experienced, bold and brave, and they would observe the battlefield in a wider and more comprehensive way than us.

But then, as our force arrived in front of the bunkers, at the point we were planning to split into two teams according to the plan, we found out that the intelligence information about the area that we had in our hands, as well as in our memory, was wrong. The distance between the three bunkers and the main upper bunker was different from what we had been told, and the upper bunker was not in fact connected to the other three bunkers by a trench. In addition, the area around the three bunkers was covered in dense thicket bushes, and the bunkers themselves were surrounded by tangled vegetation of dried-out tree branches and thorns that looked very much like rusty metal barbed wire. This meant we would have great difficulty in being able to see the target with a clear line of vision. Worst of all, the route leading up to the main bunker was blocked by large boulders that had probably been brought there from a quarry in the Lebanon Valley. This meant a change in our approach to the bunkers was drastically and swiftly needed and that the plan to split into two forces was impossible.

During the practice stages, when we had been going through the decoding of the aerial photographs taken by our Air Force over the area a few days before the operation, no one had spotted any rocks or tall vegetation near or around the bunkers. The aerial photographs we received were always accurate. The only plausible explanation was that the terrorists had laid these rocks earlier that same day, after the aerial photographs had been taken.

The feeling was of terrible frustration mixed with momentary confusion. I, as a young rookie warrior, began to learn one of the basics of war; the plans you make prior to the operation are not necessarily the actions that will take place on the battlefield. In war, you know how you get in, but you never know how you will get out. You can know how, when, and where the war began, but you can't know where and when it will end. Commanders and planners of an operation can only speculate and evaluate the outcome of the battle, but there has never been accuracy in the final results as it is never clear how the conflict will develop. However, to me, the momentary confusion that followed the changes in the field being revealed to us was actually challenging and exciting. As a child, I became quickly bored with games or situations whose outcome was known in advance, or that I found too easy. This trait still remains with me to this day.

'How can this be possible?' I muttered to myself. We all felt that we had possibly made a mistake in navigating to the destination and had been brought to a different place. The riddle was solved only after the end of the operation when we returned to the base for the post-battle briefing.

It was revealed that the rocks and vegetation had indeed been brought to the compound on that morning, the very day of the operation. It was a pure coincidence, and not because they had known we were on our way.

Whether it was an error in navigating, or incorrect intelligence, the changes in the topography of the target did not lead us to consider cancelling or postponing the operation. It was clearly not on our force commander's agenda who was indoctrinated to adhere to the mission despite difficulties, obstacles, or any nasty surprises. Perseverance and determination, along with the ability to withstand any kind of pressure until the goal was reached, certainly contributed to our capabilities as a commando unit. In this particular operation, our perseverance and determination were highly charged due to the characteristics of the target. It was a terrorists' nest, from where they were constantly terrorizing Israel and harming innocent civilians and children.

The mission continued.

Our commander noticed that just to the side of the leftmost bunker of the three, almost hidden among the vegetation and rocks, was a small path leading upwards behind the bunkers that had probably been cleared by their builders and used by the occupants to bring supplies, as well as for any emergency escape. It was decided to use this path to carry out the attack, even though originally we were supposed to carry out the attack on the bunkers through their access trenches. Our experienced force commander estimated that the terrorists would not be expecting an attack from a path that they used in their daily routine. We, with our developed senses, could read his thoughts. Tricks and deception in battle are necessary to deceive the enemy in such situations where you feel almost lost, trapped, and unable to press ahead with your task due to changes or surprises in the field. These techniques were not invented in recent times, nor even during the extensive battles of the Roman Empire or the Mongol Empire of Genghis Khan. They have been ingrained in man since the dawn of history during hunting, in times when hunting animals was the only way for man 'to put bread on the table'. It can be seen in nature when watching a beast pursuing its prey. If Charles Darwin's theory is correct, then it is clear from where we humans have inherited this trait. The Israeli army managed to achieve victory in all its wars, in spite of being greatly outnumbered, only because of its way of thinking. Throughout my training period, and after each operation in the post-battle debriefing process, I learned a lot about methods of deception and tricks, even though they have been used in much more dangerous and frightening situations. The necessity of using tricks and deception during combat can even outweigh the greater risk to the safety of the fighters. One example out of hundreds is Operation Entebbe, a daring operation that stunned the world in 1976 when Israeli commandos landed in Entebbe, Uganda, to rescue over 100 Israeli hostages who had been highjacked on a flight to Paris by terrorists. The brilliant trick they employed was the use of a black Mercedes car in which the Israeli fighters disguised themselves as Ugandan soldiers, supposedly accompanying their president Idi Amin, who regularly used a similar black Mercedes.

Our strike was about to happen. We quietly made our way towards the left-hand bunker. We were so close that we could clearly see the trenches that connected the three bunkers. Our aim was to surprise the occupants of the bunkers from behind. The force commander, along with eight fighters, began to creep quietly, hunched over, towards the path. My team was ordered to remain where we were in front of the bunkers. Our task was to attack the bunkers from the front and also to serve as a blocking force in case the bunkers' occupants would try to escape. But then, out of the blue, came another unexpected incident. Our commander noticed one of the terrorists standing by the side of the vegetation and urinating. This amusing but disconcerting fact became known to me only when we had returned to our base and I really wish I had seen it.

While peeing, the terrorist spotted the commander force moving towards the path. He immediately picked up his Kalashnikov rifle and began firing and shouting in Arabic to his friends in the bunkers.

The battle had begun.

The terrorists who were inside the three bunkers immediately realized what was happening. They noticed not only the force moving down the path above them, but they were also able to see us, as we were literally standing before their eyes, in front of their bunkers. We found ourselves trapped by firing from all sides. The terrorists, in addition to firing from their Kalashnikov rifles, began throwing grenades at us and shooting shoulder missiles. We threw ourselves down on the ground behind rocks for cover. I tried to lift my head above the rock but could not see anything.

Our concern was that the shooting would hit our three fighters who were carrying the explosives to be used for blowing up the bunkers. If this were to happen, the explosions would kill not only the fighters on whose backs the explosives were being carried, but all of us.

The force commander acted fast. He shouted his commands and instructions to us but we couldn't hear them clearly due to the cacophony of the gunfire and grenade blasts. When he realized this, he shouted the orders intermittently, in the pauses between a grenade or a missile explosion, but in spite of that, we were able to hear only fragmented instructions. We had to bring our combat intuition into play. Even though it was my first baptism of fire, I felt an urgent need to initiate a move without waiting for an order or guidance. I assumed the tangled shrubby area, which made it difficult for us to see clearly, would have the same impact on the bunker's occupants who may not be able to easily identify the sources of fire. Also, our helmets were covered in shreds of grey-green cloth for camouflage, meaning we could assimilate successfully into the tangle of vegetation. I decided to get up on my feet to create a strong burst of fire that would silence for a few seconds the occupants of the first of the three bunkers on the left, behind which, by the path, were my force commander with his fighters, waiting for a suitable moment to break into the other bunkers. I had a MAG machine gun that fired bullets of 7.62 mm in diameter, so I was sure that a massive round of fire from such a gun could definitely do the job.

Shooting from such a heavy machine gun is carried out with the assistance of one of the fighters. He is known as a 'MAG 2', and his job is to load the bullets into the machine gun while the combatant is shooting. The machine gun operator would not be able to fire the weapon alone. He needs help from his MAG 2, who does the loading at the correct speed for the shooting.

The advantages of this MAG are its reliability and great firepower. Its disadvantages are its relatively heavy weight and its heavy 7.2 mm diameter ammunition, which can be a limiting factor for the infantry operating it. When used by infantries, the MAG would play two roles during the battle. One role is for 'suppressive fire' and the other is 'covering fire'. 'Suppressive fire' is when you are firing at the enemy to stop them from firing back at your force. The enemy is paralyzed by the fire and this facilitates the assault of the attacking forces. 'Covering fire' is a backup firing, when you are firing at the enemy to allow your own troops to advance towards the enemy targets.

I got on my feet, aiming the machine gun towards the bunkers, squeezing the trigger to the maximum while maintaining the gun's stability and precise height. I could not see clearly but used my senses to direct my shooting towards the left-hand bunker to paralyze its occupants. My shooting was strong, continuous, and ferocious, but my machine gun was becoming red hot, as if the metal was about to melt from the heat generated by the massive round of fire. Luckily the bipod with which I was gripping the gun was designed and shaped for this situation, so I did not feel any burning of my left hand throughout the shooting. My intention was only to paralyze the bunker's occupants, as I was well aware of the fact that my shooting alone would not destroy the bunker. This would be done later on by our three fighters carrying the explosives.

The rest of my team noticed what I was doing and used my covering fire to advance towards the three bunkers simultaneously, coordinating with the commander's team. I kept up the firing with my MAG, while my No 2 was slowly and carefully pulling the chain of bullets out of its bag, placing them into my machine gun's chamber at precisely the right pace for my shooting, as calmly as if he was back at an exercise training at our base. For my part though, I was becoming crazily high and my adrenaline was spiking to a superhuman level. It felt like I was in the middle of a hallucinogenic dream. This was the first time I had fired at such a speed from a machine gun, or from any automatic rifle. I would never have believed I could keep up such a pace.

In a matter of seconds, the terrorists began to ease the rate of their firing to the point that was nowhere near as strong as when it had started. We assumed they were by now running out of ammunition, so MAG 2 and I raced to join the rest of the team who were busy storming the three bunkers, facing the firing coming at them head-on.

Our force commander, who had also noticed the lessening of the enemy fire, shouted an order, and all of us, as we had been trained, jumped into the trenches that were connecting the three bunkers and began inching towards the bunkers. Our progress was made slowly and cautiously, but all the while we were keeping up our massive fire. Around the bunkers we found several more trenches, so we divided into small groups and scattered throughout them as much as possible.

For some incomprehensible reason there was no response of fire coming from the main upper bunker. 'The silence of the upper bunker' as we described it when we returned to our base after the battle. We were worried about the ominous lack of response from the upper bunker, the one which we were most wary of. Our fear was that its occupants would suddenly overwhelm us with a massive round of firepower and that they were just waiting for the moment we would all be in their range of fire. Our commander got up out of the trench and started climbing towards one of the bunkers, calling his team to follow him. The rest of us continued edging our way inside the smaller trenches. These were extremely narrow, barely half a metre wide, which meant that while we moved along them, only the fighter at the head of the line could fire. The trench was uncomfortably small and gave us a feeling of being trapped and confined. We felt that this form of fighting, where only one fighter could shoot forward, was a dangerous situation in which we were all perilously exposed to an enemy shooting at us.

Every second counted. I felt I had to do something radical.

I jumped up out of the trench and quickly crawled alongside the route of the trench towards a nearby rock. When I got to the rock, I hid down behind it, raised my head slowly, and aimed my MAG directly at the centre of the bunker's opening. This time, I was firing my MAG and loading the chain of bullets completely on my own, as my No. 2 had suddenly disappeared. I swung from my back the spare bag containing a long chain of bullets and put it on the ground beside me. After placing the top end of the chain of bullets into the feeder box of my MAG, I straightened my body, shouted the words 'Suppressive fire', and started shooting towards the bunker. At that moment, some of our fighters emerged from the narrow trenches and started running towards the bunkers while shooting. One of the fighters knelt down, aimed a shoulder-fired missile directly at the middle bunker, and hit it directly.

My spontaneous suppressive fire action was indeed helping the onslaught on the bunkers, however, like everything else that has a limit, so too did my MAG machine gun. I estimated that my bullets were about to run out. What was more worrying was that more terrorists had begun to arrive in the area. As they started adding to the firing on us, I realized that my huge shooting machine was no longer of use due to lack of ammunition. Although the rest of the fighters were successfully advancing towards the bunkers, the battle had become even more intense and was by now at very close range. Two of our fighters whose mission was to storm the upper bunker were wounded, but even so continued firing at the bunker as they advanced with the fighters inside the trenches. One of the fighters from our other team quickly crawled towards me carrying a green sack. When he reached me, he immediately opened it and pulled out a chain of bullets and put its tip into my hand. 'You must continue what you're doing. Stay here and keep shooting,' he shouted. I nodded while loading the chain into the machine gun and continued firing.

Suddenly there was a loud explosion, and immediately following that a huge blast that almost blew us off our feet. From the intensity of its blast, we could assume it was a booby-trapped explosive device placed just in front of the bunker's entrance. Two of our fighters dropped to the ground, but I could not tell if they had been hit or were just taking cover; I was busy firing towards the bunkers from behind the rock.

I felt a stream of warm liquid trickling down from my head to my neck, but I could still continue to function and shoot with my machine gun. I was sure it was blood but there was no pain. I did not have the time or opportunity to touch it and check, as I was so madly engaged in my powerful firing which required both hands and huge concentration. If the injury is in my head I thought, then it's better that I continue my 'suppressive fire' shooting until I fall and lose consciousness. Because of the colossal amount of enemy fire, the machine gun I was holding could contribute to the success of the battle, so I was determined to continue as long as I was able to function. I was literary counting the seconds until I would collapse.

One of the two fighters who were lying on the ground was my No 2. He had been hit in the head. The other was one of the squad whose job was to break into the upper bunker.

I tried to get closer to pull them out of the fire zone and back into one of the trenches, but the commander threw two fresh sacks of bullets towards me.

'Don't stop, keep firing!' he shouted.

I returned to my position behind the rock and continued to shoot towards the bunkers, facilitating the way as much as I could for my fellow fighters.

The battle was heating up as the seconds passed, with the unremitting shooting by us and from the terrorists' direction getting ever stronger. Our shooting was accurate and incessant as we were determined to reach the bunkers, but the terrorists showed no sign of surrendering. We felt we were literally fighting for our lives. It was no longer the conquest of the bunkers and the elimination of terrorism from southern Lebanon, it was in all regards a battle for life or death. The fire coming at us was becoming more accurate and threatening. Even our paramedics were participating in the firing and were ordered not to attend to anyone who got hit until the battle was over. The three fighters with the explosives on their backs were also firing from their position on the back path. They had been ordered not to advance with us during the onslaught but to remain where they were and hide behind the nearby bushes until told to run towards the main bunker and blow it up.

This is done to avert a major disaster. If they are hit by a terrorist's bullet, all of the explosives on their backs would detonate, causing a calamity.

The noise was deafening. Thick clouds of smoke and dust were billowing up. There was a feeling of being involved in a world war, and that all the armies of the world were taking part in this one fierce battle. 'These are the scenes of real war,' I muttered. It was definitely my baptism of fire. I was extremely scared. Terrifying thoughts of parting forever from my family were going through my mind. I even saw my military funeral. My heart was beating so fast that I could hear its loud pulse. I was sure the pressure in my chest would tear my heart and lungs apart. I had no air. I felt I was suffocating and couldn't inhale any air. Suddenly a smoke grenade was thrown and it was unclear where from. The purpose of a smoke grenade is to create camouflage. But who the hell among us would want camouflage now when we were all in the fateful seconds of storming the bunker?

A few seconds later, the mystery was solved. We noticed two terrorists emerging from one of the bunkers and running towards the bushes behind it, just by the path used by the terrorists to access the bunkers. They wanted to obscure their run. One of our snipers opened fire, killed one and injured the other, who vanished into the bush. Our three fighters carrying the deadly explosives, who were still by the path, spotted the fugitive terrorist. Without waiting for an order, they began chasing him, and thanks to the light of the moon, they could follow the trail of blood he left behind. Within a few minutes, they had reached and eliminated him.

Our assault on the bunkers continued to intensify. A colossal amount of fire was coming from both sides. I was continuously squeezing the trigger of my machine gun so as to provide cover for my friends who were advancing towards the bunkers. But then, my heavy gun went silent. I had run out of ammunition. In a matter of less than sixty seconds, I had gone through a sack of 500 bullets.

I put the MAG on the ground, grabbed my automatic rifle and loaded it. Then together with my squad ran fast towards the three bunkers. Within seconds we reached the bunker on the left. I found myself the first to reach one of the bunkers, so I decided to use my grenades to try to paralyze the terrorists inside before we all sprayed it with my rifle, so that we could advance towards the rest of the bunkers easily. I pulled out the two grenades from a pouch in my vest and removed their safety pins, one with my hand and the other with my teeth. Then I got myself as close as possible to the bunker's opening, the two unpinned grenades in my hand, counted to three, and shouted 'Grenade!' as I slid the two grenades into the bunker.

When using a hand grenade, there are four and a half seconds from the moment the safety pin is removed until the grenade explodes. The count to three prevents those in the bunker from throwing the grenade back at us. Despite the risk involved, if you are cool and skilled, then it would be best if you throw the grenade after three seconds and not before.

I managed to slide the grenades into the bunker. The paralysis of this bunker was a significant step in the battle to further disable the other two, so we could make our way to the upper bunker and end the battle. However, later, as we approached the bunker's entrance, we discovered that the door was wide open and it was completely empty. I felt like an idiot. I thought I had performed a daring move and even risked myself to make sure it was as close as possible to the enemy, but I failed. I did not have time to think about whether there were actually any terrorists in the bunker when I threw the grenades in, or that they could have fled when they saw the grenades rolling on the ground in front of them. Because of the noise of the shooting and the explosives, the commotion of the battle, and the darkness of the night, I could not determine where we were being shot from. Only as we were coming to the end of the raid, when we reached the upper bunker, did it become clear to us that there had been no firing coming from the bunker into which I had thrown the grenades. I wanted to bury myself in shame. The embarrassment was great, even though the fact that the bunker was empty had helped hasten the onslaught toward the rest of the bunkers and complete the mission. I found that to be a consolation.

After a further strenuous and stubborn battle, we managed to get to the other two bunkers.

The battle was over. Mission completed.

We were ordered to start preparing for our retreat back to base. The three fighters who carried the explosives began the demolition of all the bunkers, placing the explosives carefully around them, while we all made our way down towards the path. On the way down, I collected my machine gun I had left near the bunker.

Only after the explosives had been placed, and we had scanned the entire compound to make sure there was no living terrorist left, was the final order given to head back towards the base.

As we retreated, I could not miss the opportunity to watch the demolition of the bunkers. I asked one of the men who had placed the explosives how long he had timed them to detonate. He smiled at me as he walked quickly, 'Three minutes.'

I estimated the distance and realized I could be safe from harm at about fifty yards. I ran those yards like a child involved in an exciting new playground game and stood up tall. I looked back at the rest of the fighters, who were indifferent to what was about to happen and could not understand what I was so excited about. It turned out later that none of them had been aware that this operation was my first 'baptism of fire'.

The explosion was stunning, illuminating the sky with flashes of red-orange-yellow, followed by black smoke rising up and billowing over the ruins. I, an enthusiastic child, continued to stand upright watching the flames and tall mushrooms of dense smoke that reminded me of photos of Hiroshima. As I stood upright, admiring the amazing sight, I said to myself, 'So this is what real war looks like, these are the sights and sounds of a real battle.' I felt like everything that had happened was a thrilling dream. I did not believe it was real, it seemed to me more like I was in the midst of a terrifying nightmare, or I had stepped into a scene from a Hollywood movie. The fact that I was not hurt added to my joy and satisfaction.

The operation was crowned a success. Ahmed Jibril's terrorist network realised that we could reach them anywhere and, in any way, they tried to hide. It had been vital for us to destroy these bunkers and their occupants as, according to intelligence, the PFLP-GC organisation was planning a special deployment to north Israel through southern Lebanon with only one goal in mind – killing as many Israelis as possible, and harassing Israel with terror attacks.

Chapter 18

The Israeli-Palestinian conflict

Children and youth, both Palestinians and Israelis, did not get the chance to experience a normal childhood because of the constant bloody conflict between two obstinate nations. The war between the Palestinians and the Israelis is not over valuable oil or diamond resources but over religion, the Holy Land, and Jerusalem. These children were exposed, defenseless, and helpless, doomed to a lengthy bloody conflict that wrecked the lives of millions of Israelis and Palestinians, Muslims and Jews, all descended from the same biblical ancestor. Children who suffer immensely as a result of their elders' craziness, and who are unable to deal with the horrific brutal conflict that has been decided by adults, who are considerably better qualified to deal with its ramifications.

My heart empathizes with the situation of the Palestinians, and my sympathy towards them has grown over the years. I fought them. They were my enemy. But my aching heart goes out to them. They live in poverty and without hope, only because they are constantly in fear of their 'Hamas' leaders, not of the Israeli tanks. The Hamas terror organization forced the Palestinians to vote for them. The corrupt leaders of Hamas use the many millions of dollars they receive from the world to continue the war with invincible Israel. They build tunnels and purchase weapons, instead of building universities, schools, hospitals, infrastructure, and most importantly, investing in education. They do not encourage children to choose academic studies and better their lives. Instead, they are poisoning their minds with false promises of defeating Israel.

Many countries, including the United States, that have realized this stopped their financial aid that was flowing into Gaza for many years.

Here is a summary of the events and background that have led to one of the longest conflicts in the history of war:

For nearly 700 years there was a harmonious and amicable coexistence between Arabs and Jews, who lived together as good neighbours in Palestine. They traded with each other, ate together, and danced at weddings together. What ended this idyll was the UN's decision in 1947 to divide Palestine in two, one part for Jews and the other for Arabs.

Prior to that, back in 1917, the Ottoman Empire, which had ruled Palestine for 400 years, was falling apart, and Britain took over its rule. The British Foreign Secretary Arthur Balfour had written to Lord Lionel Rothschild, a leader of the British Jewish community, expressing the British government's support for a Jewish homeland in Palestine. This letter became a landmark document, also known as the 'Balfour Declaration', offering hope of a sanctuary for the Jews who had suffered European antisemitism and pogroms. However, the British government's support caused anger among the Arabs who feared losing their land. They felt threatened by the arrival of waves of Jewish immigrants chiefly from Eastern Europe, building on and cultivating the land they had lived on for generations. The Jews subsequently became the majority in Palestine. On the other hand, many Arabs actually welcomed the Jews, as they were convinced that the Jews could contribute greatly to the development and prosperity of Palestine, a neglected region, but they did not have the power to do anything about it. They were even afraid to say it publicly. Thus, just a few days after the Balfour Declaration was published, the Arabs in Palestine began terrorizing their Jewish neighbours, with whom they had coexisted for decades. Some of the Arabs did not feel comfortable about this, but their leaders wanted to send a warning message to those Jews in Europe who were planning to immigrate to Palestine.

The Jews, supported by the British, were determined to implement the Balfour Declaration and emigrate to Palestine, which they saw as the Holy Land, the land of their ancestors, Abraham, Isaac, and

Jacob. The Arabs who lived in Palestine were stubborn and very willing to fight them. They committed dozens of attacks on Jews living in Hebron, Jaffa, Haifa, Tel Aviv, and Jerusalem. Hundreds of Jews were massacred during these bloody pogroms, many of them children. This was a war of existence for Jews who had been persecuted for centuries and believed that they were returning to their long-promised Holy Land. Likewise, it was for Arabs too, who had believed in their own right to Jerusalem, from where, according to their faith, prophet Mohammed ascended to heaven.

The war intensified. Neither the Jews nor the Arabs showed any signs of relenting.

Only after thirty years of bloodshed and a persistent war between the two sides, did an international body decide to intervene. After instructing the British to bring to an end their mandate over Palestine, the newly created United Nations held a vote. Thus, on 29 November 1947, the United Nations General Assembly voted by two-thirds in favour of adopting Resolution 181 (the UN Partition Plan for Palestine), calling for the dividing of post-Mandate Palestine into two areas, one for the Jews and one for the Arabs. Israel had agreed to the partition arrangements for Palestine and welcomed the idea of coexistence with the Arabs, even though the Arabs received a larger share of the land. However, the neighbouring Arab countries rejected the UN partition of Palestine and chose instead to go to war, initiating a bloody confrontation that became an ongoing war between Jews and Arabs for many years into the future.

In the eyes of the Jews, the partition of Palestine between the two nations was implemented legally and officially in 1947 by an international body, the United Nations. However, to the neighbouring Arab countries, it was an act of appropriation and occupation of land.

Years later, as the twentieth century was drawing to a close, some senior Arab figures spoke out in the media that the war of 1948 was in fact initiated and led by the leaders of the neighbouring Arab countries, and not necessarily supported by the Arabs living within Israel. They disclosed that the war had happened against the will of the majority of the Arab population who lived and flourished in Israel. Just from these testimonies, it became clear that most of the Arabs who had lived in Palestine during the British Mandate and during the 400 years of Ottoman rule, had coexisted with the Jews, and considered the Jews as a force for good that could only help bring about improvement to the neglected Holy Land. They were proved right when Israel not only managed to revolutionize the agricultural output of the difficult terrain but also succeeded in becoming a world leader in advanced technology.

The conflict between Israel and the Palestinians is and never was Israel's war against the Palestinians but on Palestinian terror organizations only. The terrorist groups started their war on Israel after the Six-Day War of 1967 'to liberate Palestine from the Jews.' The Palestinian terrorist organizations had one goal and that was the destruction of Israel in order to liberate Palestine and the holy city of Jerusalem.

On 14 May 1948, on the final day of the British Mandate for Palestine, the declaration of the establishment of the State of Israel was officially announced to an ecstatic Jewish nation by its newly appointed Prime Minister David Ben-Gurion. The following morning the brand-new Israeli nation had a sober awakening from its night of celebration. Egypt, the largest Arab country at that time and de facto leader of all the Middle East Arab countries, had vehemently opposed the partition of Palestine and was the first to attack Tel Aviv with an aerial bombardment. Simultaneously, it shelled the area of southern Israel bordering Egypt with artillery fire. Egypt was able to persuade other Arab states to join it in the jihadi war against the Jews. Syria, Jordan, Lebanon, and Iraq agreed immediately, and together with Egypt, they stoked up a massive and bloody war, one that has become an ongoing bloody conflict between Arabs and Jews over the Holy Land to this day. The British, who still maintained a presence in the new state of Israel beyond the end of their Mandate, chose not to interfere in the war between the Arab and Jewish nations. They instead focused on maintaining public order among the citizens of the divided state until each side established their own civilian law enforcement agencies, such as police and community wardens.

Israel was determined not to surrender to its enemy neighbours. Its people fought stubbornly and resolutely, spurred on by the brutal fact that they had nowhere else to go as so many of them were survivors of the Europe-wide Nazi Holocaust. Most of them had already witnessed the annihilation of their families and communities and had experienced the torture, starvation and humiliation of the concentration camps. Prime Minister David Ben-Gurion was about to complete the process of integrating all the Jewish underground forces who had fought the British during the Mandate to form one strong and cohesive army, to be known as the IDF, the Israel Defense Forces. In spite of having the benefit of a newly organized army, for Israel, this was a war against all odds, a war of the numerically few against the many, and of a huge imbalance in terms of equipment and weapons. However, the stubbornness of the Jews, which had brought David his famed victory over Goliath, resulted in a different outcome. Highly motivated to survive because they had nowhere to go, the Jews were in a position to fight to the death, a fact that shocked and weakened the Arab states. Israel, in the years to come, would regularly prove that neither the sophisticated tank nor the modern fighter jet is the element that wins the war, but more the individual soldier's assets and qualities. This desperate motivation of the Jews can be said to have made them bold and tough fighters, and the trigger that helped them build the best army in the world.

When the young Jewish state began to build its own army, the founders of the military were strongly influenced and helped by a British officer named Orde Wingate, who had served in Palestine under the British Mandate. Wingate had invented the concept of 'Defence and Retaliation'. The principle underlying this form of military action was to take action against the enemy who had first taken action against you, but your action against the perpetrator would be seven times stronger than his. This is for deterrence purposes and to make the enemy think twice before planning any further attacks. Another principle of fighting Wingate taught the Israelis was to be more daring during the advance, to move the combat 'across the fence and over the border' into the enemy's territory in order to widen the range of attacks on enemy targets. In addition, Wingate placed an emphasis on the efficient and smart use of the 'surprise factor', an important component for success when venturing deep into enemy territory. It involves moving quietly and stealthily and striking before the enemy is able to respond. When Orde Wingate explained to them these methods of warfare, the founders of the Israeli army, who gladly embedded all of Wingate's advice and methodologies, realized that neither the tanks nor the jet planes could apply these methods better than a commando unit that operates on foot, quietly, and uses a precise short-range hit. This understanding led the Israeli army's founding fathers to establish its special commando units, among them, the legendary unit I was privileged to serve in for three years for my compulsory service period, plus another 28 years in its reserve force.

Following their defeat in the war of 1948, Israel's four bordering countries, Egypt, Syria, Jordan, and Lebanon, relented to a degree and began to talk about peace.

On 22 October 1948, after negotiations, the UN Security Council declared a ceasefire, but this was in fact never to take effect as the future showed it was soon to be disregarded by the Arab states. The armistice agreements with the four bordering countries, Egypt, Syria, Jordan, and Lebanon, were soon to be broken. Gamal Abdul al-Nasser, the Egyptian president, who was the leader of the Middle East Arab countries in their war against the young country of Israel, determined to drag Israel into a continuous war. He managed to persuade Syria to attack Israel from the north, and Jordan to attack from the east, while he and his mighty Egyptian army, would attack the Jewish state from the south. Israel fought on three fronts with determination, and at this time, public opinion around the world, and in particular the UN and

Saving the enemy. Rescuing the wounded by helicopter

As a reserve combatant in an arduous journey of forty kilometers

The map of our main war zone in southern Lebanon

On the way to a mission behind the enemy line in south Lebanon

Oslo Accords 1993: Signing of the peace agreement in 1994

Along the border fence with Lebanon

The morning after an operation in Lebanon. Mount Hermon in the background, 1977

As a reserve combatant in full combat gear preparing for another battle in south Lebanon during the Lebanon War, 1982 (me standing back right)

On a shift defending our base in south Lebanon, 1977

Minutes after the operation in Damour, south of Beirut, 1976 (my first baptism of fire)

Me on an outpost along the border with Syria and Lebanon, 1977

Leaving after a fierce battle during the 1982 Lebanon War

Defense Minister Ariel Sharon and Cabinet Minister Shimon Peres visit us during the Lebanon War, in 1982

Assault training in rocky terrain on a fortified target

Southern Lebanon – awaiting an order to raid a stronghold of terrorists

On our way to a raid on a stronghold of terrorists in Naqoura, south Lebanon, 1978

the United States, was firmly on its side. This helped the besieged Jewish state to receive military assistance that increased its operational ability to defeat its attackers. The IDF managed to occupy the entire territory of the Upper Galilee in northern Israel and to remove the Egyptian forces from the Negev in the south.

On 16 November 1948, the Security Council called on all the parties to open ceasefire negotiations, and on 29 December, it adopted a resolution calling for a ceasefire between the State of Israel and the Arab states, under the auspices of UN mediator, the American political scientist Ralph Bunche (Bunche would win the 1950 Nobel Peace Prize for this work). The armistice talks at the Rose Hotel on the Greek island of Rhodes began in January 1949 to set the boundaries of the Jewish state according to the UN partition. Only a small part of Jerusalem was to be included within the borders of the State of Israel. The talks, which became known as the Rhodes Agreements, lasted six months and ended on 20 July 1949 with the signing of the agreement with Syria, which was the last of the agreements signed. With all the agreements signed, the war between Israel and her Arab neighbours was considered over. However, the reality was different, as the Arab countries seemed to be playing a game of deception. When they had agreed to a ceasefire, they did so only to gain time to allow their armies to re-arm themselves. This time, the aggression came from Egypt only. The frustrated Egyptian president Nasser could not withstand the fact that such a small army had managed to defeat him and his great army in several battles. This time he initiated a war of a different kind, a guerrilla war that would exhaust the Israelis and bring them to despair.

Armed guerillas from Egypt, known in Arabic as *Fedayeen*, started a campaign of nightly insurgencies in southern Israel to carry out murderous attacks on its civilians, including women and children. The terrorist *Fedayeen* was made up of a few hundred disgruntled young Arabs, who together with their families, had fled Palestine during the 1948 War of Independence between Israel and its neighbouring Arab states. As refugees, they had settled along the Egyptian-ruled Gaza

Strip to the south of Israel, and in Jordan on Israel's eastern border. These were some of the thousands of Arabs who had hastily left their homes during the war, promised by the Egyptian leaders that they would be able to return to their homes in just a few weeks after their powerful army had exterminated the Jews. The Egyptians promised them not only a return to their homes and the repossession of their land and property, but they would also receive a special permit allowing them to loot all the empty Jewish homes that would be at their disposal. After Israel's victory in the 1948 war, the refugees realized that the Egyptian promises were hollow. Not only in that the Jews had not been wiped out but also that the promise of a return to their abandoned homes was now impossible.

The Egyptian government led by Gamal Abdul al-Nasser took advantage of the Palestinian refugees' living conditions, as well as their dream and desperation to return to their homes. They could be useful as armed insurgents to carry out terrorist attacks on Israel, and he promised them financial support if they would agree. Jordan's King Abdullah initially saw no need to send insurgents from among the refugees he was hosting in his country, but few a years later, he agreed to participate with Egypt, and Jordan began to train its own teams of armed insurgents to be sent from Jordan into Israel. Egyptian intelligence officers, who had been trying in different ways to gather intelligence on what was happening inside Israel, also recruited some of the disaffected young refugees. They were trained and sent unarmed into Israel for intelligence-gathering missions, impersonating local Arab residents, those of the half a million Arabs who had chosen not to flee Israel during the war and remain in their homes.

In spite of their anger, frustration, and the harsh living conditions of the thousands of refugees, only a few hundred of them agreed to the Egyptian president's request. Those who refused were constantly harassed by Egyptian soldiers threatening their families. Nevertheless, these brave refugees adamantly refused to surrender to the demands of the Egyptians and, as they were in a majority, confidently persisted in their refusal. They also believed that Israel would welcome them back to their homes if the neighbouring Arab countries would one day agree to sign a lasting peace agreement with the Jews. Indeed, Prime Minister David Ben-Gurion had explicitly mentioned this during the peace talks between Egypt and Israel, assuring the Arab refugees that they could return to their homes to live in peace with the Jews. But Nasser and the rest of the neighbouring Arab countries thought otherwise. They did not want the Jews to be co-existing partners with them under any circumstances.

In light of this, there was huge pressure on the government from the Israeli public to react to these new and brutal attacks. Prime Minister David Ben-Gurion demanded action from his army Chief of Staff. He called his senior army commanders for an urgent meeting at which they urged him to establish more small commando units. The Chief of Staff, who was already well aware of the value of the small commando units, instructed his senior commanders to start. The first to be formed was 'Unit 101' under the command of Ariel Sharon and his deputy Meir Har-Zion.

Sharon was a legendary warrior with unique strategic skills and extraordinary courage, and in later years became Prime Minister of Israel. 'Unit 101' was assigned most of the operations to deal with the insurgents' problems. The unit's already extensive experience helped bring about good results. They would trace the insurgents, calculating their route and the pace of their advance from the point of penetration, then setting ambushes to surprise and eliminate the insurgents. During one of these ambushes that took place in 1951, after the insurgents were discovered, the unit's force commander rose up, opened fire, and while running towards the surprised terrorists, he shouted the word *'Aharay'*, which means 'After me' in Hebrew. This order, *Aharay*, is calling the fighters to advance towards the enemy while their commander is leading the advance completely exposed to the enemy fire.

Due to this incident, an IDF doctrine was born around a single word of command, *Aharay*, encompassing a principle that has been used by the Israeli army for many years and taught to all the ensuing generations of soldiers. This principle is that the commander will give an example to his soldiers and lead them fearlessly into the fire. This is upheld in all situations, such as when the area is aflame and the enemy fire is getting stronger or when the enemy fires from inside a ditch or bunker. In the case of an enemy being concealed, the commander may decide to storm the source of fire. He will lead and be followed by his soldiers who create a powerful stream of firepower to protect him and paralyze the source of the enemy shooting. Many commanders of the Israeli army have been killed over the years when applying this principle in battles and operations. Nevertheless, this sad outcome has not deterred IDF commanders from shouting the word *'Aharay!'* during a tough battle.

The wars between the Arab countries and Israel intensified greatly.

The Sinai War of 1956 broke out in response to the nationalization of the Suez Canal, and the closure of the Straits of the Red Sea to Israeli ships. Israel coordinated its operations with British and French forces in the war with Egypt.

The Six-Day War of 1967 began in response to the closure of the Straits of Tiran in the Gulf of Eilat to Israeli ships, and the conclusion of an Arab military alliance against Israel, who moved their armies towards Israel's borders. The war ended in a brilliant Israeli military victory and this is still considered one of the most glorious victories in the history of warfare. The results of the war changed the map of the State of Israel: Jerusalem, the Golan Heights, the Jordan Valley, Judea and Samaria (the West Bank), the Gaza Strip, and the Sinai passed to the State of Israel.

But six years later, the war of 1973, known as The Yom Kippur War, broke out.

Egypt and Syria could not bear the humiliation of the fiasco they had suffered in a war lasting only six days, in which the small army of a small country managed to defeat them against all odds. They sought revenge. Thus, Syria from the north and Egypt from the south, surprised Israel. The Egyptian army crossed the Suez Canal at the same time the Syrian army was striking Israel from the Golan Heights. After several difficult days of fighting, the IDF managed to stem the invading armies and moved to counter attack and defeat their attackers. But with a heavy toll. 2,300 Israeli soldiers were killed, and many were wounded. The Egyptians achieved their goal of inflicting a shocking blow on Israel.

In 1978 came the Camp David Accords and the 1979 signing of peace agreements between Israel and Egypt. However, the peace agreement with Egypt did not stop the terrorist organizations from fighting Israel. Jordan assisted and financially supported the PLO (Palestinian Liberation Organization), encouraging them to instigate a war of terror against Israel. This would be a war conducted on a different front, which would intensify over the years, even though the Jordanians stopped their support and expelled the PLO from Jordan in September 1970, which Palestinian terrorist organizations would henceforth refer to as 'Black September.'

In 1982, following the increase in terrorism on Israeli and Jewish targets, Israel launched an operation in southern Lebanon, targeting Palestinian terror organizations, mainly the Abu Nidal Organization, and the PLO Organization, who had been welcomed in Lebanon after being expelled from Jordan. The PLO terrorists, led by Yasser Arafat, were well armed and trained, having enjoyed the open-armed support of Syria, and managed to base itself in southern Lebanon from where they began launching terror attacks on Israel, mainly against civilians and children.

The operation in southern Lebanon brought significant achievements to Israel. The PLO was expelled from Lebanon and established its new headquarters in Tunisia, and most of the military forces of the other small Palestinian organizations were eliminated. However, the operation which had been planned to take no more than a few days, was expanded and lasted much longer than originally planned, deepening the polarization between the left and the right in Israeli society.

But the terror continued against Israeli citizens: on buses, in schools, in markets, and in every possible place inhabited by civilians, resulting in the death of hundreds of Israeli women and children. The Israeli army reacted harshly, but this did not deter the terrorist organizations from continuing to harm Israeli citizens. Then, in 1993, some faint hope appeared on the horizon, the Oslo Accords.

Signed in 1993, the Oslo Accords were designed as confidence-building measures to create trust between Israelis and Palestinians and bring peace to the region. Palestinian expectations were in the main twofold. The first expectation was that the Oslo process would bring to a halt the construction and expansion of Israeli settlements in the West Bank and the Gaza Strip. Israeli withdrawals were to proceed according to a fixed schedule leading to Palestinian Authority control over more than ninety percent of the Gaza Strip and West Bank, setting the stage for a final Israeli withdrawal, all the way back to the 1967 borders.

The second expectation centred around increased economic development in Palestinian society, lifting Palestinians out of crushing poverty and narrowing the gap in living standards between them and the Israelis, which many Palestinians thought humiliating and enraging.

The Oslo Agreements were to assuage these fears by establishing a Palestinian Authority that would consider organizations such as Hamas and Islamic Jihad as a threat to its own existence, thus aligning Israeli interests in fighting terrorism with the interests of the Palestinian leadership.

Yitzhak Rabin, Israel's prime minister when the agreements were signed (who was assassinated in 1995 by a right-wing Jewish Israeli), put it rather inelegantly when he stated that the Palestinian Authority would fight terrorism more effectively than Israelis ever could because it would operate without constraints imposed by 'human rights groups and the Israeli Supreme Court.' In that statement, he was expressing the hope many Israelis pinned on the agreement for an anti-terrorism alliance between Israel and the Palestinian Authority. The Oslo agreements even established joint patrols involving Israeli and

Palestinian soldiers patrolling side by side to prevent terrorist attacks. Initiated and mediated by senior Norwegians, the agreement was signed on the lawns of the White House under the broad umbrella of Mother America. Yasser Arafat, Yitzhak Rabin, and Bill Clinton were all seen beaming, new hope spread across their faces. But in reality, that optimistic hope morphed quickly into hell as the region was already mired in war. Terrorism on the part of the Palestinians not only did not decrease but even increased. All this with the encouragement and supervision of Yasser Arafat who showed two faces; one, loyal and sticking to the Oslo Accords, and the other, a supporter and initiator of terrorism against Israel, continuing to raise funds for that purpose from Arab countries, including Iran and Syria. In the light of this alarming development, the inevitable happened: the collapse and failure of the Oslo Accords.

Palestinian spokesmen repeatedly explained to the world that the collapse of the Oslo peace process was due first and foremost to the expansion of Israeli settlements and the disappointing level of the territorial control of the Palestinian Authority. On the other hand, Israel claimed that it was not the settlements but the security of its citizens that was its main concern. Israeli officials made clear to Arafat before signing the accords that Israel's expectations would mostly be centred on security. Decades of Palestinian terrorism had led many Israelis to fear that relinquishing control over the West Bank and Gaza Strip would leave Israel dangerously exposed to hostile Palestinian movements, who would use the territories as springboards from which to launch terrorist acts well within Israel. The failure of the Oslo agreements can be ascribed to the same reasons that are usually the cause of most agreement failures: both parties felt that Oslo had not delivered what they had expected from it. Besides, this agreement was weak, as it was from the start meant to be an interim agreement, as a prelude to the expected more difficult negotiations towards a final agreement. An important component of it was that peace could be spread by goodwill on the part of the leaderships of both peoples.

The implementation of the Oslo agreements actually started quite well. The first Israeli withdrawal from Palestinian territories in the Gaza Strip and in Jericho on the West Bank was conducted smoothly. The establishment of the Palestinian Authority and Yasser Arafat's installation as its President followed. Then, after a good deal of tough negotiating, a second Israeli redeployment occurred outside of the larger Palestinian cities and towns in the West Bank. Unfortunately, the upbeat mood of confidence-building in both the Israeli and Palestinian public was short-lived, as each side began to perceive the other as violating its agreements.

Palestinians believed the Oslo agreements included a firm Israeli commitment to halt the expansion of settlements and even begin dismantling them. While there was no such explicit commitment in the signed agreements, the Palestinians maintained that this must have been understood by the Israelis as entirely self-evident and that such conditions would be a minimally necessary precondition for Palestinian assent to any agreement.

An Israeli 'third redeployment', that was expected by 1996, was not carried out. The West Bank was divided in a complicated arrangement into three zones, labelled Areas A, B, and C, with complete Palestinian Authority control in Area A, complete Israeli control over Area C, and 'joint responsibilities' in Area B, which was intended to provide civilian Palestinian rule alongside Israeli security control. The Palestinian Authority was thus confined to about fifty percent of the West Bank, far less than the ninety five percent or more that they had originally expected.

A 'free passage' route connecting the West Bank and Gaza Strip by running through Israeli territory was never realized, but instead, Israeli military roadblocks were established on the roads between Palestinian cities. While Israelis cited 'security concerns', these moves were interpreted by much of the Palestinian public as an Israeli attempt to create separate Palestinian cantons without territorial continuity, in order to strangle any possibility of a viable future Palestinian state.

For the Palestinians, this was seen as the ultimate Israeli betrayal, indicating that Israel never intended to come to a peace agreement.

From the Israeli perspective, the dynamics of Israeli–Palestinian relations since the signing of the Oslo Agreement confirmed their worst fears: that the Oslo process would give a militant enemy the tools and launch opportunities for bloodthirsty terrorist attacks against Israelis. Very early on during the establishment of the security services of the Palestinian Authority, it was noted by Israeli observers that the number of armed Palestinians and the types of armaments being brought into Palestinian Authority territory were significantly exceeding the limits established by the agreements. This led to the suspicion that Arafat was constructing an offensive army rather than a police force. However, the greatest Israeli anger was elicited by the fact that the Palestinian Authority was doing very little to prevent terrorist attacks emanating from its territory. It refused to take steps towards disarming terrorist militias, permitted terrorist organizations to operate overtly in offices within its territory, and either refused to arrest terrorists or would adopt a policy of 'revolving door' arrests, i.e. detaining terrorists in prison for a handful of days and then releasing them.

As terrorist attacks against Israelis exacted an increasingly heavy toll in civilians killed and wounded, the entire concept that had been presented to Israelis — of the Oslo process creating efficient Palestinian security teams who would be better than Israeli soldiers in combating terrorism — collapsed. Palestinian explanations that they 'can't be expected to be collaborators and fight against our own people' rang hollow to Israeli ears in the face of civilian deaths.

A series of incidents caused the Israeli public to wonder whether Arafat and the Palestine Liberation Organization (PLO) had ever truly intended to lay down their arms and seek negotiated peace agreements rather than armed struggle: the immense number of arms being supplied to the Palestinian Authority were made public; captured documents indicated Palestinian Authority support for terrorist infrastructures; and

Palestinian policemen took up arms against Israeli soldiers. For Israelis, this was the ultimate breach of the agreement, rendering it moot.

From an economic perspective, the reconstruction of the Palestinian territories was to be handled by internationally respected Palestinian economists and business people working along with the World Bank and enjoying the financial support of Western donations. Toward this end, as early as November and December 1993, potential donor nations were gathered to commit large sums of money. The economy of the Palestinian Authority was, since its inception, run as if it were a syndicate, with monopolistic control over sectors granted to individuals or institutions in return for percentage kick-backs paid to figures in authority, in a pyramid going all the way to Arafat's office. These public figures operated under no requirement to use the funds at their disposal, whether public money or 'kickback payments' in an accountable or transparent manner – a state of affairs generally described as corruption.

The success of the Oslo process was predicated on a beneficial progression of confidence-building measures that would bring Israelis and Palestinians ever closer to trusting in the possibility of peaceful co-existence. In actual fact, Oslo led to a series of claims and counter-claims of breaches of the accords that formed a negative spiral of mistrust and feelings of enmity.

In light of these facts, it might be said in hindsight that Oslo ultimately failed because while its fashioners set in motion a process that could potentially lead to trust and confidence, they did not establish mechanisms for monitoring violations or ensuring that claims of violations could be arbitrated and corrections could be guaranteed. Without such safeguards, the dynamic of the Oslo process fell prey to longstanding sentiments of mistrust and anger between Palestinians and Israelis. Arafat's death in 2004 changed the leadership of the Palestinian Authority. Israel unilaterally pulled out of the Gaza Strip in 2005, and soon after this, the terrorist group Hamas assumed control, sparking two wars. Israel and the Palestinian Authority have returned to the negotiating table, most recently for talks that fell apart in 2014, but the hopes of peace and security that the Oslo Accords offered have still not been realized.

After the 1993 and 1995 peace agreements were signed between Israel and the PLO, a vacuum was created in Lebanon. Hezbollah filled it with the encouragement and support of Syria and Iran. The picture that emerged was sad. It seemed that Israel would have to continue to fight terrorist organizations, which sprout like mushrooms after the rain, as a result, the reality had been altered. Israel's war today is no longer between countries. Peace agreements have been signed with Egypt and Jordan. Syria is engaged in an internal civil war and has forgotten Israel for the time being, and Lebanon is completely shattered, with no stable government with which any peace agreement can be signed. It seems that the wars with Arab countries have been easier than the never-ending war with terrorist organizations. Wars with Arab countries had a schedule, and allotted time periods, whereas the war with terrorist organizations is endless.

When I am asked in interviews, or during my lectures on the Israeli-Palestinian conflict, if there is any possibility of a resolution and peace between Israelis and Palestinians, I present the following possibility: peace between the two sides is possible only when today's Palestinian leaders have left the world. Today's generation of leadership is used to war because it grew up on it, hence in these leaders' eyes peace is something that is far from achievable. Compare this to today's children who will not grow up only seeing war and conflict, but peace as the most suitable and reasonable option. Palestinian children today are more exposed than ever to the world through the internet, where they see opportunities to succeed and make money, study or learn a profession, and touch the existence that is happening in the Western world. They will strive to implement this out of self-interest and for their personal ego and well-being, not because of nationalism. They will also understand from history that in all the decades of conflict between the two sides, the Palestinians have never defeated the Israelis. They will ask themselves what the point is of continuing to fight.

Chapter 19

Children in war zones

Many children in conflict areas face unimaginable challenges and suffer from the devastating consequences of armed conflicts. Their stories are often heart-wrenching and serve as a reminder of the devastating impact of armed conflicts on innocent lives. Their stories emphasize the urgent need for international efforts to protect and support children in war zones. Organizations like United Nations Children's Fund, UNICEF, work tirelessly to provide aid, education, and psychological support to these vulnerable children, but much more needs to be done to ensure their well-being and a brighter future. More efforts are needed to protect and support children affected by armed conflicts, to ensure their rights are upheld, and to work towards a more peaceful world where children can grow up without the horrors of war. Addressing the needs of children in war zones requires a concerted global effort to prevent conflicts, protect children's rights, and provide humanitarian assistance to those affected. It also involves supporting initiatives for post-conflict recovery and the reintegration of children into society. The protection and well-being of children in conflict zones are essential for building a more peaceful and just world.

Here are a few stories that highlight the experiences of children in war zones:

Malala Yousafzai

Malala, a Pakistani girl, became a global symbol for girls' education when she survived a Taliban assassination attempt in 2012. The Taliban had banned girls from attending school in her region, but Malala continued to advocate for education and was shot in the head while riding home on a school bus. She survived and went on to become a Nobel laureate and a prominent advocate for children's rights.

Omran Daqneesh

In 2016, a haunting image of five-year-old Omran covered in dust and blood after his home in Aleppo, Syria, was bombed shocked the world. His image served as a stark reminder of the suffering endured by Syrian children during the ongoing civil war.

Ishmael Beah

Ishmael Beah, a former child soldier from Sierra Leone, wrote a memoir titled 'A Long Way Gone', in which he detailed his experiences as a child forced to fight in a brutal civil war. His story sheds light on the recruitment and manipulation of children in armed conflicts.

Syrian Refugee Children

Millions of Syrian children have been displaced due to the ongoing Syrian civil war. Many of them have lost their homes, families, and access to education. Their stories of resilience and determination are both heartbreaking and inspiring.

Children of Yemen

Yemen has been devastated by a protracted conflict, leading to a humanitarian catastrophe. The children of Yemen face extreme food shortages, lack of access to healthcare, and the constant threat of violence. Their stories highlight the dire consequences of war on innocent lives.

Rwandan Genocide Survivors

The Rwandan genocide in 1994 left many children orphaned and traumatized. Survivors like Immaculée Ilibagiza, who hid in a tiny bathroom for ninety one days to escape the violence, share stories of resilience and the long road to healing.

Kurdish Children in Iraq

During the conflict with IS (Islamic State) in Iraq, Kurdish children were often caught in the crossfire. Many were displaced from their homes and faced the horrors of war. Their stories highlight the importance of humanitarian aid and support for conflict-affected regions.

Bosnian War Children

During the Bosnian War of the early 1990s, countless children were affected by the violence and ethnic conflict. Many lost their homes and loved ones. The story of Elmina Kulašić, known as the 'Sarajevo Rose', symbolizes the resilience of Bosnian children. She survived a mortar attack and became a symbol of hope for the city.

Child Soldiers in Uganda

Joseph Kony's Lord's Resistance Army (LRA) in Uganda abducted thousands of children, forcing them to become child soldiers or sex slaves. The story of Dominic Ongwen, who was once a child soldier but later faced trial at the International Criminal Court, illustrates the complex experiences of children caught in the web of conflict.

Children of Gaza

The ongoing Israeli–Palestinian conflict has had a devastating impact on children living in Gaza. Many have experienced trauma from repeated conflicts and have limited access to basic necessities like clean water, food, and education. Their stories reflect the challenges of growing up in a conflict zone with little hope for a peaceful future.

Child Refugees in Europe

The Syrian conflict forced millions of families to flee their homes in search of safety. Many children embarked on dangerous journeys to reach Europe. The image of Alan Kurdi, a Syrian toddler who drowned while attempting to reach Greece, brought global attention to the plight of child refugees.

South Sudanese Child Soldiers
The civil war in South Sudan has involved the recruitment of child soldiers. Many children were forcibly conscripted or joined armed groups out of desperation. Organizations like UNICEF have worked to rehabilitate and reintegrate these children into society.

Afghan Girls' Education
The Taliban's rule in Afghanistan in the late 1990s and their resurgence in recent years has severely limited girls' access to education. The bravery of young Afghan girls who continue to seek education despite threats and violence serves as an inspiration.

Sudanese 'Lost Boys'
During the Second Sudanese Civil War (1983-2005), many children, mostly boys, were separated from their families while fleeing violence. They became known as the 'Lost Boys of Sudan.' Their long and perilous journey to refugee camps in neighbouring countries and their resilience in the face of adversity is a testament to the strength of the human spirit.

Children in the Democratic Republic of Congo (DRC)
The DRC has been plagued by conflict for decades, and children are among the most affected. They face the risk of recruitment by armed groups, sexual violence, and displacement. Organizations like War Child work to support these children and provide them with education and psychosocial support.

Child Survivors of the Hiroshima and Nagasaki Atomic Bombs
The bombings of Hiroshima and Nagasaki in 1945 during World War II had devastating consequences for the children who survived. Their stories serve as a reminder of the long-lasting physical and psychological impact of war on innocent civilians.

Child Refugees from Central America

Gang violence and instability in countries like El Salvador, Honduras, and Guatemala have led many children and families to flee their homes in search of safety in the United States. Their dangerous journey through Mexico and their experiences in US immigration detention centres highlight the challenges faced by child refugees.

Child Victims of Landmines

Landmines in conflict zones like Afghanistan and Cambodia continue to pose a threat to children. Many have lost limbs or lives due to landmine explosions while playing or traveling to school. Organizations like the International Campaign to Ban Landmines (ICBL) work to clear landmines and support survivors.

Child Survivors of the Rwandan Genocide

Many children who survived the Rwandan Genocide in 1994 lost their families and witnessed horrific violence. Their stories of resilience and the process of rebuilding their lives in post-genocide Rwanda show the strength of the human spirit in the face of unimaginable tragedy.

These stories underscore the importance of protecting children during times of conflict, providing access to education and healthcare, and addressing the long-term psychological and emotional trauma they endure. Efforts to promote peace and security in regions affected by war are essential to ensure a better future for these children and prevent the cycle of violence from perpetuating.

Chapter 20

The tragic death of Yoav

Yoav was not a member of our gang and did not participate in our petty thefts. This was not because he had a stronger sense of morality than us, but because he didn't have the same struggles we did. He was not desperate and hungry like the rest of us, and didn't have to share a bed with his siblings since he was an only child. Even though he wasn't a part of our gang, I spent time with Yoav nearly every day, outside of my gang activities. Our friendship was unique, with a special bond between us.

I had first met Yoav on a summer day in 1963. I was six years old. A group of us were playing a game of hide and seek at the ravine, and we were joined by a boy of my age who informed us his name was Yoav. The fauna at the ravine teemed with lizards and snakes in a variety of sizes and colours, as well as spiders, butterflies, locusts, snails, worms, grasshoppers, and other small inhabitants of our wildlife. There were rumours that jackals and even one lonely tiger roamed the area. On that afternoon, I had found an ideal spot to hide beneath a protruding rock. While making myself as undetectable as possible, I glanced up at the rock above me, and there, basking in the sunshine about a foot above my head was a snake. I heard Yoav calling but I kept ignoring him as I was mesmerized by this beautiful creature. I found myself having an imaginary two-way conversation with it and totally forgot about the game. According to the game's rules, if the seeker stops calling, it means he has failed to find the hider and thus, the hider wins the game. But the game no longer interested me. I kept my eyes peeled on the vividly colourful snake as I whispered soothing words to it. Then, to my surprise, Yoav found me. I was sure he would panic and run away, but he started approaching slowly and quietly until he got really close to me. We both found ourselves staring admiringly at the snake. Yoav did not seem to be afraid of it either. At that moment I realized I had found a friend. A courageous and special soulmate with whom I could have fascinating experiences. Someone with whom I could at last materialize my dreams, which usually included dangerous and menacing situations, since all the other children in my circle, both at school and in the neighbourhood, did not dare to consider dangerous activities. They preferred to play their boring game of soccer.

Yoav did not like soccer.

Together, we would train ourselves to overcome fear. Sometimes, we would stand in the middle of the road in front of a car that was speeding towards us, and only at the last second would we jump aside. The loud curses of those angry drivers still resonate from time to time in my ears. We would compete between ourselves on who would dare climb onto the roof of the town hall and stand as close as possible to the edge, and for how long. On particularly windy days, the fear was sevenfold. From the first day we met, we sensed an amazing connection between us. Unlike the adults who would put on a mask of pretense just to impress or be liked by others, we kids had none of those concerns. We had not been spoiled yet. Yoav and I felt we were different from all the other children in the entire world. As our childhood friendship developed, I noticed we shared the same traits and characteristics; we were both rebellious, charismatic, brave, adventurous and good-looking. Yoav, without intending to, carried about him a melancholy look, as though he resided on the verge of tears. But when someone addressed him, he would seem to perk up from his dejection and change his demeanour. He had the instincts of a child who was raised in a jungle. He rarely made mistakes and had a quick grasp of sudden changes of circumstances. And he could come up with a solution to any thorny situation he got himself into.

Yoav did not have to make any effort to attract attention or get compliments. During a lesson in class, when the teacher would ask us to come up with the correct answer to his question by raising our hand

and waiting for permission to speak, Yoav would nonchalantly scribble down the answer on the notebook in front of him.

'Why don't you give the answer to the teacher?' I once asked him.

'What's the point?' he shrugged indifferently. 'I already know it. Maybe it's better to give others a chance too.'

Yoav was modest. I felt I had things to learn from him about human behaviour.

At the end of the school day, Yoav and I shared a regular habit: instead of running outside happily like the other kids, we would remain in class and get on with our homework. It was not because we were both outstandingly diligent pupils. It was just a profitable calculation. Firstly, this would give us more time to play in the ravine which entailed a long walk there and back. Secondly, it was easier to do our homework when the material we had learned that day was freshly planted in our brains. Either way, one thing was always certain; our teachers, as well as our parents, were impressed with us and were convinced that we were unusually diligent.

When I was about nine, I wrote a short story. It was the first time I had dared to write a story. When I asked if I could read it to my father, he looked at me indifferently. When I turned to my mother, she told me she was busy cleaning the house. There was never any encouragement to engage in arts or culture in the home I grew up in, nor in the town where I lived. I loved writing stories. My mind was constantly whirling and inventing characters, places, and plots. The problem was that in the Israeli south of the 1950s and 1960s, it was not easy to dream of being a writer or a poet. Anything related to art or literature was considered a frivolous luxury. If you did not hold a full-time job, preferably in one of the factories in the industrial area, people would look down on you and break your spirit, until you began to believe that something was wrong with you. If you tried to read to them from the poems or short stories you had composed, they would look at you with contempt and laugh at you.

Yoav was my only audience. And he did not force himself just to be nice.

Yoav had blue eyes. Although they were sad most of the time, they always shone with their azure beauty. 'He inherited them from his father,' Alice, his aunt, once told my mother. 'His father looked like the French actor Alain Delon,' she proudly added. Although I had never seen Alain Delon, as my childhood taste in movies was more American Westerns rather than French sophistication, I figured that Monsieur Delon must have been very good-looking. Sometimes I wondered if Yoav was at all aware of his remarkable blue eyes. I reassured myself that when he grew up, he would probably become a heartthrob among the girls of Netivot. Apart from his melting eyes that made him stand out from the crowd, Yoav had lustrous black hair, which he kept well-groomed and anointed with scented oil brought for him from Paris by his aunt. A small but charming dimple was imprinted on his cheek, and when he smiled, he would bear healthy white teeth, even though he did not like milk and dairy products. I actually loved dairy products. Not because they were tasty and healthy, but because there was nothing else to eat in our poor household. Yoav, on the other hand, did not suffer from a lack of food. According to rumours, Alice had a lot of money stashed away in a safe in a bank in Paris. Whenever I was hungry and found nothing in our own kitchen, I would go to Yoav's home under the pretext of doing homework or just playing. Even if I missed their early dinner, I would treat myself with chocolate and sweets made in France, or one of Alice's delicious homemade cakes.

Yoav was orphaned when he was only a few months old. Alice, his only aunt, had adopted him. As an orphaned child, he felt the absence of his parents' love every day and every night. In contrast, I actually had my biological parents, a father and a mother. However, from the age of two, I never received love from them. I was one of nine children. From the moment the next baby came along after me, I stopped existing. In a family with two children, the attention lavished on the younger child after its birth would balance itself out in due course. However, in my case, attention was shifted to each new baby, who appeared on average every eighteen months. The same thing happened to the baby who was born after me and to the one who came after him.

As religiously observant Jews, my parents felt they were pleasing God by bringing a large number of children into the world, regardless of their inability to provide them each with adequate love and attention. 'This is what God commanded us to do,' is how they would excuse it. When we were fifteen, Yoav and I mocked them for it. We believed the obligation to produce babies was just an excuse for horny men who wanted to enjoy as much sex as possible. In the absence of contraception in those days, the result was a proliferation of children in every home, with the accompanying lack of attention and love. People bring God into their homes only when they wish to benefit from it.

Yoav did not suffer from a lack of pocket money. His aunt Alice had some savings and a steady job and had only one extra mouth to feed. Yoav and I found ourselves spending most of our time together without giving much thought to it. We felt drawn to each other like a magnet. We did not understand the meaning of this connection between us. We were just kids. I never heard him complain about anything. I never saw him cry, even though he had good reason to cry about the absence of his parents' love. I loved Yoav so much. I once told him I loved him more than I loved any of my brothers. Yoav would then blush and bow his head. In breaks between the often physically tiring games, I would try to guess if Yoav was thinking about his dead parents. I could not really know what he was thinking or feeling. If I asked him, he would draw in his slender body and fall silent. Much like a frightened turtle who would retract into his shell as soon as he sensed danger.

'Do you love your Aunty Alice?' I once asked him softly, as if apologizing for my intrusive question.

'Yes…of course,' he replied enthusiastically. 'She's my mother.'

One rainy day, we could not go to the ravine, nor wander around the town looking for somewhere to commit our brand of mischief. Yoav suggested that I come round to his house to listen to some French songs on the new record player Alice had bought on her recent visit to France. Alice, as usual, greeted me with a genuine smile and a welcoming hug. She took my coat off and hung it to dry next to the oven that served as a heater, a cooker, and as a toaster in the mornings.

Alice then made us hot chocolate, added some milk, blew on the two glasses several times and set them down in front of us. I stared at a framed black and white picture in the corner of the living room.

'Are those your parents?' I asked Yoav. Yoav bowed his head and said, 'Yes,' almost in a whisper.

'Now I can see where you inherited your melting eyes,' I said, trying to cheer him up, to put a smile on his face. Yoav went silent. Alice sat down next to him and hugged him. Yoav buried his head between her breasts. I felt embarrassed for a moment. Maybe I should not have said what I did. The glass of hot chocolate I was holding was scalding my palm, even though I was blowing on it constantly.

'Boys, would you like to watch TV?' Alice asked sweetly.

Yoav, who by the slowness of his movement clearly would have preferred to continue to bury his face between Alice's breasts, mumbled 'Yes,' or something like that.

I moved myself over to the other side of the couch so as to get a better view of the tiny TV screen.

Alice did not have to ask us which channel we would like to watch. In 1965 there was only one channel in our small country. Luckily, our favourite programme was on: heavyweight boxing. That evening, our hero, the Black American Cassius Clay, was fighting. It was a rematch between Clay and Sonny Liston, in which Clay defeated Liston again, this time by a knockout in the first round, making him the undisputed world heavyweight champion. His technique was to dance around his competitor, wear him down, then overcome him with a punishing knockout blow. Yoav never liked those knockouts. He was always frustrated and annoyed by them. To him, a knockout meant the end of the show.

To sate our appetite for combat sports, we later watched wrestling. The fighters would brutally beat each other about without any protective gloves on their hands. We felt this was a competition of life or death. Sometimes they would break each other's bones. Yoav and I would feel sorry for the competitors. The sight of blood and pain saddened us. We were sure that the vanquished competitor would die from his wounds. Alice could resist no more and burst out laughing. Only when she had calmed down a bit and wiped her wet lashes, was she able to explain to us that the wrestlers we were watching so avidly in the ring were play acting. They were not really competing with each other. They were just putting on a show, a dramatic performance. The beatings were not real and the howls of pain were nothing more than an act. Yoav and I were so embarrassed and ashamed, to the point we prayed that the earth would swallow us. From that incident, the pleasure of watching wrestling matches was taken away, and we never watched them again. The truth revealed to us had destroyed the illusion that had given us pleasure.

Alice used to photograph us hugging, fooling around, sparring, and eating together, when we would sometimes throw vegetables at each other. Yoav did not like carrots. Alice was among the few people who could afford a camera in those years of the early 1960s. She had studied photography and art in Paris and brought with her not only a sophisticated camera but also expensive perfumes and cosmetics that caused envy among the women of Netivot. As a child, I never saw a camera at home, not even the simplest one. My parents could not afford such a luxury. That's why I don't have any childhood photos. When she was photographing us, Alice would keep asking us to smile. Yoav and I did not feel comfortable about that, in actual fact, we felt ridiculous.

'Why don't you photograph us naturally?' I asked shyly. I always despised those who would direct a fake smile towards someone or a camera.

'Why take a picture at all?' Yoav responded with his sweet rolling laugh and threw half a tomato at me. Surprisingly, Aunty Alice replied to him very seriously, sounding almost like our teacher Shalin, who always used to bring live frogs, spiders, and reptiles to class instead of relying on showing us pictures and illustrations.

'To preserve your memories, your past,' said Alice softly. 'A person without a past is a dead person. If you know your own history, then you will know who you are and where you came from.'

I could not understand what that meant but had to comply with Alice who had always been very generous to me, and not just with her delicious cakes.

Alice couldn't find a husband. She would dismiss any guy who showed interest in her if he wasn't tall, the common issue that exists among millions of women in the world who find themselves alone because of the excessive importance they attach to a man's height. However, if you have wealth, then height is no longer a factor. The double standard of women.

Alice put her faith in the stars. She believed that the position of celestial bodies at the time of our birth affected the course of our lives. In addition, Alice was extremely superstitious. She thought if you hung an iron horseshoe above your door then you would be forever protected from evil and illnesses. And if a bird pooped on you, it was a sign of good luck and money would fall out of the sky. As the years passed and she reached the age of forty, and no potential husband was in sight, she believed that a curse was placed on her. Once a week she paid a visit to Aisha, the witch of Netivot, to help her remove the curse from her with some of her silly witchcraft. Because there wasn't a single person in the whole town who didn't have problems with livelihood, everyone desperately flocked to Aisha even though she never produced any positive results. Aisha made a lot of money from the stupidity of others.

Aisha was not as old as one might expect when describing a witch. She was about forty-five, slim and pretty, but she had an air of mystery about her. She would listen to other people's troubles and make a living from it, but never shared anything personal with others, and never took part in the gossiping that was prevalent among the women of Netivot. Her face was perpetually sad, and she rarely smiled or laughed. She was a widow who typically wore all-black clothing, apart from Saturday, the holy day of Shabbat. She obscured her face by way of a faded chiffon veil covered in gilt pins and her earlobes were adorned with two green metallic earrings. The veil was tied with a rainbow of coloured beads that had a magical meaning she alone could decipher. Every Saturday, Alice would pack up her belongings into three large suitcases, place them in her doorway, and sit down next to them, dressed in her best clothes. She would then quietly mumble vague prayers and entreaties in perfect Moroccan French, asking God to transport her back to Morocco, a place she missed dearly.

Yoav was always very supportive of my creative ideas on how to survive poverty. Although there were dozens of situations where he knew that those 'creative ideas' were not exactly legal, sometimes even immoral, he never dipped out of being my accomplice in a crime or ran away from the scene. When I asked him to join me, he always replied in the affirmative. Sometimes I would ask myself if he did that just to please me or because he saw it as the adventurous thrill he craved. I had the feeling that he would be willing to die for me. In every situation where I landed myself in trouble, he would stand by my side. He never once snitched about any of the naughty things I did, and boy, I was very naughty, oh, how naughty. Another one of my tricks was to get into the cinema for free. The cinema in Netivot was a vast dimly lit building and had a smell of mystery and suspense.

Once a week, on a Tuesday, at three in the afternoon, a film would be shown that was considered suitable for our age group. As a gesture for children only, the mayor, who owned the 'Orion', the town's only cinema, would open its doors to the local children. The mayor would also occasionally donate money from his own pocket to the needy of the town, and certainly there were many of those. It was only in the summer that we were allowed to go to the cinema, the magical privilege where we were given the opportunity to dream, fantasize, and escape to faraway places.

Yoav didn't really like movies but I would drag him with me every Tuesday. He never objected. I felt he was there just to be with me. Visiting the cinema was for me an escape from my miserable reality at home. A painful need for escapism that was bubbling inside me. There was one movie about a family that lived in a large farmhouse in rural Arizona and was subjected to constant harassment by Native American warriors who demanded they vacate the farm they had built on land they rightfully owned. In a particular scene, the father is seen playing with his son on the lawn. Later in the evening, the mother is shown sitting beside the child's bed and reading him a story. After he falls asleep, she tucks him in, caresses his head, and gives him a goodnight kiss.

I cried, but not about the injustice that had been done to the Native Americans. I was crying because my father never played with me in the yard and my mother never told me a bedtime story.

The lack of pocket money never stopped me from realizing my love for the cinema. I always managed to be among the audience, thanks to all sorts of clever ruses and petty thefts. Yoav would join me in the adventure of entering the cinema for free by performing illegal tricks, even though he could easily afford to pay for both of us. This was my inner problem with Yoav. I always felt poor next to him. He seemed to have everything. Money, toys, plenty of food in the fridge, hugs and attention, and a bedtime story.

Anyway, I had devised a scheme to get into the cinema for free. My idea did not involve any sneaking in, but getting in with actual tickets. The trick was simple:

Admission tickets to the cinema were divided into two parts by a perforated line, which the usherette would use to tear a ticket into two. The main part of the ticket would be handed back to us, the audience members, whilst the smaller stub would be retained by the usherette as a record. During the movie, while everyone was glued to the screen, Yoav and I would sneak into the ticket booth of the cashier, who would be relaxing in the refreshment kiosk enjoying a beer or two. We then raided the drawer where he kept the stubs that the usherette had ripped from the tickets at the entrance. At the end of the show, after most of the audience had left the theatre, Yoav and I would go around collecting the main ticket parts that lay discarded on the floor. Fortunately for us, trash cans were rarely seen in Netivot.

Once home, we would diligently glue the two parts of the tickets together with a thin paste that we concocted from flour and water. We would place these between the pages of a thick book for a few days in order to firmly secure the parts together and give each one the appearance of a brand-new ticket that would not arouse any suspicion. Then, in readiness for Tuesday's afternoon movie, we would pull out our tickets from the book and go off to the cinema.

Pale with excitement and fear that the scam would be discovered, Yoav and I slowly made our way towards the entrance, approached by a row of long, rusty iron pipes that always reminded me of a horse's stable. Yoav and I were nervous, glancing at each other in trepidation and debating whether to give up the daring attempt and instead head to Revivo's grocery store, which was only a few metres away, and pinch enough empty bottles to purchase two tickets. But the line moved quickly. There was no time to think. The ticket collector's face got closer and closer. I focused on his eyes to see whether he was meticulous, or indifferently ripping off the ticket without checking the date stamped on them. Within a few seconds, we found ourselves standing right in front of him. Still pale and panting we would hand him the two carefully ironed tickets while greeting him with a trembling smile. It seemed to work. We got in. The seconds between handing over the tickets and running into the movie hall seemed like an eternity to us. We expected a shout behind us, but it soon became clear that there was a God who had mercy on needy children.

'It's because we're kids,' Yoav giggled as we sat panting. 'No one believes that children could be capable of coming up with such a sophisticated trick.'

I laughed. I felt a stream of momentary pleasure searing across my chest. At that moment I felt like I was God myself. Realising that my trick was successful, and hearing Yoav compliment me on it. I had never received any encouragement or compliments from my parents in my gloomy home. I heard only negative criticism and reprimands. Yoav was my mental balance.

It was indeed a brilliant trick, but eventually, it was cut short because of my greediness. I tried to make money by selling glued tickets to other children. One day, one of the children was caught and tipped me off that he had been forced to divulge where he had got his ticket from. He was the weakest boy in the class, one who would have been immediately broken in interrogation if he had been captured by the enemy. I kept Yoav out of it and took the whole blame upon myself. To my relief, the generous cinema owner refused to involve the police. I learned a valuable lesson; a secret can be kept as long as it is between you and yourself, or at most, with one other person whom you blindly trust. Someone like Yoav.

Even throughout the sweltering summer, when children often fainted, our tricks continued.

One very hot day, Yoav and I strolled lazily along the main road that stretched between the row of houses and Revivo's grocery store. We started discussing ideas on how to get some delicious cooling ice cream without having to pay for it. Yoav suggested we go to the store and simply tell Mr Revivo the truth. I lost my nerve all of a sudden. Yoav laughed and climbed with the agility of a monkey up onto the stone wall that separated the main road from the houses.

'Are you crazy?' I shouted and hoisted myself onto the wall, though not with the same agility as Yoav. 'You don't understand,' Yoav smiled and started walking along the wall, stabilizing his balance by swinging both arms. I stood up and kept quiet. Yoav continued to walk along the wall, then stopped, looked back, and turned around towards me.

'We won't tell him about our thefts,' he said and jumped down onto the road. 'We will tell him that we have no money to pay for the ice cream today, but that we will pay him tomorrow.'

I jumped down from the wall and joined Yoav, who had already started walking towards the grocery store.

'I like the idea,' I said as we continued to walk on the main street with our arms around each other's waists. Suddenly, terrified cries were heard from behind us. We looked back and saw a horrified woman running towards us with a baby in her arms, shrieking loudly, 'My house is on fire. Please help me.'

People started coming out of their houses to find out what was happening. Two men who were close to the burning house started running towards it to try to put out the fire. The heat was unbearable. Their firefighting efforts were not much help. The fire continued to lick the walls of the house and black smoke billowed over towards us. In the absence of a fire truck, the kind of well-equipped red trucks we had seen only in the movies, more people came to the scene and started pouring water from buckets and jerrycans.

One of them shouted at us to move away from the threatening flames and suggested we take shelter inside the grocery store, which was only a few yards away. Yoav smiled and looked at me. He did not have to explain much. The telepathy between us never ceased. We went inside the store. Mr Revivo was on his way out holding two buckets of water.

'Keep an eye on my store,' he called back to us and ran quickly towards the fire.

At that moment Yoav and I felt there was a true God who must have been watching us scratching our heads in a desperate attempt to find a way we could enjoy some ice cream for free.

While a small group of heroic people were busy undertaking a serious and dangerous task inside the burning house, Yoav and I headed straight to the little blue freezer containing ice creams. We felt like two kids who had got lost in a large toy store where we were allowed to pick whatever we wanted for free. After devouring a sizeable ice cream cone apiece, we carefully positioned ourselves by the front door, so that we could carry out the duty of protecting the shop from any potential mischievous kids who might exploit the fire.

After hard work and impressive cooperation, the fire was put out. The fire was an incident that was headline news in our small town. People were talking about it non-stop.

When the Six-Day War broke out in June 1967, Yoav and I were ten years old. We spent most of our days and nights in the shelter during that war. The adult males were drafted into the war and we, the little ones, were huddled together with the women and elderly. From the outside, there were noises that further intensified the women's cries. These were the deafening rumble of fighter jets and helicopters speeding in the direction of Gaza. And as if that weren't enough, the chilling wails of the sirens did not stop. I started to invent games in my imagination to escape to another reality as far away as possible. But the sounds of the war happening outside and the crying of the babies inside distracted me. I began to feel I was suffocating. Instead of fresh air, I started to inhale the air that the people around me were exhaling. I shouted, 'Someone open the window please!' but everyone looked at me as if I was crazy. I decided to look for Yoav. I had to climb onto a wooden crate to find him standing next to his aunt Alice, clinging to her long legs. Alice had kindly given her seat to an older man holding a walking stick.

I looked at Yoav and smiled. It was my way of checking on how scared he was. Yoav smiled back. The whiteness of his teeth stood out even in a dark, musty, and suffocating place like this oppressive shelter. I kept looking at him and he kept his gaze on me. It seemed like we were silently communicating with our thoughts. 'It's amazing how strong the telepathy is between us,' I mumbled to myself.

'I want to stand near my friend,' Yoav said to Alice while pointing his finger in my direction. Alice, beautiful Alice, looked at me and waved. Yoav then walked over to me. Had Alice known what I was planning, she probably would not have allowed Yoav to move out of her sight. Without saying a word, Yoav and I crawled on the floor towards the shelter's front door. We made sure there was no one by the entrance and immediately ran out towards the street. Luckily, my parents did not notice my absence because often members of our large family would disperse into different shelters, depending on where we happened to be when the siren sounded.

Yoav and I were the only living creatures on the street. Not even a single cat or a dog. The noise of the planes in the sky continued, and the pungent smell of charred fuel rose up our small noses, causing them to twitch uncontrollably.

'Yoav, this is what war smells like,' I shouted with a strange excitement, while we both ran along the empty street. A spring breeze caressed our faces, filling our lungs with much-needed fresh air. We ran without knowing where we were headed. We ran aimlessly, as if we wanted to rebel, to protest our incarceration in the crowded windowless shelter.

Yoav was the first to stop. I stopped too, both of us expelling air in short panted breaths. Still employing our amazing telepathic communication, we stared together at the round white building that stood in front of us. It was the community centre. We knew every corner of this building. After all, this was where I ran away from my impoverished home to, usually dragging Yoav with me.

Despite its appearance as a neglected building in the industrial area, I spent long hours in it, participating in enrichment classes, playing music, and learning a smattering of English from a volunteer teacher who gave up his luxury life in America in favour of volunteering for the needy children of a poor country.

Yoav suggested we go behind the building. There was a metal ladder attached to the wall from which we could climb onto the roof. Soon we found ourselves standing on the roof, each of us wiping the sweat from our forehead with the sleeve of our shirt. It was so hot that June. Suddenly, without warning, we found ourselves caught up in a terrifying and challenging situation. Taking place in front of our eyes was real-life air combat. Two Egyptian fighter jets had entered the southern Israeli air space. Israeli fighter jets were scrambled, and an air battle began in the skies above. It was amazing to watch, but at the same time very frightening. The noise was so deafening we had to hold our hands tightly against our ears. I thought that at any moment one of the jets would come crashing down on both of us. Yoav kneeled down and covered his face.

'You're missing the action,' I shouted. 'Come and stand next to me.'

'The jets are shooting at each other…we might get shot,' he screamed.

Strangely, I had never seen Yoav scared. He was not scared of anything. I was having the best time of my life. Trembling with both fear and excitement, I was experiencing a genuine moment of sheer pleasure. 'This is what real war looks like,' I mumbled to myself.

Suddenly, there was a huge explosion. A bomb had been dropped by one of the Egyptian jets and landed in the wheat field by the ravine. Red flames licked the wheat field and black smoke billowed up and obscured the horizon. It seemed as if the Egyptian pilot was trying to hit the houses alongside the wheat field but missed. A burning smell of dried shrubbery was pervading the air. A nearby wooden hut was damaged and went up in flames, and shrapnel flew across the field and hit an army truck parked nearby. By then I was starting to get scared, and while I was debating whether we should get down from that exposed roof and get ourselves to the nearest shelter, Yoav jumped up and shouted 'Wow!' His face beamed with enthusiasm and excitement. For a moment I was not sure it was Yoav, I thought it was another rebellious kid who had joined us on that roof. I could not understand how Yoav's reactions had changed so dramatically. But it didn't matter. We both felt like we were in a movie theatre watching a Hollywood action movie. I put my arm around my friend. I could not determine if it was just my instinct to shield him, or because I was so glad that he was not scared anymore. A few seconds later, the Israeli jets managed to force the Egyptians towards the Mediterranean Sea, about six miles away, where we watched them disappear. We both let out a loud cheer and hugged each other.

Over the following days, the war continued. We children were ordered to spend more and more time in the shelters. When it came to Yoav's tenth birthday, one of our teachers suggested that the party being prepared by Alice be postponed. But Yoav insisted on it going ahead. He cried and refused to eat to make his point. The teacher eventually acceded and decorated the shelter with the colourful decorations that we had all prepared. The grey concrete walls and ceiling of the drab-looking shelter were transformed into a much more attractive sight. Multi-coloured balloons were hung, and an iced birthday cake stood invitingly in the centre of the shelter. I could swear there was not one pair of eyes that was not staring and drooling at the cake. And so, while outside the shelter the echoes of falling shells and the wail of sirens were heard, we celebrated Yoav's birthday. Life is stronger than war.

Yoav and I felt like we had already tried every trick and antic in the world. We believed that compared to other children our age, we had already experienced things ten times over. Yoav even claimed that we had more experiences than most adults. We kept our naughtiness a secret. No one else in the world would ever know what we did. We kept this vow throughout our childhood until the tragic day he was found dead in the ravine.

As someone who had developed a deep passion for the natural world, Yoav spent countless hours exploring the ravine, collecting rocks and leaves, and marvelling at the wonders of nature. When I asked him why he didn't suggest I join him, he would bow his head and say sheepishly, 'I'm going to study, not play.'

One fateful summer day, two years after the war of '67, the war that brought a brilliant and sweeping victory, the year in which we all felt that hope had begun to appear on the horizon, tragedy struck us all. Yoav had been on one of his nature expeditions. Unbeknownst to him, a sudden storm had begun to brew in the distance. The sky darkened, and thunder rumbled ominously. Yoav didn't notice the approaching danger until it was too late.

A lightning bolt struck a tree nearby, sending a shockwave through the ravine. The deafening crack and blinding flash of light sent Yoav, who was only twelve years old, tumbling to the ground.

News of the accident spread quickly throughout Netivot, and the community rallied together in a desperate attempt to rescue Yoav and rush him to the hospital.

It was the ill-tempered but kind-hearted Marco who was the first to discover Yoav's lifeless little body. He was lying beneath a gnarled oak tree, his well-groomed dark hair cascading around his pale face like a ghostly shroud. For days, he fought for his life in the intensive care unit, surrounded by the love and support of the whole community. Alice couldn't stop sobbing. It was a heart-wrenching sight, something you don't see any more these days. The entire town held its breath, hoping and praying for his recovery.

That's how it is in small towns, where everyone knows everyone. Sometimes that's good, and sometimes it's bad, like if you get caught stealing. But despite the best efforts of the medical team, Yoav's injuries were too severe, and he slipped away from this world, leaving a void in my heart that could never be filled. I was shrouded in sadness. I felt helpless, too weak to cope with the loss of my beloved brother. The only one in Netivot with whom I could share my very essence. As time passed, the pain of losing Yoav began to heal, though the scars would forever remain. His memory has always lived on in my heart.

We all met in the sweltering summer of '71 to mark the second anniversary of Yoav's awful death. Alice was shattered. She could not accept the passing of the endearing, intelligent boy she had adopted with such love. I could no longer take the anguish. I left the cemetery and started walking towards my house. Tears were choking me up as my face was buried in the ground. But when I arrived at Bar Ilan Street, I noticed something that transformed my gloomy mood. It was Sima, Netivot's most stunning girl. It was Friday, the day when Netivot was preoccupied with preparing for Shabbat. I didn't get a chance to talk to her, but in the few seconds she stepped outside to grab a few heads of garlic from the bunch hanging beside the front door, I was captivated by her stunning appearance. That was the day I fell in love for the very first time. It looked like my angel had sent me something to lift my spirit after returning from the cemetery.

Over the following years, my love for Sima grew into a genuine adult relationship, capable of overcoming any obstacle or challenge that might come my way in the forlorn town of Netivot. 'If my love for Sima comes to fruition,' I cheered myself up, 'Then it will grow stronger and stronger, despite the torments surrounding both of us in this wretched place. A place where despair and hopelessness, and the boundaries of possibilities, were etched in stone.'

When I saw her that day, I felt I was ready to embark on a journey into the realm of teenage love. All I needed to deepen our connection was the chance to spend some time face-to-face with her, even just for an hour a day, during or after school. The problem was the lack of opportunities I had to let her know about my existence and how I felt about her. I did not have the option of courting her; if I sent her flowers, or if I attempted to serenade her under the bedroom window, her father would kill us both.

Anyway, I was told I was skilled with words, and this gave me an idea. Girls love to hear romantic words, I was a man of words, then I should write Sima a heartfelt poem that captured the essence of my love for her. My writing talent was discovered when I was nine years old. It was after I had won the first prize at school for writing the best story. One of my teachers, Mr Danon, went to the trouble of buying me second-hand books out of his own pocket after realizing my parents' financial situation. He always encouraged me and this boosted my low confidence. Sometimes he would assign me tasks of writing songs for a summer camp or a *Chanukah* party, or he would ask me to sit next to a pupil with difficulties and assist him with his homework. I loved writing stories. My mind was constantly whirling and inventing characters, places, and plots. Sadly, in Netivot of the 1950s and 1960s, which was populated entirely by people with daily hardships, it was not easy to dream of becoming a writer or a poet. Everything that had to do with art and literature was considered a distant luxury. If you did not work in a permanent job, preferably as a school teacher or a rabbi, or at least a worker in one of the factories in the industrial area, you were not considered a man among men in their eyes. If you asked to practice art, they would look down on you and break your spirit, until you began to believe that something was wrong with you. If you tried to read out poems you had written or a short story you composed, they would look down on you, and from that day on you would be considered an idle and daydreaming young man who didn't like to work.

But it was not only writing that I loved. I liked studying and I liked school. While most of the children in Netivot resented having to attend school, I found myself impatient to enter its gates each morning, carrying books and notebooks that weren't on the list of lessons scheduled for that day, memorizing the material eagerly, as happily as if I were savouring a delicious ice cream cone. Despite this, I never received acknowledgment or compliments from my parents for the good grades I obtained so easily in school. Instead of words of encouragement, they were preoccupied with their own survival and their unceasing worry about feeding us. There were many moments of thirst for attention. I cried and pushed myself into my mother's arms, but they were too busy with the new baby that had been born just a few months before. To keep me from demanding attention, I would often be put in the 'coop', the barred wooden bed where mothers imprison their toddlers while doing their household chores. I was a helpless child in a family with many children. I felt forgotten and abandoned, so I started improvising creative solutions to get attention and love. One of them was honing the art of lying. And not only was it my childhood that was crappy. Even during my teenage years, I felt I was living in an abandoned and desolate small town that seemed to have been forgotten by the government and its fat officials. The men of my small town Netivot were mostly labourers who were compelled to engage in menial work to provide for their families. When they walked through the murky streets, their demeanor was stooped, slow, and hesitant; most of the time, their lips were tightly pursed, and their eyes were suspicious and tormented as if they were angry at the whole world. Towards nightfall, they would lock themselves inside their homes and escape to sleep, even though it was only seven or eight in the evening. It was as if they were impatiently waiting for the night to come and sleep was a momentary balm for them, an escape from their harsh reality.

The only sports hall in the town was used not only for gymnastics and various sports activities but mainly for celebrations such as bar mitzvahs and weddings. Celebrations like a birthday party or the anniversary of a happy marriage were considered a luxury. The esteemed mayor, who focused only on the public's interest and certainly not on his own, kindly gave permission for families to use this hall for free. Two years later, he was sent to jail for corruption.

The hall didn't supply tables and chairs but was large enough to accommodate more than three hundred guests. Chairs and tables would be borrowed from the nearby synagogue. The tables would be covered with white cloth, improvised from used sheets donated by relatives of the celebrant. You would never see a live band playing there. It was cheaper to simply install a record player in the corner of the hall and connect two speakers to it. The role of DJ was taken in turns by willing volunteers, teenagers who wished to draw attention from the girls. We, the children who were not invited, took advantage of these celebrations to try to sneak inside. Our intention was to sate our hunger rather than enjoy the music and dancing, even though there were some children among us who had already had their supper at home. They wouldn't want to miss the delicious Moroccan dishes that were arrayed on those white tables; the slow-cooked stews made with a variety of ingredients such as poultry, fish, vegetables, and marinated with olive oil, garlic, lemon, cinnamon, saffron and other herbs and spices. Due to their high prices, the inclusion of lamb or beef was rare. For dessert, there would be luscious Moroccan doughnuts dipped in honey.

If we didn't manage to sneak in, we would wait for the festivities to end with the patience of a carnivore stalking its prey, and we would then pounce on the leftovers before they vanished from the tables. There was a kind of unspoken, informal understanding that guests would be allowed to take home some of the leftovers. We took advantage of the leniency shown by the adults towards us and would storm the tables while they were busy scooping up the remains of the feast. This did not cause any embarrassment among the guests, who were all dressed to the nines; they would brazenly fill their pockets with the leftover meats and sweets. One of them, Aboudi, would go so far as to pack his spoils into a large plastic bag that he had taken the trouble to bring from home, especially for this purpose.

Outside the sports hall, Limping Elisha, the beggar of Netivot, would stand by the entrance and pester the arriving guests.

'Please, a few coins for the poor, please for the family. I'm unemployed and have five hungry little children at home.'

Elisha the Limper had no physical problem. He earned the moniker 'limper' because of his propensity to drag his right leg when walking in an effort to win sympathy from onlookers. This trick of his didn't last long. It was revealed to be a fraud when he had to run away from one of the market vendors, who was chasing Elisha after he had taken a bag of almonds without paying for it.

'Please, I have five hungry little children at home. I'm unemployed,' he said over and over like a mantra.

'How long have you been looking for work?' I quizzed him. 'Oh, for more than eight years, my son.' His expression was troubled as if he was sure that I, a boy of barely nine, would throw him a coin.

'How old are your little children, sir?' I queried.

He didn't answer as he was focused on trying to get money from Victor Ben-Atar, one of the latecomers, who ignored Elisha as he made his way to the entrance. Victor Ben-Atar was a wealthy contractor from Beersheva, the nearest city to Netivot. Apparently, he was an important person because only important people arrive late for celebrations.

'My little one is one,' Elisha smiled longingly. 'The others are between two and seven. I don't know exactly.'

'If you don't work, then why did you bring five children?' I asked. I thought he would treat my question with the respect that such a question deserved. Instead, he slapped me round the face. 'Go home you brat!'

In 1955, the first prime minister of Israel, David Ben-Gurion, had a plan to colonize the southern part of Israel with the thousands of new immigrants arriving from North Africa. My parents were among them. This region was essentially a barren desert, but his aim was to create a band of new towns stretching from east to west, populated by vigorous young immigrants who would help make the desert flourish. As waves of new arrivals set foot on the land of Israel, asking to be taken to the cities of Jerusalem and Tel Aviv, they were loaded onto trucks and driven south, according to Ben-Gurion's plan to settle the desert. Arriving at their destinations of unfamiliar 'towns', they found makeshift military tents and huts awaiting them, with no urban infrastructure. Such was my town of Netivot, as well as others like Sderot, Ofakim, Yeruham, and Dimona, where the atomic reactor is situated today. These naive immigrants, who believed the idle promises of Ben-Gurion and his friends, were unceremoniously forced off the trucks and left to find accommodation for their families in those improvised tents and huts. My disappointed parents, on seeing what was to be their new home of Netivot, were extremely reluctant to get off the truck. They agreed to disembark only after being urged by my grandfather, a fervent Zionist, who told them, 'We are pioneers and will help build the state of Israel where Jews will, at last, have a safe haven from persecution.' But in reality, the living conditions were very harsh, with no running water, electricity, or indoor sanitation, and worst of all, there were no jobs or any sources of income to feed the many mouths. And as if that weren't enough, they had to suffer a bloody ongoing war with the Arab neighbours. The Zionist dream began to evaporate, leaving behind a bitter taste of frustration and regret.

To build hundreds of properly designed houses in the hot desert conditions in the south of Israel, David Ben-Gurion himself appointed dozens of engineers and professionals in the field from Tel Aviv. The labourers were all locals, the same pioneers who poured out of the trucks late at night in the name of Zionism. Sometimes two or three contractors from the area would be appointed to work with the engineers of Tel Aviv. One of them was Victor Ben-Atar from Beersheva who would come almost every day to Netivot to collect workers in his van to man his construction sites.

Ben-Atar was a thirty-eight-year-old bachelor, desperate to get married, but he had a problem. His personality was difficult; he had feelings of inferiority even though he was a successful contractor who owned two cars, a van for work, and after work, to impress the women in the area, a Cadillac shipped from America, equipped with leather seats, air conditioning, and a sophisticated radio.

Victor the Builder, as everyone called him, was an absurdly over-groomed man who placed a significant emphasis on his personal appearance, thinking it would boost his chances of finding a wife. He always wore stylish and well-fitting clothes that were of the highest quality and he scrupulously followed the latest fashion trends. His hair always looked perfect. He probably visited the barber every day to keep his hair in such optimal condition.

His meticulously maintained moustache and French 'Chapeau' hat gave him the image of an English gentleman from the eighteenth century who occasionally visited the impoverished to observe their suffering. As opposed to what was commonly thought, he would not readily open his wallet nor would he approach those in need to offer some assistance. He would walk down the street with his annoyingly upright stature and wait for the people to come to him. Victor the builder was a type whose modesty was as foreign to him as East is from West.

Always inflated by excessive self-importance, always rushing to some place or other, or to a meeting he had arranged in order to appear an active and eminent man. As it turned out, these meetings were not those that could yield him large construction deals or occasional property acquisitions, but rather inconsequential meetings that he himself would inflate and glorify just so that the people would treat him with respect as an industrious businessman. In his shirt pocket were at least ten pens of all colours and types. He believed this would give him the appearance of being a respectable and well-educated man. It was rumoured that the man was actually illiterate and that the pens were intended to mask his ignorance. Sometimes he would immerse himself in a long conversation with strangers just to appear to be an interesting person whom people would wish to engage with. He made a big deal out of everything, even simple questions like what drink he wanted. He would take an excessive amount of time to answer as if he had been asked how much it would cost to build a six-story building or an asphalt road that would connect Netivot to Tel Aviv. However, despite his shortcomings, Victor Ben-Atar possessed significant financial clout and was able to employ numerous Netivot boys in his many ventures. That's why everyone was pleasant towards him, even though most of them had to put up a front in order to tolerate his whims and odd behaviour.

Chapter 21

The Lebanon War of 1982

The 1982 war in Lebanon was inevitable. The number of Israeli and Lebanese children affected by it was increasing. Their childhood was completely taken away from them as they were forced to spend nights and days in shelters. Their routine was disrupted and most of them developed anxieties that got worse even in their adulthood. What began as a 40 km-wide Israeli military operation against the activities of terror organizations based in Lebanon evolved into an eighteen-year bloodbath on Lebanese soil, claiming the lives of thousands, including innocent children.

On 3 June 1982, three members of the Abu Nidal Organisation ambushed Shlomo Argov, the Israeli Ambassador to the United Kingdom. One of the three terrorists, Hussein Ghassan, shot Mr Argov in the head as he was getting into his car after a banquet at the Dorchester Hotel in central London. Argov was critically injured and remained in a coma. Israeli intelligence discovered that the attack, carried out by the ANO, was in fact ordered by the Iraqi Intelligence Service.

On 4 June, one day after the assassination attempt, the Israeli Air Force attacked the Abu Nidal Organisation in southern Lebanon. However, this counter-attack did not deter the terrorists from continuing their bombing raids on Israeli civilians along the northern border.

The Israeli Defense cabinet ordered the army to prepare an operational plan to eradicate terrorism from southern Lebanon, in order to restore peace for both the Israelis and the Lebanese civilians who were suffering from a situation imposed on them by the terrorist organizations, that were being equipped and armed by Syria and Iran. The Israeli army submitted an operational plan to Defense Minister Ariel Sharon, who in turn presented the plan to Prime Minister Menachem Begin. Sharon had no idea of the hornet's nest that was about to burst open before our eyes, the fighters. Thousands of missiles, bombs, and grenades came to be discovered in schools, clinics, hospitals, and anywhere where civilians, especially children, could be found. The terror organizations exploited the fact that the Israeli army would hesitate in opening fire on such places. This caused not only a difficult moral dilemma for us fighters but also greatly endangered our lives.

The war began with a massive bombardment by Israeli jets on targets that, according to accurate intelligence, were being used as terrorist bases. This forty-five-minute attack served as a 'softening assault' in order to prepare the way for us, the ground forces.

I was a twenty-four year old reservist, assigned to a reserve battalion composed of twenty-two to twenty-five-year-old fighters, men of my age group, who found themselves once more being sent into Lebanon's fields of fire. We were joined by younger Golani fighters who were still doing their mandatory service, and by the Galilee Division (91), which consisted of brigades and battalions of infantry and artillery, plus platoons of engineering and sabotage forces, intelligence personnel, and medical teams.

I was already married to Sima and father to one-year-old Daniela. I had a part-time job at the local newspaper and attended the university for my political science studies. While juggling my parental responsibilities, my job and my studies, I volunteered in the community to support teenagers who had dropped out of school and were facing financial troubles at home.

As our 'limited operation' progressed, we found ourselves advancing to a far greater distance north, due to the discovery of numerous well-fortified terrorist bases and headquarters hidden in houses within the civilian population. Although the two groups, the Abu Nidal Organisation and the Palestine Liberation Organization, were in constant conflict with each other, they each carried out terrorist attacks against Israel to an equal extent. In response, Israel's reactions against the two organizations were equally tough, as they had been with all the other organizations in the West Bank and Gaza Strip operating at the same time. The instructions we received at the briefing before entering Lebanon left no room for doubt about the level and intensity of the action we were about to embark on. We were ordered to hit the terrorists as hard as possible, no matter which faction or organization they were from. We, the reservists, prepared ourselves well for combat contact with the enemy and also advised and helped prepare the younger members of the infantry force who were aged just nineteen and twenty, and were about to enter Lebanon for the first time to carry out the dangerous and complex ground battle.

After the bombardment by Israeli jets was completed, we crossed the Lebanese border and headed north, through the southern part of the Lebanon Valley, towards the town of Damour, and then onwards towards Beirut following the Beirut-Damascus Road. In the blue skies above us, we noted the presence of Israeli jets and armed helicopters that instilled confidence in us.

Apart from our main objective to halt the constant bombarding of Israel from the southern Lebanese border, our other goal was to capture a wide stretch of land, extending to 45 km into Lebanon, to have better control of the area that was being used by the Palestine Liberation Organisation and the Abu Nidal Organisation to attack Israel. However, in practice, we found ourselves advancing much deeper into Lebanon, well beyond the distance of 40-45 km in the original plan. We gained control of the coastal towns of Tire and Sidon, after fierce house-to-house battles where we came face to face with PLO terrorists, who were embedded in these urban areas and using civilians as human shields. War plans were drawn up and studied daily because it was not clear how the battles would unfold. You know how the war starts but there is no way of knowing how it will end.

We didn't feel comfortable during a war that lasted longer than planned. We were promised that we would return home within ten days at the most. But the deeper we went into the blazing but beautiful country of Lebanon, a different reality from that which our brilliant intelligence services knew dawned on us. We discovered unimaginably huge arsenals of weapons that were donated by Syria and Iran, and a large number of terrorist groups consisted of trained recruits from Gaza and the West Bank and mercenaries from other countries.

As we marched towards Sidon, we unexpectedly ran into Syrian commando and armoured forces, as well as a group of PLO terrorists who were sheltering like cowards behind the Syrians.

'This is going to be a war, not an operation,' I muttered out loud as I fired wildly at the house where a group of terrorists were firing at us.

The Syrian force was well-trained and lavishly equipped. But it was not their impressive equipment that prevented us from fighting them. It was politics. Israel did not want to be dragged into a confrontation with Syria. She only wished to eradicate terrorism from Lebanon, which was mostly carried out by terrorists from its various factions. We fighters were ordered to dig into a hideout and hold our fire until the parliamentary cabinet decided what to do. However, the other side showed absolutely no interest in Israel's political talks with America and with the Syrian President Assad himself. Their commander ordered his forces to open massive fire on us. It felt like hell. We had to literally glue our faces to the ground. The noise of the radio communications grew louder. Our commanders spoke to their senior commanders who were monitoring the war from Tel Aviv, and they spoke to those across the political spectrum, who were divided in their opinions. Meanwhile, we the fighters, were attacked by fire from all possible types of weapons, as if these stupid Syrians did not think that one or two grenades would be enough to eliminate us, the skilled commandos whose hands were tied and did not fire back.

One of us threw a few grenades at the Syrians but was immediately reprimanded by our commander, Omri.

'Aren't these clowns in the government aware of the hell we are in?' we shouted to our commander. And when we didn't get a response, we started sharing jokes about politicians and politics in general.

Sometimes it seemed that our raucous laughter even reached the ears of the Syrians. When flipping through the historical battles with Syrians, a picture emerges of stubborn, skilled fighters, and above all, filled with an abysmal hatred towards the Israelis. In their many battles with Israel, they demonstrated devotion and adherence to the mission and showed courage and perseverance. However, they always lost in the end. They would win battles but lose the war. During the 1967 Six-Day War and the 1973 Yom Kippur War, the Syrians reportedly demonstrated professionalism and praiseworthy commando fighting in the Golan Heights battles. However, despite this, they lost the wars and failed in their goal to control the Golan Heights. The Golani fighters fought like lionesses protecting their young, persevering with their stubborn fighting and brave professionalism until a total victory was achieved.

After the peace talks between the suit and tie wearers reached an impasse, we were given the order to act. We felt like beasts that had been chained and suddenly released. We noticed some additional forces from the Galilee Division (91) had joined us. The noise was deafening. In addition to the mutual fire between us and the Syrians, helicopters were circling overhead and firing heavy machine guns. We could not hear Omri's orders, so we decided to act independently based on instincts and experience. The battle was fierce and uncompromising. The Syrian commandos fought with much more professionalism and bravery than their terrorist comrades did. They fired RPG, rocket propelled grenade, missiles. One of the missiles hit our sniper. His head was torn from him and flew into the distance. After the battle, we started looking for his head and came across a torn and bloody hand. It was the hand of one of the Syrian commando fighters. The sight was gruesome. One of our fighters picked up our headless sniper's body with both hands and gently placed it on a stretcher. The entire body was intact. There was not a scratch or a single drop of blood on it.

This sight did not leave me for many years.

The fight turned into close-range combat, almost face-to-face. The adrenaline surge was sky-high. Ilan, our medic, ran towards some of those lying wounded under fire. He managed to save one and then ran back into the inferno to save others. But then, he was fatally hit by the Syrians. It was hard not to admire what Ilan did. You save one wounded perhaps out of instinct, but if you return to the same inferno to save another, then you are undoubtedly applying the value of brotherhood that is ingrained in every commando fighter.

At some point, Menashe, the commander of the 3rd platoon, took a bullet in the head and collapsed. Only after the battle was over, did we begin to treat Menashe, who was lying unconscious. We put him on a stretcher and started moving quickly, to an area where we could evacuate him by helicopter – a matter of a few kilometres on rough ground. It was not an easy task. We were being hit by mortar bombs and could not land a helicopter. We put him on a jeep and drove to a more convenient point, and from there he was taken to a hospital. With a lot of hard work and a strong will, he recovered, got married, and started a family.

After almost fourteen hours the battle was over. The Syrian force had been weakened and lost its ability to continue fighting due to the heavy losses it suffered. This is in addition to running out of ammunition due to a lack of supplies. The Syrian president seemed to have sent this commando force of his on a suicide mission. Our successful battles with the Syrian commandos embarrassed the Syrian president, Hafez Assad. It was all over the world's media. He scolded his senior army officers and in a moment of rage and desperation for revenge ordered his air force commander to launch an air attack on us. However, to his disappointment, his jets failed in their mission. About twenty Syrian artillery and air missiles were destroyed, and forty-seven Syrian fighter jets were shot down by the Israeli Air Force over the Lebanon Valley in an astonishingly brilliant operation during which not a single Israeli jet was lost. This remarkable operation emphasized Israel's absolute air superiority over the Syrian Air Force. This battle significantly shaped the character of the Israel Air Force.

After vanquishing the Syrian commandos in a long and stubborn battle, we left the area and started marching north, towards Sidon, our next target. On the way to Sidon, we arrived at an agricultural farm on the outskirts of the city. The sheep and cows were locked inside their pens. The smell of war was in the air in every corner of Lebanon. After we came across some water pipes, probably used for irrigation, our commander ordered everyone to shower. It was a mixed feeling of apprehension and relief. On the one hand, we were in the midst of a war in enemy territory, but on the other, our bodies were dirty and smelly after many days of not being able to wash. It was spectacularly surreal to see how everyone was jumping about naked under the water pipes as if we were all in one of the parks in Tel Aviv. It greatly improved our morale.

As we marched toward Sidon, we learned through the communications between the commanders of the forces that some members of the Galil Battalion 91 had reached the Beirut-Damascus Road. Others had already entered Beirut itself, after a bloody battle to destroy the PLO's main bases and drive out the Syrian forces stationed there. We then received an order to move speedily westward towards the outskirts of Sidon, where a battle had broken out between fighters from a paratrooper battalion and terrorists who had ambushed them. After helping them destroy the terrorists and the house where the paratroopers had been ambushed, we remained there for twenty-four hours engaged in continuous fighting in the crowded and densely populated refugee camps around the town, mainly inside the Ein al-Hilweh camp. The camp was established in 1948 by the International Committee of the Red Cross to house refugees from Arab villages, who flocked to it during the war between Israel and the neighbouring Arab countries. Initially, most of the refugees were Lebanese, but soon thousands of refugees from Syria, Jordan, and Palestine arrived and settled there. Within five years, the camp's population reached 70,000, making it the largest refugee camp in the Middle East.

The battle in the camp was, as we had expected, complicated by the presence of Lebanese civilians and children who found themselves trapped between us and the terrorists who were shooting at us from their houses. It was later discovered that these civilians had been held captive in their homes against their will by the terrorists, who took advantage of the fact that Israeli soldiers would not shoot in any direction where they suspected the presence of unarmed people. Our moral dilemma intensified once inside the notorious Ein al-Hilweh refugee camp. Not only was the dilemma of firing on civilians doubled, but became even more complicated. It turned out that not only were the terrorists using civilians as human shields, but there were also civilians, including children, who had agreed to pretend they were being held against their will in return for a considerable sum of money. This was proved to be correct after external, non-Israeli sources examined some of the incidents that took place in Lebanon during the years 1980 and 1981. It was a UN delegation that was investigating war crimes against children allegedly committed by the Israeli army. To their surprise, they discovered the opposite. Not only did the Israeli soldiers, and I can testify to this, not shoot these children, but they even risked their own lives by avoiding shooting back at those who were firing at them. What most amazed the members of the delegation was the discovery that it was not the Israelis who had committed war crimes, but the terrorists who had done so by using their own children as human shields.

"I wonder if the outside world knows about these situations," I said to my comrade Oded, as we advanced through Ein al-Hilweh. We were moving at a slower pace than usual taking extra care, shooting single bullets instead of rounds, and avoiding as much as possible the use of grenades that could make it easier for us to clear the target. Measures that caused us to further endanger our own lives.

'I doubt it," he replied. "The world only sees the bodies of those children through the media, who never tell the whole story."

Oded was generally a quiet person, the type who did a lot but said little. He excelled in all of his tests. He refused to settle for average grades. Every small deed or task seemed like a challenge to him. He had a constant sadness in his expression and rarely smiled. In 1974, when just a teenager, he lost his mother in a terror attack. He never admitted it, but we all assumed that he enlisted for the unit mainly to avenge his mother's death. This is why he would challenge himself not to fail, so as to avoid being thrown out of the unit.

That particular year, the northern part of Israel had been suffering greatly from incessant shelling by terrorist organizations based in southern Lebanon, as well as from the ongoing incursions of terrorists into Israeli territory. Many innocent and defenseless civilians, including dozens of children, had been killed. Among them was the Kiryat Shmona massacre on 11 April 1974, during which eighteen Israeli civilians were killed, half of them children, and a mother with her four-month-old baby who happened to be walking past the school that was attacked that morning. Then, only a week later, came the Beit She'an attack, during which four children and two women were killed, one of whom was Oded's mother who was on her way to work at the local school.

Those attacks were not carried out by the PLO as we all assumed, but by the most prominent of the terror groups at that time, the Democratic Front for the Liberation of Palestine (DFLP), which had split from the larger Popular Front for the Liberation of Palestine in 1969. This group based itself along Lebanon's border with Israel, from where they carried out many brutal terrorist attacks on Israel. These combined atrocities all proved too much for the Israeli government to continue to act with restraint. It called on its army to suggest a plan for an effective operation deep in Lebanon. In just forty-eight hours, the army came forward with 'Operation Three Rings', an operation involving forces of the navy, the air force, undercover fighters, agents from *Mossad*, and commando fighters from the Golani brigade. The objectives of the operation were:

1. To destroy the DFLP's houses and bunkers which served as their headquarters in the Lebanese coastal city of Damour, 20 km south of Beirut.

2. To capture three wanted leaders of the DFLP who were the main planners of the massacre in Ma'alot, bring them back to Israel for interrogation, and extract valuable information from them about the organization's activities. For this task, six cold-

blooded warriors with absolute control over their reactions and movements were chosen.

3. Following the completion of the infantry operation and once the forces were back safely on the naval ship, air force jets would bomb and destroy other targets in the area that housed the DFLP, eliminating as many terrorists as possible.

The Cabinet gave the green light. Late at night, the operation began. An elite force of thirty-six Golani fighters, together with nine fighters from their undercover unit dressed in civilian clothes, were brought to the waters off Damour by an Israeli navy ship. This was equipped with spare ammunition and an improvised operating theatre, along with medical staff. Above them a helicopter, with a rescue force on board ready to act if needed, was hovering and monitoring their movements. The entire assault force was collected from the ship by six commando boats and brought to shore. Arriving on the beach of Damour, they split into two teams. One, the Golani force, swiftly boarded a truck displaying local identity plates which had been prearranged for them by a *Mossad* agent. They were immediately transported to the area where the bunkers and houses they had been sent to destroy were located.

The other force, the undercover unit, quietly got into the three civilian cars that were waiting for them, also hired locally by a *Mossad* agent. The drivers, who just so happened to be *Mossad* agents too, drove them to the address of the house where they would find the wanted terrorists, as well as the documents they needed to seize. When they reached the area of the house, the undercover unit fighters calmly got out, making sure their weapons were well hidden under the civilian clothes they were wearing as a disguise, and slowly walked towards the target property. The drivers kept the engines running, waiting for them as if they were simply local taxi drivers.

Mission completed and along with the captured terrorists and documents, the fighters climbed back into the waiting cars and were driven away inconspicuously at a normal speed towards the sea and to the ship waiting for them. Ten minutes after the forces had left the area, including the *Mossad* agents who disappeared back to their rented apartments somewhere in Beirut, Israel Defense Forces' planes bombed the offices and training bases of the DFLP and PFLP terror groups, eliminating at least twenty-seven terrorists and destroying bunkers and houses that had served as their headquarters. The operation was crowned a success. All the forces involved had met the mission goals faultlessly, with no mishaps and no casualties.

Back to the Lebanon War of 1982

On 13 June, after our complex and extra-cautionary fighting in the Ein al-Hilweh camp was completed, we arrived in Beirut along with the other forces from our division that had been separated at the beginning of the war. We were ordered to besiege the city. During the seventy-day siege, we endured fierce battles all over Beirut, including in some very crowded residential neighbourhoods where it was difficult for us to distinguish between the enemy and innocent civilians, since everyone was wearing civilian clothes. The cowardly terrorists chose not to dress in their combat fatigues so they could deceive us, as we, from our experience with them, knew for sure that they possessed uniforms. Yet despite the challenging limitations of fighting with civilians nearby and the mounting numbers of dead and wounded among our force, we continued to tighten our grip on the city of Beirut and clear the terrorists out of the city, eventually forcing Yasser Arafat to consider surrendering. During the course of the fighting, Beirut Airport and many buildings throughout the city were destroyed. At the end of three months of fierce combat covering almost all areas of Lebanon, many terrorists from all the factions and organizations established in the country had been killed. The IDF lost 368 soldiers. The organization that suffered the most losses was the PLO. Not only did Arafat lose a lot of his fighters, including many commanders, but he also suffered a bitter insult when he was expelled from Lebanon to Tunisia. In the light of the resulting situation, especially after it became clear to Yasser Arafat that he had lost more than a thousand of his fighters and most of his infrastructure had been destroyed, he expressed his readiness for negotiations. The United States was required to mediate and called for the PLO to withdraw completely from Lebanon. Arafat, for his part, agreed to negotiate in an attempt to rescue his forces from this political disaster; an attempt that resulted in the arrival of an international force that evacuated the PLO fighters from all Lebanese territories.

In mid-August, an agreement had also been reached to expel the Syrian and Palestinian forces from Beirut, a move that left the city under IDF control until the area could be stabilized by diplomatic means. While waiting for the evacuation process to be carried out during the agreed period of between 31 August and 10 September 1982, the Lebanese Christian leader Bashir Gemayel was elected president. Israel saw his election as a political breakthrough and Israeli Defense Minister Ariel Sharon stated that the signing of a peace agreement with Lebanon was imminent. Gemayel himself did not get to sit in the presidency for long. By 14 September, Gemayel had been assassinated. By way of revenge, Christian Phalangist militia entered the Palestinian refugee camps of Sabra and Shatila and killed hundreds of local Muslim civilians. During that volatile period, we, the exhausted reservists stationed at our makeshift base in southern Beirut, were receiving hints that we were about to be sent home and released from duty, perhaps as early as 13 September. While waiting for our discharge, we were patrolling and protecting the locals from Muslim militants who were willing to kill anyone who looked Christian.

Israel had gone to war in Lebanon in the summer of 1982 for three principal reasons:

a. The largest terrorist organisations Abu Nidal and the PLO had taken over Lebanon and made it the main base for Palestinian attacks against Israel.

b. The bloody Lebanese civil war in 1975 between the Christians and a coalition of terrorist organizations and Muslim radical groups, plus other factions and groups, ultimately led to the collapse of the Lebanese government and its army. This created an existential threat to the Christian population in northern and southern Lebanon and to the Christian political hegemony. Israel had looked on the Christian militias as a partner in the war on terror and had therefore armed and assisted them. When the terror from southern Lebanon intensified, Israel felt that the Christian militias would not be capable of fighting the terrorist organizations alone, hence the invasion of south Lebanon with the aim of eliminating the growing terror infrastructure there. There was another symbolic reason why Israel chose to assist the Christian militias. This dates back to 1948 and the early months of the Jewish state. Israel always appreciated the aid it had received from the Lebanese Christians when they helped to smuggle weapons and equipment through southern Lebanon into Israel in exchange for sums of money. Czechoslovakia in the days of its Communist leader Marshal Tito, as well as France and Britain, had agreed to sell Israel obsolete weapons that were stored in warehouses after the end of World War II. Delivering these weapons via the sea or by air was problematic, almost impossible. The only viable option was to smuggle them to Israel by land, and the only friendly soil Israel had in those days was Lebanon. Egypt, Jordan, and Syria were all at war with Israel and sought its destruction rather than its receipt of armaments. In those years, the Christians completely controlled Lebanon. Beirut became known as 'the Paris of the Middle East', with millions of tourists visiting it each year to enjoy its beautiful beaches, luxurious hotels, and vibrant nightlife. Israel, which had just been established, desperately needed these weapons to deal with the threat from its three belligerent neighbouring Arab countries.

c. In the thirty years between 1975 and 2005, Syria deepened its presence and influence in Lebanon, taking advantage of the punishing civil war that had caused huge chaos and disrupted the Lebanese establishment. The Lebanese army was easily crushed due to the defection of fighters and officers who had gone to join the dozens of different militias and groups fighting each other for control of Lebanon. Syria understood very well how to fill the vacuum by asserting her presence and promising to help return the order to Lebanon, but in actual fact, Syrian intentions were not solely to help the fractured country, but also to take control of it. Syria had proclaimed many times that historically the land of Lebanon had actually belonged to her since the dawn of history. However, Israel was not interested in historic territorial claims nor in the ownership of Lebanon, but simply wanted to ensure peace and security peace for its citizens in the north suffering from the incessant terrorist attacks coming from Lebanon. Israel was aware of Syria's support and encouragement for the terror organizations that attacked her, hence Israel's intention was to weaken, even if just temporarily, the Syrian presence and influence in Lebanon, and if necessary, to remove all Syrian forces from Lebanon, either militarily or by diplomatic efforts. Nevertheless, despite Israel's warnings, the Syrian influence in Lebanon did weaken the Christian militias, including by the assassination of the Christian-elected president, Bashir Gemayel. Syria also managed to strengthen the power of Lebanon's Shiite Muslims, who were Syria's dependents and doers. This subsequently led to the birth of the brutal Shiite terrorist organization Hezbollah, which filled the void created in southern Lebanon after the 1982 war once the two dominant terror organizations, the Abu Nidal Organisation and the PLO, had disintegrated. While Yasser Arafat and his organization were deported to Tunisia, the ANO fighters fled east to Iraq. Once there, its founder and leader Abu Nidal set up another terrorist organization after major disagreements with Yasser Arafat. Nidal even tried to eliminate his rival when Arafat hinted that Nidal had been willing to negotiate with Israel, which the extremist Abu Nidal saw as an unwarranted betrayal. In August 2002, Abu Nidal was assassinated by Saddam Hussein's soldiers in Baghdad.

The issues outlined above left the State of Israel with no choice but to go to war in Lebanon.

However, before the Israeli cabinet would agree to enter Lebanon to conduct a full-scale war, the IDF tried to deal with the terror issue by conducting a series of short military actions. There were numerous raids both in southern Lebanon and in the capital Beirut (many of which I took part in with my battalion) during which we targeted and destroyed the terrorists' bunkers, at the same time eliminating some of their senior leaders. However, these actions failed to completely paralyze the terrorist activity. Syria's deepening involvement in Lebanon and support of the terrorist organizations, aided by the collusion of Iran in this, made our short military actions less effective.

In the spring of 1976, the United States tried to mediate between Syria and Israel to reduce the Syrian military threat created by Syria's growing involvement in the unfolding Lebanese civil war. This succeeded in bringing reconciliation talks between then-Israeli Prime Minister Yitzhak Rabin and Syrian President Hafez Assad. Israel demanded that Syria must not increase its hold on southern Lebanon nor send its army into that area. Assad agreed to this in order to prevent any possible confrontation with the Israeli army, which needed to control southern Lebanon to purge it of terrorist activities. Syria was aware of the importance Israel placed on supporting, arming, and training the Christian militias, particularly those based in the south of Lebanon. Surprisingly, the Syrians tended to endorse this. Without officially acknowledging it, Syrian President Assad understood the necessity of Israel controlling the south of Lebanon, as the terrorist organizations favoured this region for two reasons. Firstly, this area was what we had termed the 'Wild West of Lebanon', as the terror organizations were rampant and it was too chaotic for the Lebanese army to control. Secondly, this was the part of Lebanon closest to the Israeli border, making terrorist attacks on northern Israel easier and faster.

However, in the spring of 1981, relations and implicit understandings between Syria and Israel deteriorated. This was after the Israeli Air Force had shot down two Syrian helicopters in the central Lebanon Valley. Israel mistakenly thought these Syrian helicopters were on their way to attack the fortified Christian headquarters on a mountain east of the town of Zahala. Once it realized its mistake, Israel immediately sent an apology to the Syrians, which was rejected. Syria was convinced that it was a provocation by the Israeli army to prove its supremacy and control over southern Lebanon. The Israeli prime minister at the time, Menachem Begin, who had promised the Lebanese Christian leader, Camille Chimoun, complete protection from the Syrians and the terrorist organizations, had, in this case, relied on Israeli intelligence reports confirming that Syrian helicopters were on their way to attack the Christian headquarters. Prime Minister Begin reiterated, both in an official statement and in a media interview, that he felt obligated to protect the Christian militias in Lebanon and therefore the downing of the Syrian helicopters was justified and even necessary. Many years later, in his autobiography, Menachem Begin wrote that he would regret until the day he died granting the permission to shoot down the Syrian helicopters and that the last thing he wanted then was to worsen his country's relations with Syria. Thus, on 29 April 1981, after feeling that their honour had been trampled, the Syrians decided to respond to the loss of the helicopters by deploying long-range SA–6 surface-to-air missiles to the Lebanon Valley. These missiles had the capacity to reach any corner of Israel and beyond. Israel felt seriously threatened and could not countenance this aggressive move by Syria which, in addition to the physical presence of the missiles, sent a strong message throughout the media of a possible war against Israel.

A crisis was beginning to unfold.

The presence of the Syrian long-range missiles obstructed the Israeli Air Force's ability to control the airspace of south Lebanon and to continue its mission to clear out terrorism in the area. The IDF's ground forces were now also limited in their protracted actions against terrorist organizations, not only around the Lebanon Valley but all over the south of Lebanon. What made the situation worse, and prompted great concern on the Israeli side, were the public statements by Syria encouraging terrorist organizations throughout the whole of Lebanon to intensify the armed struggle against Israel, and that they, the Syrians, would be happy to support them with unlimited financial resources. Israel's Cabinet was convened at night to discuss the Syrian threat. One of the ministers expressed concern that a war on the Syrian front could only be a matter of hours. The Israeli army began preparations for war.

At the same time, US President Ronald Reagan sent his special envoy Philip Habib to the area to try to (a) persuade the Syrians to remove the missiles from Lebanon, and (b) persuade Israel not to invade Lebanon and certainly not to attack the Syrian missiles. But Syria stubbornly refused to accede. Not only did they close their ears to what the US envoy Habib presented to them, but they continued to issue explicit threats against Israel. In one of their threats, they even suggested they would welcome a comprehensive war with Israel in order to take advantage of the opportunity to conquer the Israeli part of the Golan Heights.

This rejection by the Syrians led the following year to its military confrontation with Israel during the 1982 Lebanon War. Prior to that, on 9 June 1981, Israel forcefully demonstrated its military capability to Syria when Iraq's nuclear reactor was destroyed by the Israeli Air Force.

A few weeks after this audacious Israeli attack on the Iraqi nuclear reactor, in July 1981 the relentless war between the IDF and the terrorist organizations in southern Lebanon stepped up another notch. The terrorist organizations, who feared losing control over southern Lebanon, now began to use a method of attack not seen before, that of long-range artillery. By this time, having completed my mandatory three years of service, I was serving in a reserve battalion composed of several companies of infantry. We were constantly having encounters with terrorists and nearly every night we had to infiltrate southern Lebanon to carry out raids on terrorist targets scattered throughout the area. We were aware of the new weaponry the terrorists were using, thus most of our raids were to target their locations and destroy their artillery. It turned out that the terrorist organizations, which for years had only been using bazookas and Katyusha rockets to attack Israel, had received a gift from the Syrians.

As part of its unlimited and broad support, the Syrians provided the terrorists with cannons that had far-reaching artillery capability. This method of attacking Israeli population centres by artillery has since been adopted by all terrorist organizations and would go on to be used by Palestinian organizations operating in the Gaza Strip and by Hezbollah in Lebanon. In recent years, southern Israel has suffered from rockets and explosive balloons launched from Gaza. These attacks not only caused panic and large numbers of casualties among Israeli civilians but also completely disrupted their daily lives to the point that a significant number of Israelis in the northern region were forced to leave their homes. Israel escalated its response and sent fighter jets to bomb terrorist bases throughout southern Lebanon. However, the attacks on northern Israel did not diminish, despite the extensive destruction of the terrorists' headquarters by Israeli jets. Instead, they increased, with the encouragement of the Syrians and the support of several Arab countries that were providing the terrorist organizations with ammunition and large sums of money.

An atmosphere of war pervaded the entire region covering the north of Israel and the south of Lebanon. Military vehicles, including tanks, plus infantry forces, began to flow into the area.

We, the young reservists, were observing everything from our lookout point high up on Mount Dov, the outpost from which we conducted our operations in southern Lebanon. The terrorists insisted on continuing their belligerent acts, feeling compelled by the generous and extensive support they were receiving. From my past experiences of engagement with them, I can say that I did not consider these terrorists to be brave warriors or admirable fighters. On each encounter, they would flee the battlefield, surrender immediately, or use children as human shields. I can only count a few cases where I saw some of them behaving like fighters, squaring up to us, the armed soldiers. Their 'heroism' manifested itself by dominating the weak in society, the civilians, children, and unarmed women.

For three consecutive weeks, we found ourselves engaged in a war with the terrorist organizations, sometimes having to use guerrilla tactics. In such cases, they had the advantage over us because they were familiar with the topographic conditions in the area of operation. But we learned that guerrilla warfare doesn't always have to be to the advantage of the terrorists. This type of engagement can also serve to benefit the attackers as long as they are able to call on their personal skills and not just the weapons at their disposal. We proved this when we came under fire from the terrorists, including from close range, and defeated them by way of tricks and deception. Sometimes we had to stop ourselves from bursting into laughter during the battle itself when we saw the terrorists' reactions to our wily stunts. Encounters with these amateurish fighters could make us laugh, but on the other hand, they caused us great stress and misery. Not only were we in intense combat activity and not able to sleep more than three hours a night, but we were saddened to hear the continuing news about the wounded and killed from the civilian population of northern Israel who were still being incessantly shelled.

The heated situation led to a further flourish of diplomatic activity, thus, on 24 July 1981, after many weeks of negotiations, the American mediator Philip Habib succeeded in breaking down the stubbornness of the terrorists. The fighting ended through a ceasefire agreement between Israel and the terrorist organizations in Lebanon, especially the PLO. Sadly, it turned out that this agreement was a smokescreen, as the terrorist organizations had no real intention of implementing it. They had agreed to the ceasefire to buy themselves some time to reorganize and re-arm. After the Israeli success of Operation Litani in 1978, when the PLO's morale and operational capacity had been totally undermined, Arafat and his organization managed to equip, rearm, and re-establish themselves in southern Lebanon. Now they enjoyed the support of Syria, Iraq, and Iran. Arafat chose to violate the ensuing ceasefire agreement after he 'discovered' a loophole in the agreement, which he cunningly exploited. It turned out that this ceasefire agreement was proving to be problematic in the way it was interpreted.

The agreement signed was aimed to ensure a state of non-combat between Israel and the PLO. It was understood that the ceasefire agreement covered all territories and that it was not the location that mattered, but the cessation of hostilities, no matter in which geographical location. Thus, while Israel argued that the PLO should be banned from mounting attacks against Israel from any country, Arafat's interpretation claimed that the terms of the ceasefire agreement were valid for its attacks on Israel from the soil of Lebanon only, and still allowed the PLO to attack Israel from non-Lebanese territory, such as Jordan or Syria. Moreover, although Arafat explicitly undertook that he would condemn any act of terrorism against Israel, it turned out that his promise was false. Arafat constantly refused to condemn many of the acts of terror that were carried out from south Lebanon.

Emboldened by the ambiguity of the agreement, the PLO began to encourage terrorist activity from Syrian territory and renewed their terrorist attacks against Israel, this time with increased force and the use of more sophisticated weapons. Israel saw this as an example of Arafat's duplicity and felt not only betrayed but also threatened. This signaled the first steps leading to the 1982 Lebanon War.

After many discussions in the Israeli Cabinet, it was agreed to deploy an extensive military force and enter Lebanon from its south to eradicate the terrorist threats from there once and for all. Prime Minister Menachem Begin, together with Chief of Staff Rafael Eitan, and with the encouragement of Defense Minister Ariel Sharon, recommended to the Cabinet to approve Sharon's plan to invade southern Lebanon. The goals were:

1. The elimination of the terrorist organizations' headquarters throughout Lebanon and thus remove the constant threat to the citizens of northern Israel.
2. To hit and cause severe damage to the Syrian military force. The Israeli Air Force would destroy the Syrian armaments and missiles in the Lebanon Valley, thus ending the Syrian influence in Lebanon and its support and arming of terrorist organizations.

3. To help the Christian militias end the civil war within Lebanon, and establish a westernized Lebanese state with a stable regime that would agree to sign a peace agreement with Israel.

At the same Cabinet meeting, Ariel Sharon revealed that he had been in contact over the recent months with a Christian leader in Lebanon named Bashir Gemayel who was planning to run in the forthcoming presidential election. The Mossad, which had begun developing these ties a year earlier, had helped to strengthen Gemayel's status in Lebanon. Sharon, who was a dominant force in the Cabinet meeting, recommended the Israeli government help prepare Bashir's path to the presidency. Sharon saw him as the most favourable candidate due to his westernized views, and as someone who would sign a peace agreement with Israel, whom he did not regard as the Zionist enemy to be eliminated.

Indeed, on 23 August 1982, Bashir Gemayel was elected president by the Lebanese parliament. Israel did not conceal its help and support in this, including transporting voters to the polls in military vehicles as protection from the Syrian and terrorist organizations' threats to kill anyone who voted for Gemayel. Those threats did not hurt the voters, but unfortunately, they hurt the candidate himself when he was assassinated three weeks later. The assassin, Habib Tanius Shartouni, had been sent by the Syrians to send a clear message to all Christians that the control of Lebanon would remain in their hands. Israel hoped that the successor to the murdered president, who would undoubtedly be a Christian too, would continue on the westernizing path and sign the anticipated peace agreement. But the reality took an unexpected turn. Bashir Gemayel's brother Amin, who took over from him, was too weak to implement the accords with Israel as he was in fear of the Syrians and other Arab countries. Amin excused this by the inability of his fractured country to defend itself against interference, due to its dependence on the Muslim Arab world. Therefore, Lebanon could not afford to deviate from the Arab consensus regarding its relations with Israel. Amin felt he could not sign a separate peace agreement with Israel because in doing so he could find himself 'facing the firing squad'. Amin did not wish to suffer the same fate as Egyptian President Anwar Sadat one year earlier, who was assassinated because he had dared to sign a separate peace agreement with Israel.

Fearing for his life, the new Lebanese president cancelled the peace agreement drawn up by the Americans that Israel had hoped to sign with his late brother Bashir. This move spurred the terrorist organizations in Lebanon to continue attacking Israel, and subsequently, strengthened the rising Hezbollah organization, which was supported by the Syrians and Iranians. Above all, it increased the power of the Shiite Muslim majority in Lebanon, who traditionally maintained religious and cultural ties with their Iranian brethren. With the backing of Iran and Syria, it was the Shiite community that gave birth to Hezbollah, a development that forced Israel to remain in southern Lebanon for eighteen years, with the loss of hundreds of its soldiers. Only after public pressure within Israel did she withdraw in 2000 under the leadership of Prime Minister Ehud Barak, leaving Lebanon in the hands of divided and conflicting organizations that are fighting each other to this day, Hezbollah being the dominant one among them.

In conclusion. the Lebanon War was waged by Israel against two terrorist organizations, the PLO, led by Yasser Arafat, who had come to find refuge in Lebanon after being expelled from Jordan during 'Black September' in 1970, and the Abu Nidal Organisation, a splinter group of the PLO set up in 1974 by its eponymous leader. These terrorist groups, who were supported by neighbouring Arab states, notably Syria, saw their presence in Lebanon as an opportunity to fight Israel from close range. They therefore chose to locate their bases scattered around southern Lebanon, as close as possible to the northern Israeli border, from where they had been mounting hundreds of deadly terrorist attacks on the beleaguered civilians of northern Israel, many children among them. With the support of Syria and Iran, they were able to establish an extensive infrastructure and stockpiles of weapons.

This led to vigorous retaliation by the Israeli army in which the PLO was almost obliterated. Despite this, these organizations showed no sign of ceasing the fight against Israel, and worst of all, they repeatedly declared that their main goal was the elimination of the Jewish entity and the destruction of Israel. These announcements, which were accompanied by severe terrorist attacks against Israel, were of great concern to the Israeli cabinet.

The 1982 Lebanon War was inevitable. In the light of the continuation of the terrorist attacks, Israeli Defense Minister Ariel Sharon worked on plans for an attack on Lebanon which aimed to finally expel the PLO from its bases and eliminate its leadership and control in Lebanon, and in particular in southern Lebanon. From the point of view of the supporters of the Israeli invasion and especially its architectural planners, the war brought significant achievements. The Syrian army in southern Lebanon was hit hard, the PLO was expelled from Lebanon and established its new headquarters in Tunisia, far away from Israel's borders, and most of the military forces of the other small Palestinian terrorist organizations were eliminated. Many terrorists were killed, thousands were arrested, and the IDF seized most of their weapons.

To close this chapter on the Lebanon War, here is a tragic occurrence that can only occur one in a million:

In war, there are many heartbreaking situations involving loss and enduring pain, but we seldom encounter tragedies caused by improbable coincidences, such as for example two close family members dying in the same battle. The following story and its sequence of events, including all the stages that took place during the twenty-four hours in which the drama unfolded, is an especially rare one; an unfortunate coincidence that resulted in a devastating human error. This extraordinary event united two families, who had never known each other before, in a double tragedy. The story concerns two Israeli soldiers with exactly the same name, who happened to live in the same neighbourhood of Jerusalem, just a few houses away from each other. These two young men were both killed in action during the same week, in the same battlefield location of the Ein al-Hilweh refugee camp during the Lebanon War. The name they shared was Yuval Harel. One was Yuval Harel who served in the Armoured Corps, and the other was Yuval Harel from the Paratroopers' force. Both were aged nineteen. The tragedy in this sad story was not about the coincidence of two killed soldiers having the same name and living in the same neighbourhood, but in the way their families learned of the death of their loved one, and the unnecessary grief each of the families had to endure. It was the unfortunate set of events that caused immense grief to both families when military representatives came to inform them about the death of their beloved sons and the news of the death of one Yuval Harel became a source of hope for the parents of the other Yuval Harel. Yuval the paratrooper was killed on Thursday, 10 June 1982 at 12.55 pm, when Israeli Air Force jets erroneously bombed his force on the eastern side of Ein al-Hilweh. Thirty-four Israeli soldiers were killed in this terrible catastrophe.

I was only 100 metres away from the incident and could hear the bomb landing, followed by the pitiful screams of the wounded. My platoon could do nothing to help them since we were engaged in an intense face-to-face battle against dozens of armed terrorists in the crowded alleyways of Ein al-Hilweh. Yuval was a soldier in the force of paratroopers whom we were fighting alongside in the refugee camps around Sidon. In Ein al-Hilweh, we were fighting inside the south section of the refugee camp, while Yuval and his force were in the eastern section. They too became involved in a difficult and complex battle due to the overcrowded conditions of the camp and the large number of civilians out on the streets, as they were reluctant to stay inside their shattered homes and there were no shelters for them to find protection. Many of these people were being used by the terrorists as human shields, as they knew the Israeli soldiers would not shoot if unarmed civilians could be endangered. Only half an hour after the bombing, we were shaken by hearing from one of our paramedics about the death of Yuval and the other thirty-three soldiers. The news spread fear and concern among us. How could our revered Israeli Air Force make such a deadly mistake? Our unit was in deep shock and our morale and confidence in our own air force descended to our boots. Would we be the next unit to be attacked from the air by our own fighter jets? Nonetheless, we continued with our mission, fighting in the hellish conditions of the crowded camp. Meanwhile, Yuval Harel from the Armoured Corps had been killed two days earlier on Tuesday 8 June at 2.30 pm, when a missile hit his tank as it was breaking through into the terrorist strongholds in the same camp.

On Friday 11 June, two separate IDF teams, comprising men specially trained for the sensitive role of breaking the news to a family of the death of their loved one, were sent to Jerusalem to inform each of the dead soldiers' families. To prevent panic in the quiet neighbourhood, the teams were instructed to perform their delicate tasks at different hours. One team would inform the family of Yuval from the Armoured Corps in the morning, while the other team would inform the family of Yuval the paratrooper at five in the afternoon. But when the two teams of military representatives arrived in the neighbourhood to bring the sad news to the men's parents, they encountered a problem that caused confusion and embarrassment and which turned a routine event into an almost biblical saga. The team that arrived in the morning to inform the family of Yuval from the Armoured Corps had some difficulty in finding the house, so they asked a couple of local residents to guide them to the Harel household. But the residents mistakenly guided them to the house of Yuval the paratrooper, coincidentally just a few blocks down the road from the house of Yuval from the Armoured Corps. The first team of army representatives did not know about the death of the other Yuval, the paratrooper, and were not aware that another army team was supposed to arrive later that same day to inform his family about it. Following the instructions given by the locals, the army officials knocked on the door of the home of Yuval the paratrooper, and told the young man's family the terrible news. The family collapsed in grief and began the process of mourning their dead son. One hour later, after studying the details properly, the army officials realized to their horror that they had mistakenly gone to the wrong house. They immediately rushed back to the house of the paratrooper's family, informed the grieving family of the good news, and apologized to them profusely for their awful mistake. After leaving, they headed immediately to the house of Yuval from the Armoured Corps and informed his family about the death of their son.

This double tragedy, already shocking, now worsens.

Five hours later, while the paratrooper's family was still recovering from their shock, but yet, feeling elated and relieved to hear that it was not their own beloved son who had been killed, the second team of army officials knocked on their door. This time it was not by accident nor by error. They had come to inform the family that their son Yuval had in fact been killed.

Throughout all the years that have passed since then and even today, I have not been able to stop thinking about what this family went through on that day.

The two soldiers from the Talpiot neighborhood of Jerusalem, who in life had shared the same name, were buried near to each other in the same row of the military cemetery on Mount Herzl in Jerusalem. About a year later, a son was born to another family named Harel who lived in the neighborhood. He was named Yuval, after the two fallen soldiers.

Several documentaries and songs have appeared in Israel over the years to tell this remarkable story. One film relates a minor, but telling, incident from Yuval's (from the Armoured Corps) life. When he was just four years of age, the Harel family was living in Canada as his father was working there temporarily. One day Yuval became separated from his parents in a crowded shopping mall. With great resourcefulness, little Yuval managed to locate the 'Lost and Found' office in the mall. Once inside, the tiny boy grabbed the announcement microphone and addressed his father in Hebrew, 'Dad, I'm at the Lost and Found'.

Chapter 22

The aftermath of Lebanon

In October 1982, about three months after we were drafted into the war in Lebanon, we received the message we were eagerly awaiting; we were going home! The moment to be released from the Lebanese mud had arrived. It seemed like someone in the high windows finally realized that we reservists had done enough and that we needed to quickly return to our studies or to work. There was life after war after all. I was newly married, and the father of a two-month-old baby girl, Daniela. I had to postpone my university studies for a year because I needed to put food on the table. Sima did not want to work even though she was offered an office job, the kind of job that was the ultimate dream of every girl in Netivot in 1982. She wanted to fulfil her role as a devoted full-time mother. Fortunately, Hanania, the owner of the only local paper in Netivot, agreed to accept me back to work, but on the condition that in addition to writing articles and news and gossip, I would have to run between the two arms of the business to sell advertising space for the paper. I didn't like it but had to agree just so I could keep my job as a young journalist.

Only seven weeks later, to my surprise, it became clear that this was an opportunity for a side income. I received bonuses and percentages from each sale I made and even got paid extra for writing the ads' content more creatively. What's more, I discovered skills about myself that I was not aware of – the ability to sell!

When Sima and I thought it was time for us to take the next step in our relationship and get married, she was already two months pregnant. We were not a couple of means, and our parents had minimal financial resources. So, a grand opulent wedding was simply beyond our financial reach, and in contrast with the residents of Tel Aviv, our wedding ceremony and celebration were conducted on a limited budget. However, while a poor wedding like ours may not have all the lavish elements of weddings in Tel Aviv, it was, to us, a meaningful and joyous celebration filled with pure love, the seeds of which were planted when we were just teenagers.

The preparations for the wedding began four weeks before the set date. That's how it was in Netivot. There was no need to give people much advance notice. They weren't too busy in the evenings anyway. Besides, they would not want to miss a celebration where they had the opportunity to have a much more satisfying dinner than the kind they had at home.

To keep the costs down, we of course chose to host our wedding at the sports hall in town that was used for celebrations such as bar mitzvahs and weddings, in addition to gymnastics and various sports activities. To decorate the sports hall, we enlisted the help of friends and family, and collectively, we crafted homemade centrepieces and adorned the area with vibrant paper lanterns. Then we gathered a plethora of colourful ornaments, which people typically use to decorate their Sukkah (a temporary hut constructed alongside one's home for use during the Jewish festival of Sukkot), and hung them from the ceiling. Pieces of fabric decorated in Moroccan style were used to cover the graffiti on the walls as the content of their messages did not really match the event.

Our attire may not have been extravagant, but it suited us perfectly and made us feel comfortable and beautiful on our special day. Sima decided to wear a simple yet elegant off-the-rack wedding dress that made her radiant, I wore a well-fitted suit that I borrowed from my friend Amir, who had gotten married just a few weeks before.

Inviting a large number of guests can significantly increase expenses. Therefore, we tried to invite a small circle of friends and family. However, in reality, invited and non-invited guests felt free to turn up. There wasn't food for everyone, of course, but still, the people, adults and children, danced and sat on makeshift chairs and it was evident on their faces that they came to rejoice with the bride and groom and not just take advantage of the opportunity of a sumptuous meal.

The wedding cake was a simple but delicious creation made by Sima's sister. However, as to food, we didn't even dare to consider hiring a catering service. Our parents and other relatives took the trouble to prepare the best Moroccan dishes and displayed them on a long buffet table that was filled with a delicious array of homemade dishes.

No matter what you wore or whether you arrived at the hall on foot or in a limousine, what was important and what you would remember for the rest of your life, was the indulgent colourful Moroccan food that was served at that wedding.

For entertainment, hiring a DJ or a live band was cost-prohibitive, so instead, LP records were played on a new record player with large speakers brought by Marco, who also played rhythmic Moroccan tunes on his violin. As the evening progressed, he plucked up the courage to sing too, entertaining the guests with heartfelt songs.

Laughter filled the air as people danced and celebrated under the hall ceiling, which was densely packed with colourful hanging ornaments.

Working at the local newspaper was not the only activity I had in mind. Bitter memories of the war would constantly flood me. Horrific dreams of bleeding corpses and explosions, and nightmares from which I would wake up screaming with my whole body covered in sweat. I decided to do something to stop the brutal war. And so, as a novice journalist, in an unimportant local paper, and as a social activist, I began my journey to become a prominent anti-war activist and an advocate for pacifism and social justice. I was involved in some acts of civil disobedience to protest war and poverty that took place in Tel Aviv, but mainly in Jerusalem in front of the Parliament. I helped organize protests and wrote hundreds of letters to ministers and members of the Parliament, and even sent a naïve letter to the International Court of The Hague, imploring both sides to cease the war. I initiated interviews with the national media and shared my personal experiences of horror to raise awareness about the human cost of war. I hoped my firsthand accounts of the horrors could be powerful as a testimony to prevent future catastrophes.

In June 1983, on the first anniversary of the war in Lebanon, which was still ongoing and claiming many victims on both sides, I got hit by a truck when sat in the middle of the road in an attempt to block the many routes used to transport arms shipments to south Lebanon. The smell of that damned war was still wafting under my nostrils. I felt an obligation to do something to prevent a long war that could wreak havoc on thousands of families and potentially have a terrible effect on the Israeli economy, which was already facing many difficulties. As a seasoned, albeit young, fighter, my senses told me that this conflict could last for at least a few more years. In my mind's eye, I could see the numerous funerals, the burned corpses on the battlefield, the sorrow of the families, and the pain of the wounded, who would likely spend the rest of their lives in a wheelchair or a deep coma. I was determined to raise public awareness to encourage the government to discuss the possibility of an immediate withdrawal from Lebanon, now that the PLO had left Lebanon. But my voice was not heard. I was nobody. I was just a tiny pawn on the politicians' game board. A small cog in a mighty octopus-armed machine controlled by politicians who were experts in lying. Not only my voice was not heard, but these official brats even sent a police officer to me at the hospital where my leg was being treated to inform me that although he would not arrest me, I would be charged with obstructing the military from performing its duty, oh, and also, I would now have a criminal record.

In 1967, when I was ten years old, I watched, in black and white, an anti-war protest in the United States during the Vietnam War. The protests, including the famous March on the Pentagon in 1967 and the Moratorium to End the War in Vietnam in 1969, mobilized millions of people and played a significant role in shaping public opinion against the war. It inspired me then. I suddenly realized that we, the ordinary people, are allowed to protest against our leaders. Then, at the age of sixteen, I came across an article about Mildred Lisette Norman, a woman who, for almost three decades, walked across the United States promoting peace and nonviolence. She never carried money or possessions, relying solely on the kindness of strangers. Her message was simple but profound, 'This is the way of peace: Overcome evil with good, falsehood with truth, and hatred with love.'

There were many stories of anti-war activists who worked tirelessly to promote peace and oppose wars that inspired me greatly. These activists and movements have played vital roles in advocating for peace, justice, and the prevention of wars. Their stories serve as a testament to the power of nonviolent resistance and the enduring human desire for a more peaceful world. Among many of them were Mahatma Gandhi, one of the most famous anti-war activists in history. He used nonviolent civil disobedience to lead India to independence from British rule. His philosophy of nonviolence (Ahimsa) and peaceful resistance (Satyagraha) inspired countless others to follow a path of nonviolence in their quest for justice and peace. There was Martin Luther King Jr. who, apart from being an activist for human rights for Black people, was also a vocal critic of the Vietnam War. He believed that the resources being spent on the war could be better used to address poverty and inequality at home. He delivered a powerful speech titled 'Beyond Vietnam' in which he called for an end to the war.

Stories of anti-war activists and movements highlight the diversity of voices and approaches in the pursuit of peace. They show that individuals from various backgrounds and experiences can come together to work towards a common goal of ending conflict and promoting a more peaceful world.

Many activists have been arrested throughout history for their dedication to various causes. But nonetheless, they didn't stop and even got stronger. My inspirational example was Nelson Mandela, the iconic leader of the anti-apartheid movement in South Africa. He was arrested multiple times during his lifetime. His most famous arrest led to his imprisonment for twenty-seven years. His steadfast commitment to ending apartheid and achieving racial equality eventually resulted in his release and the dismantling of apartheid. I first heard about this great man in 1982, the year I started my activism against war. It was when he was transferred to Pollsmoor Prison in Cape Town from Robben Island, where he had served twenty-four years of his long imprisonment.

When I was released from the hospital and my leg was completely healed, I started a series of independent trips to Gaza and the West Bank as part of my activism. I used my journalist's card and travelled without fear to talk with local Palestinians. I wanted to learn the truth from their mouths and not from the media. On one of my trips, I almost paid with my life. When I walked down the main street of the Sajaiya refugee camp north of Gaza, I was surrounded by several armed Palestinians who ordered me into the back of their van. My eyes were covered with a black rag and my hands were tied behind my back. 'A black rag is a sign of execution,' I muttered with dry lips. I started saying goodbye to everyone I knew. I was a commando fighter but what could I do against four or five hate-filled armed men with my hands tied? 'You are a Jewish spy,' one of them shouted at me while the van made its way along a bumpy dirt road that made me almost throw up the kebab I had eaten just ten minutes before at Amir Padilla's in Gaza on my way to the camp. 'I am a journalist who can help you,' I replied in a confident and steady voice. 'Even a journalist can be a spy,' another one shouted at me.

I decided to fight for my life. From my experience with these 'warriors', I have learned that strength and firmness and above all, not showing fear, is the best strategy. 'You are a bunch of idiots if you don't understand the advantage and benefit you will have from using a journalist,' I said in a firm voice. I waited a few seconds, expecting to be struck across my head with their guns. And when those questions didn't come, I continued in the same tone, 'I won't beg for my life, go screw yourselves, you bunch of morons who don't understand things deeply.' Suddenly the rag was removed from my face. One of them looked at me from zero distance; I could smell his dirty sweat and the odour of nicotine coming out of his mouth. He looked at me in silence, as if examining my reactions. I stared at him straight in the eyes and didn't move or bat an eyelid. I knew this was the game I had to play. And it helped. 'Where is your excellent Arabic from?' he asked with a half-smile. 'My parents are from Morocco. I have spoken Arabic all my life,' I replied. 'I'm a Semite like you, only a Jew, that's the whole difference, we're brothers,' I said in an authoritative voice, still firm although I must admit, the terror that surrounded my whole body was intense.

Finally, after I had gained their trust and travelled with them to visit my friends from Gaza, Said, Jubran, and Amir Padilla, who all confirmed my being a left-wing activist against the Israeli occupation, I was released and set on my way, but not before we had all sat down to a pot of steaming black coffee, of the kind that can only be obtained in the colourful and noisy markets of Gaza.

Over the next eighteen years, I continued these trips despite the warnings from Israeli security officials and threats from them that they would not provide me protection. I wasn't afraid. I was determined to study the Israeli-Palestinian conflict from a different angle, different from what we were used to and had learned through the media and politicization. I learned that the Palestinian leadership does not want peace with Israel, that the war with Israel feeds them (a) with financial support from organizations and foreign countries and (b) they are seen as the victims and martyrs, and thus they gain the sympathy of the world. During these years, I have made many friends and contacts with Palestinian journalists and intellectuals, from whom I have learned about the crisis they are facing from terrorist organizations such as 'Hamas', which is completely in control. For them, this crisis is larger and more severe than when they were occupied by Israel. This is why I risked my life when travelling to Gaza and the West Bank to spend time with Palestinians. I wanted to hear the truth, and the truth comes from locals, not from the media or any politician. My risky travelling bore fruit; I came to one solid conclusion, and that is that Palestinians want peace and need Israel, but extremist terrorist organizations do not allow it. The more I spoke with locals both in Gaza and in the West Bank, the stronger my support and sympathy for the Palestinian people grew. I learned that the majority of them want to live alongside Israel, who throughout the years of occupation provided them with work and services such as electricity and water, and free urgent medical treatment. They see Israel as a solid democratic and free state. They see it as a technologically and scientifically advanced country in which a profitable future could be planned and built. These locals were afraid to talk in public for fear of being lynched by the armed extremists.

I felt I had to do something to help. I bore a moral obligation to try to help the Palestinians break free from the extremists' shackles that have sentenced them to a life of poverty and misery. I learned Arabic and studied the *Quran* to help me communicate more easily with locals, and to better understand the conflict between the Israelis and Palestinians, and where the blame should be laid. In the eyes of my family and close friends, I was schizophrenic. To them, it was surreal, because on the one hand, I was a pro-Palestinian left-wing Israeli journalist, who developed close contacts and conversed with them, but on the other, I fought them as an Israeli soldier during the twenty-eight years of my compulsory IDF reserve service. However, what bothered me in those years was not what my family and close friends thought of me, but the search for the truth. I couldn't rely on the media reports on the miserable status of the Palestinians as it was unbalanced, most of the time exaggerated and misleading just to gain global attention and empathy. I discovered this when a Palestinian freelance journalist from Hebron whom I was friendly with confessed to me that some media reports in Arab countries, in the Palestinian Authority, and some countries of Northern Europe, are written in a non-objective and biased way and without any pretence of accuracy.

Here are two examples:

During the 1987 Intifada, images were broadcast around the world showing IDF soldiers firing rubber bullets at Palestinian children.

The Intifada was a violent uprising during which Palestinian residents in the West Bank and Gaza Strip revolted against Israeli occupation using stones and other improvised weapons. It began on 9 December 1987 and officially ended with the signing of the Oslo Accords in 1993. The images of children fleeing Israeli soldiers shooting at them were shocking, but the truth was that IDF soldiers shot at armed Palestinian demonstrators who threw stones at the soldiers and wounded some of them. It turned out that the images of Palestinian children fleeing were taken from a different incident, from another location, in which IDF soldiers had chased the children without firing on them. The biased media took two videos from two different incidents and edited them into one clip, resulting in a fake drama that made every viewer empathize with the Palestinians. Furthermore, during the investigation of the event, it was revealed that many of those spontaneous 'Palestinian demonstrators' received cash from Palestinian leaders to 'demonstrate'.

Another example is one in which I was involved and witnessed during my reserve service in Gaza. It happened near the Al-Shifa Hospital, the main hospital in Gaza. My platoon and I were on a routine patrol. We heard an ambulance siren and immediately helped clear the road from cars to allow the ambulance quick access to the hospital. When the ambulance doors opened, several Palestinian children covered in blood were taken out of it and admitted to the hospital. My heart shook. It was not a pleasant sight. My patrol commander instructed us to continue the patrol as usual. My patrol headed off in the direction of the rear side of the hospital. When we got to the back entrance of the hospital, we were amazed to see those children who had just been taken out of the ambulance covered in blood, coming out through the hospital's back entrance, walking on their feet, taking off their blood-stained shirts and putting on fresh ones that were handed to them by three men. When we checked the stained shirts and questioned the children, we discovered that the Hamas organization in Gaza had used these children to deceive the world and embarrass Israel. It turned out that their 'blood' was the blood of slaughtered animals.

I could not blame these Palestinian children because I knew they were sent by Hamas. They were devoid of political views. They just wanted some pocket money, and God I know how they felt. I felt how jarring it is when you don't have pocket money as a kid. To me, they did not represent the Palestinian people, most of whom wished to put an end to the conflict with Israel, which only worsened their situation.

Hamas, the brutal terrorist organization that did not hesitate to kill Palestinians as well, is the one to blame for the sad and desperate life in the Gaza Strip because Hamas chose violence and the destruction of Israel, instead of choosing to live side by side and wisely exploit its help and support, as the residents of the West Bank chose to do and are now benefiting greatly from Israel. The Palestinians in the West Bank enjoy a life of prosperity in business and commerce with Israel and the world, low unemployment, academic studies, profitable tourism (for example to Bethlehem), and in general, most of the residents are satisfied and live well. There is development and building, and in the case of the West Bank, they really use construction materials for buildings, rather than for tunnels as routes to attack Israeli civilians. Half a million Palestinians in the West Bank make a living from working in Israel in agriculture, restaurants, industrial plants, and food. Hamas lies and misleads the world only to gain sympathy and to continue receiving the financial aid they annually receive from the Red Cross and some of the Arab Gulf states. Hamas uses millions of dollars for war purposes instead of improving the living conditions in Gaza. Most Gaza residents do not agree with 'Hamas', but are afraid of their threatening and intimidating control.

I spent many months in Gaza and what I heard from the people was that they need Israel and that only Israel is giving them hope for a better future. Many of those who were not scared to oppose Hamas and revealed the truth on social media have been persecuted, and tortured, and some were executed publicly in the town square to set an example to intimidate others. Only a small number of these courageous dissidents managed to escape from Gaza, and with the help of human rights organizations and Israel, they were able to find refuge in European countries or the United States. There have been dozens of online clips in which they explain they are Palestinians from Gaza, revealing the truth to the world in a fearless manner, praising Israel and condemning Hamas. One of them, Yousuf Karim, said these words in a video on YouTube:

'Life in Gaza is difficult and unbearable, and it's easy to think that Israel is to blame for it. But let me tell you that they lie to you. I was one of them. I wanted to blow up all Israeli soldiers, but then I began to read objective material from other sources in which I learned that the ongoing terror against Israel served only the Hamas leaders' comfort, and they did not really care about the Palestinian suffering. They are all self-appointed. When I heard that Israel was being accused of apartheid, I laughed. I have never visited Israel, but from many phone calls with my relatives who live in Israel I understood that the two million Arabs living in Israel enjoy equal rights, work, academic studies, and business, and many of them thrive in diverse fields. They live in excellent harmony with the Jews of Israel. Some are business owners, and some professionals hold jobs in Israeli institutions. Why is Gaza sinking into despair? Because Hamas, which controls Gaza, has chosen violence and the destruction of Israel instead of choosing a life of prosperity alongside Israel. Since 2007, the United States, the United Nations, Saudi Arabia, Kuwait, and the European Union have tried and are still trying to help Gazan residents build infrastructure and develop businesses and jobs, but they delay this support whenever Hamas fires rockets at Israel. And what does this rocket fire on Israeli civilians actually accomplish? Nothing. Hamas understands that, but keeps firing those amateur rockets just to show the residents of Gaza that they are fighting the enemy called Israel to justify their status and huge salaries. Meanwhile, Israel continues to exist and prosper, and Gazans continue to suffer.'

These were the words of the son of a Palestinian terrorist who carried out many attacks against Israel and served many years in an Israeli prison. They are the words of a potential terrorist who chose not to follow in his father's footsteps. Instead, he faced the truth and revealed the lie of the Hamas leadership that has cast fear over the Palestinian majority, decent people who are more interested in a life of peace than endless bloody conflict.

These realizations led me to continue my activity and even encouraged me to expand it further. Within a few weeks, I found myself travelling to and from Tel Aviv almost every day for meetings with other left-wing activists, some of whom were veterans in wheelchairs. But then the acquaintance I had longed for happened; my meeting with Uri Avnery who was the embodiment of leftism in Israel of those years. The most hated person in Israel because of his opinions, which he expressed with great courage. People spat on him in the street, defamed him on the national TV channel, and abused his two children at school.

Uri Avnery was instrumental in the establishment of '*Gush Shalom*' (Peace Bloc), which has since become the leading (and often sole) voice in Israel calling for the creation of the State of Palestine throughout the West Bank and the Gaza Strip, the release of all Palestinian prisoners, the dismantling of all Israeli settlements and the recognition of Jerusalem as the joint capital of both states. Since its creation, it has organized hundreds of demonstrations, mostly together with Palestinian activists, and numerous other political actions. On 3 July 1982, when Avnery crossed the lines at the height of the battle of Beirut and publicly met the leader of the 'enemy', Yasser Arafat, several cabinet members demanded that Avnery be put on trial for high treason. The government adopted a resolution calling upon the Attorney General to open proceedings. The head of *Mossad* at the time decided to take advantage of the event and ordered his agents to rush to Beirut and eliminate Arafat even at the risk of harming Avnery. Fortunately, common sense prevailed; the Ministry of Justice decided that Avnery had not committed any crime in talking to Arafat, and *Mossad* withdrew their intention due to fear of criticism in case Avnery was indeed harmed.

The more I continued with my activism, the greater was the hostility towards me in a small place like Netivot. I was fired from my job at the local paper, I was a joke to my friends, and half of my family didn't want to see or talk to me anymore. I was called a traitor. A waitress at the only cafe in Netivot refused to serve me, and my landlord asked me to look for another place to live. The fact that there was a one-year-old baby involved didn't bother him at all. That was the last straw for me. I decided to leave the damn town for good. I drove Sima with our baby Daniela in her arms to her parents' house, where she stayed until I settled in Tel Aviv and then she would join me.

Fortunately, a relative of mine was appointed as the new manager of the municipality's housing department that same week. Within two weeks, he made her an offer on an apartment from the list of rentals the town was making available to young parents at particularly low prices.

I didn't look back. I found a small one-room apartment in Tel Aviv and continued my activities. Luckily Avnery, who owned the controversial newspaper '*Haolam Hazeh*' offered me a job as a reporter, and subsequently as an editor's assistant. During my work, I took part in all activities and protests orchestrated by '*Gush Shalom*', the organization Mr. Avnery had founded. I was detained by the police at one of these protests only because I was carrying a placard that read, 'The fate of the nation is in the hands of fools.' I was freed after eight hours spent in a filthy detention cell alongside actual criminals—those who didn't just steal food from the market.

Following the historic signing of the Oslo Accords in 1993, I received a three-minute phone call. It was Foreign Minister Shimon Peres who wanted to personally congratulate me for my selfless efforts, which began in 1982 and laid the groundwork for a potential cease-fire between Israel and the Palestinians. I, along with forty-five other peace activists, were then invited to the President's office, where we were given a letter of appreciation decorated with shimmering gold stripes.

Unfortunately, during my visits to Netivot, where I spent time with Sima and my daughter, the first cracks in our marriage began to show. Due to my PTSD, I was increasingly afflicted by anxiety attacks accompanied by outbursts of verbal violence, nightmares, and fits of rage.

In addition, there was a deep rift that opened up between me and Sima, which I could not see as a madly-in-love teenager. She wanted to be a housewife, I wanted to be strongly involved in the academic world. Our conversations were unexciting and banal. When she tried to do the weekly crossword puzzle in the newspaper, she would ask me to help because it was too difficult for her. After a few months, the inevitable separation occurred.

However, even though it was painful and sad, my divorce from my sweetheart Sima was beneficial. I left Netivot for the big city of Tel Aviv where I completed my master's degree and worked as a full-time journalist. My efforts to promote peace have not ceased. I exploited my position in the second-largest newspaper in Israel at the time to produce critical articles on the government's decisions regarding Israel's long and bloody presence in Lebanon. I joined the 'Peace Now' organization and campaigned for peace throughout Israel.

After establishing myself as a recognized journalist in a tiny nation with only six million people I started a secondary career. A lecturer. No, neither about political science and politics—two subjects in which I was well-versed and experienced—nor about bombs and battles. I dealt with anxiety and the treatments for it. It all began with one appearance on Israeli television when I was asked to talk about my experience of anxiety. I merely intended to share my experience with the viewers just once; I had no idea that this would pave the way for a new profession, and something that would inspire others. During the programme, the moderator, who himself was a war wounded, asked me to share with the viewers the techniques I used to alleviate my anxiety. Methods that have proven to be successful. Then, suddenly, things developed quickly. Hundreds of phone calls started pouring into the studio. It was before the era of email or Twitter messages. All the questions were addressed to me to elaborate on the techniques I used. A week later, I started receiving requests to give talks throughout the country to groups that included both anxious civilians and military veterans. Over the years, I've been able to help hundreds of anxiety sufferers how to get better, or at the very least, how to ease their suffering without the use of medication.

Chapter 23

How I healed myself from PTSD

In 1984 I started to suffer from severe anxiety attacks as well. It was only several years after I had agreed to go for tests, that I was informed I had contracted a condition well-known to combat soldiers all over the world. After a thorough examination of all the combat situations I was in between 1975, the day I enlisted, and 1984, when I was diagnosed, I could not put my finger on a specific event that caused me to contract this disorder. There were long conversations and further tests by my then psychologists, who were in contact with military sources that provided them with information about my activities. They were especially interested in the years between 1980 and 1984, when I was already a combat reservist taking part in hundreds of intense combat situations, the peak being the Lebanon War, where over three consecutive months I had witnessed terrible scenes of corpses and explosions. I was told that such a disorder does not necessarily happen from just one event but can be from a sequence of events over several months or several years. Thus, I learned that the disturbing phenomenon residing within me and causing me so much disturbance was acquired throughout those years from 1975 to 1984. When I was about to be discharged from combat reserve service, the psychologist suggested to me that the best treatment would be to continue my combat service in order to overcome my fears. He explained that there was a case in which a soldier who was shell-shocked was brought back later in the day to the same battlefield, and this helped prevent the development of PTSD. Thus, in spite of having nightmares and crazy thoughts, I continued my reserve service for a further twenty years.

After three years of unbearable agony, nightmares, insomnia, irrational outbursts, and even a divorce from Sima, the love of my life, I decided to fight. 'I am a commando fighter,' I would repeat to myself throughout the day, dozens of times. 'I am skilled in combat, and I know how to prevail in dire circumstances,' I kept muttering to myself like a mantra. Then, one morning, while dozing in a chair from lack of sleep, I decided to embark upon the battle of my life – curing myself of PTSD.

In order to defeat your enemy, you must thoroughly study, examine, and learn every aspect, down to the smallest detail about him. So, I decided to study the topic of PTSD. I have deliberately refrained from calling it an illness because this is part of my dealing with it. I wanted to learn more about PTSD not because I was looking for ways to heal myself, but out of curiosity, or perhaps out of my personal insight that if you discover the source of the problem, then the way to find its solution might be achievable. During my study, I learnt that the source of anxiety attacks is a disruption in the balance of chemicals in the brain due to psychological symptoms of negative and terrifying thoughts, such as fear that something bad is about to happen, a feeling of going crazy, a sense of watching oneself from the outside or feeling about to die. When these happen, the brain receives a 'false warning' of impending danger and prepares itself for dealing with a threat in a state of 'fight or flee'. This sudden preparation of the brain causes the chemical balance to be disturbed. For example, on a ship, as long as the passengers are spread out in all areas of the vessel in a balanced way, then the ship sails smoothly. However, in the case of panic following a sweeping wave or an attack on the ship, if all the passengers flee to one area in the back or the front to find shelter, this would cause an imbalance in the ship, and its sinking would be inevitable. For healthy people who do not suffer from anxiety, this imbalance can be transient, a temporary glitch in their lives when they encounter situations such as a serious car accident, or being near a huge fire. But for people with anxiety, the situation is more difficult due to the additional physiological symptoms, such as sweating, body tremors, dizziness, rapid and strong heartbeat, blurred vision, and shortness of breath, all of which aggravate the situation.

These physiological symptoms do not attack people who do not suffer from anxiety.

I realized that the key to success is the willingness to sacrifice for it. If you train yourself to think that achieving success is as critical as breathing air, or consuming necessities like food and water in order to stay alive, then the road to seeing success will be easy and short. Success can be counted not just in a career or passing an exam. Success can also be in curing an illness, or in complicated surgery that saved your life. In order to redeem yourself from anxiety attacks that disrupt your daily life, you must succeed in reducing their presence in your thoughts.

Success is driven by your will alone. The stronger and more persistent your desire along the way, the more success becomes achievable. Neither money nor social status will bring success, as a strong will and constant desire can. To deal with serious illnesses such as PTSD and other anxiety-based illnesses, you must find a key, and that key is in your head. Just as the key to success is your strong willingness, the same key can be used to treat and even completely heal your PTSD or any kind of anxiety. If I succeeded in doing it, then you can too. In this chapter, I will share with you the process I went through to heal myself from post-traumatic stress disorder without any medication, in the hope this can help others who suffer from any kind of anxiety to try to heal themselves, or at least reduce and minimize and control its attacks. This can also be helpful for partners or other family members who live with someone who suffers from anxiety.

When I was asked to describe anxiety by a friend from my platoon with whom I was talking about his and my injuries, I said, 'The problem with anxiety is that you live and feel it all the time, at almost every moment. It is with me when I smell, hear, see, feel. When I smell meat on the grill and see its rising smoke, I smell the burnt and smoking corpses that I saw during battles. When I hear shouts or sirens, or even fireworks exploding, I hear echoes of the explosions of shells and grenades. Anxiety is something I feel on a daily basis as long as I am active and alive. This is in addition to the terrifying uncontrollable thoughts that take me to dark and terrifying places.'

Anxiety and post-traumatic stress disorder is a condition that is very difficult to deal with within our human limitations. From my personal experience, over the many years I have suffered from it, I can describe it as a crippling attack of fear that causes discernible physical symptoms. The problem with PTSD is that it involves not only the people who suffer from it but also those who surround them, such as work colleagues and family members. Whenever I raised my voice or shouted in a way that seemed insane, my wife would be shocked and trembling for several hours. Only after deeply studying the subject, I learned that it was not me who was shouting at her, it was an uncontrollable urge that conveyed in my mind flashing images of violence, fire, tension, corpses, and approaching death. There would be a strange loud noise in my head, and I could not understand how it found its way into my mind while relaxing at home, and not on the battlefield.

It was only after meeting with a psychologist in one of the support groups I joined, that I started to understand that these were invisible and uncontrollable flashes and that they found their way to my consciousness when a minor unimportant trigger would occur, such as a brief argument, or a feeling of momentary chaos; normal situations in relationships that usually conclude in a short time with understanding and a hug. Not so in PTSD patients. We would get a different picture in those moments of argument confrontation or momentary chaos. We see fire and smoke and we hear noise and violence that takes place deep inside our brains, invisible to the outsider. A feeling of a fierce inferno surrounded my whole brain.

This led me to the realization that if we can divert our thoughts, we can reduce the signs of anxiety. And so, whenever an anxiety attack approached, I diverted my thoughts elsewhere. I even shouted out loud, 'Think of something else!'

Amazingly it worked. Thus began the process of my self-healing without medication and without expert and educated psychologists who would tell me what to do in such situations. This process led to the amazing revelation in which I realized that each of us has hidden powers inherent in his soul and embedded in his essence, and all he has to do is give them expression. The ability to think of creative solutions, to think outside the box, and not to be held captive by what the doctors automatically recommend, are all traits for which I was accepted to serve in a commando unit.

What made me doubt conventional treatment with drugs was the understanding that the drugs are only used for a short period to ease the problem, and cannot cure the problem itself. The conventional medical approach is based on the assumption that among PTSD patients there is an imbalance in the level of neurotransmitters in their brain - an imbalance that can be adjusted by drugs that increase the level of serotonin and inhibit its absorption and breakdown levels. Such drugs were used for twenty-four years to treat the anxiety I have suffered from, but in my case didn't help. In fact, they only helped to alleviate my situation by confusing me and displaying a different reality in my head from what was real. The drugs also caused me to run away from the problem by taking the easy way out instead of facing it head-on and dealing with it. This is not even to mention the addiction they caused me over the years. I was taking a selective serotonin reuptake inhibitor (SSRI), plus the medication Sertraline (Zoloft), both of which were approved by the Food and Drug Administration (FDA) for PTSD treatment. In addition, I took Diazepam, Amitriptyline, Phenelzine, and antidepressants such as Paroxetine or Mirtazapine. When I realized that these medications were not preventing anxiety attacks, I started looking for other ways to deal with my problem. I felt that there had to be another way to treat psychological conditions that do not require surgical intervention. PTSD is a psychological condition, and psychology is all about thoughts, so maybe I can change the way my thoughts run, or control them by diverting them to other situations and places. Realizing this, I started learning about alternative techniques for relaxation such as meditation, deep breathing, massage, yoga, or any practice connected with thought diversion while using my imagination. I found myself searching for any mind activities that could change the content of the thoughts presented in the brain at that given moment. Activities that could push those frightening thoughts into a totally different path and location, changing their colours and their scenario. This was my turning point. This understanding gave me an insight that the temptation to self-medicate my illness with alcohol or drugs would only bring a momentary relief. This significant insight was the starting point of my personal journey of self-healing from the terrible disorder called PTSD, a journey that has borne fruit and success. Thus, since 2018, I have been helping those similarly suffering from anxiety, and I hope that in this chapter I can help others or even those who know others who suffer from it. Before I detail the ways that have been proven to be effective, I would like to relay some background to this phenomenon.

Post-traumatic stress disorder, PTSD, is an ongoing stress response to a traumatic event, which includes increased agitation and avoidance of any stimuli that could be reminiscent of the traumatic event. Many people will experience significant trauma during their lifetime as a result of war, an accident, sexual assault, or other life-threatening event. However, if these symptoms persist for more than a month after the event, then it will be diagnosed as post-traumatic stress disorder. My PTSD was manifested in disproportionate panic attacks and anger, a feeling of losing my sanity or that I was about to die, a feeling of disconnection or alienation from others, an inability to feel positive emotions, irritability or aggressive behaviour, self-destructive and risk-taking behaviours, constant alertness, trouble in concentrating, and difficulty in falling asleep or sleeping continuously. And the scariest manifestation was a strange feeling that I was detached from myself, that I was not part of any existence or reality, a kind of derealization.

Anxiety is a reaction by our brain to certain situations and is essential to us as human beings. Without anxiety, the human race certainly would not have survived. Anxiety pushes us to strive, to be sharp and focused in order to achieve an important goal or to fulfil a dream. In addition, it acts as a warning mechanism against danger and causes us to be careful and take protective measures, such as escaping from a fire, or undergoing medical tests when new symptoms are felt. But on the other hand, anxiety can be in our backyard. A threat to our health. This is when it becomes a disorder or illness when it is chronically present and impairs the ability to function in daily life. Anxiety disorders are a collective name for a variety of sub-disorders such as panic attacks, social anxiety, obsessive-compulsive disorder, post-traumatic stress disorder, general anxiety disorder, and more. Anxiety affects thoughts, behaviours, and bodily sensations and can impair personal and social relationships. A study by the American Association of Anxiety Disorders (ADAA) compared people diagnosed with anxiety disorder with people who weren't. Many of the anxiety disorder participants who took part in the study testified that they do not believe they deserve to live in a healthy society, make friends, or get married. Indeed, a relationship with a person suffering from anxiety can be no easy task at all. Only those who live with such a person can really understand what the difficulties are. These difficulties can manifest themselves on several other levels, such as social, economic, occupational, and any situations that require contact with others.

From my experience, I can recommend ways and methods to deal with anxieties effectively. Before that, I would like to suggest that in addition to my tips and recommendations below, when feeling a spate of acute anxiety attacks, it is advisable to also take medication in combination with psychotherapy, but just for a short time. Medication does not cure PTSD or anxiety totally, as they usually return after stopping the medication. Psychological treatment is designed to bring about long-term changes in thoughts and inclinations to prevent the effects of anxiety that impair the quality of life. In an anxiety attack, the brain can sometimes distort reality and give it different interpretations, and different appearances, causing confusion that leads to panic attacks.

However, studies show that these imaginary and false thoughts are not harmful to you and do not physically threaten the body. It all depends on your reaction to these thoughts. If you direct and control them and convince yourself that these are just hollow thoughts and that there is no danger to your body, then in a while these thoughts will disappear. This is what a relaxing medication like Diazepam does when it is used during an anxiety attack. I once remarked that anxiety is like a wave on the sea. When it hits us, it is better to just let it wrap us within it and drift away for a short distance, rather than to fight it and be dragged exhausted underwater. Although this sounds like a highly philosophical approach that does not offer a practical way of coping, it actually makes a lot of sense. Sometimes we need to let our thoughts sink into an imaginable void, and not rush to address any problem as quickly as possible and out of stress. You will be surprised to find out how much the anxiety level of your life can drop if you simply decide, if it's possible, that you will wait a few minutes before you start dealing with crises or problems that life presents to you. You can then start solving the problem and deal with the stress, instead of fighting it and in doing so only aggravate your situation. After studying and observing the healing processes I was going through, I can recommend the following ways to deal with anxiety:

Thought diversion

I'll start with something simple that will surely seem amusing and not serious to you, but believe me, it works. To soothe an anxiety attack, pop an ice cube on your tongue. The cold of the ice cube gives the body a physical shock and helps the brain to stop getting lost in its distortion of reality by dealing with the sudden temperature change in your mouth. As for you, instead of being lost in vain thoughts that are not in any way harming you physically, your mind concentrates on the discomfort in your mouth. This is what I call thought diversion, and is at the core of dealing with anxiety which I discovered over time while studying this subject. While your mind is concentrating on the cold on your tongue, and performing the principle of thought diversion, the body at the same time is dealing with the feeling of cold. Your body sees it as a problem that needs to be addressed immediately. When we enter the 'fight or run' state, the body devotes more energy to the processes necessary for its survival, and along the way also puts us in alert. The ice cube causes dryness in the mouth that makes it start to produce saliva. Because the ice cube encourages the body to produce saliva, it actually calms the thoughts that have caused your anxiety attack. This can also apply when sucking something sharp such as a slice of lemon or eating something hot and spicy.

Cognitive Behavioural Therapy

If we can change the way we think, we can change the way we feel. If we can do both, then we are able to change the outcome of things. By using this ability, you can help clear any frightening thoughts that cause anxiety and depression. If we understand that our brain sometimes distorts reality in a way that causes us to perceive it or its consequences incorrectly, then we should address the brain and its thoughts through cognitive behavioural therapy. This is a method of treatment based on the assumption that thought patterns influence behaviour, and that emotional disorders originate in distorted thought patterns. As in the example of sucking a slice of lemon or an ice cube, in which you use both elements, your imagination, and concentration that direct your thoughts to one focus - the coldness of the ice cube, or the acidity of the lemon slice – this can also be applied in redirecting the brain's distorted thought patterns to the kind of thoughts that you want and feel comfortable with. In doing so, you are actually returning your thoughts to their normal state. By controlling and redirecting those troubling thoughts that originate in distorted thought patterns, you are in actual fact shaking their ground and weakening their influence on your behaviour. Therefore, if your behaviour due to an anxiety attack is reckless, anxious, obsessive, desperate, and panicking, then with this method of weakening the influence of those scary thoughts, your behaviour will cease to be in panic mode, and you will not feel threatened by any of the distortions in thinking that lead to anxiety. From time to time our mind wanders to places and situations against our will. For us, there is no control over the brain, but we have the ability to change the direction or the patterns of the brain's thoughts by our ability to imagine, an ability that is exclusive to humans. In doing so, you divert the direction of your thoughts that lead you to distorted places and situations that you did not want to go to or to be in.

Make changes in your behaviour

A change in your thoughts or behaviour can happen quickly, much more so than you could imagine. Simply take this project of your life seriously and be persistent. That is, use imagination and a high degree of concentration to tilt negative thoughts that cause or lead to anxiety. It takes commitment to do so not just every day, but every minute and second. Erase from your mind and consciousness any notion that it is easier to believe in the negative than in the positive. Believe in the positive, be proactive, and implement it at every opportunity you have in your daily life, not just theoretically in your thoughts. Work on building a strong mental response mechanism that will help you to control and direct your thoughts. This will help you calm down and repel anxieties that are the result of the distortion of reality created by the mind. Look at yourself in the mirror every day and say loudly that all those negative beliefs you have adopted and embraced throughout the time you have suffered from anxiety, are illogical, false, and bear no connection to reality. This can only be realized if you work on a strong and positive response mechanism that is opposite to the negative. With this kind of mechanism, you will manage to avoid those thoughts that have come from distorted thought patterns, which lead you to anxiety attacks. Remember, an anxiety attack focuses on negative situations only, such as death, insanity, fainting, loss of consciousness, paralysis, feeling worthless. When this happens, direct your thoughts to a happy event in your life that you remember well, and concentrate on all its details down to the smallest one. By doing this, you can recreate the whole event and focus on all its beautiful details, including the people who took part, the delicious food, and every good thing that was part of the event.

When your brain focuses only on negative thoughts and memories, then fears and worries become intensified. When this mental distortion occurs, you begin to lose control over your thoughts and let them lead you. When that happens, they take you to dark places and situations that bring back bad memories or fearful experiences. That's how my personal anxiety developed. If I had been told then, when it all began, I would have stopped letting my thoughts lead me and thus I could have spared myself from PTSD. This is why I am writing this chapter. I wish to warn those who are at the starting point of this terrible illness.

With all due respect to modern medicine and to the esteemed doctors and psychologists, I state here one unequivocal fact from my many years of experience in dealing with the terrible illness of PTSD, and that I direct to you if you suffer from it. Your mind deceives you! This is the fundamental principle for you to acknowledge so you can start healing yourself.

During PTSD attacks, your mind instils in you a strong belief that the reality you see is incorrect, and at the same time distorts what's really happening to you by embedding a completely different reality in your thoughts. This can also happen to those who do not suffer from PTSD or anxiety, including elderly people or children. An elderly person may have lost his self-confidence and thinks that his mind is no longer functioning as it used to because of old age, or fear that this is the beginning of Alzheimer's disease. A child is not yet experienced in life and does not know much, so he will think he is wrong and must always believe and obey what he is told.

Because he is fragile and being dominated by the forces of the illness, a PTSD patient tends to believe any reality or thought that his mind presents to him. By controlling your thoughts through thought diversion and by cognitive behavioural therapy, you will be able to interpret reality to the way you wish to see it, and not the way your mind wants to. Your mind deceiving you during an attack is easy because of the tendency of the average person to think negatively rather than positively. Few are the people in this stressful modern society who live and think positively all the time. So, remember that whenever you apply the method of diverting and controlling your thoughts, always do so while calling up good memories from your past to your consciousness.

This mind distortion during a PTSD attack is actually an auto-generated action, not triggered by an external event or witnessing something distressing that is happening, such as a car accident or devastating fire. Because you are surrounded by anxiety, you subconsciously surround yourself with dramatic events that are not happening at that moment and relate them to you. Sometimes you even amplify them as a cry for help. And what kind of help are you looking for in those seconds? A chemical medical miracle that you convince yourself when swallowed, will help you escape the threatening inferno. And that is the trap you are caught in and start drowning; a trap that you have dug by your own actions. The addictive use of drugs, which in some cases makes the illness worse. It is not far from the truth. I have been there.

It is difficult to change familiar behaviour patterns and it is very easy to succumb to negative moods and avoid action. When difficult times engulf us - whether due to events in our daily life, feelings that have begun to attack us, or due to the general situation around us, it is easy to succumb to depression and fall into a black bile. I too have experienced this many times in my life and have reached the brink of depression more than once - but each time I have discovered that there is one thing that helps me and is not related to such and such drugs, but simply in encouraging the mind with one mantra that boosts my ability to overcome my anxiety, and that is, 'These scary thoughts are about things that do not exist, I am OK.'

Memorizing this mantra and bringing it into my everyday life has made a huge difference for me even when I seemed to be on the verge of despair. They can do the same for you.

Epilogue

Over the decades since those days of my childhood, the small town of Netivot has grown and developed into a thriving business and retail centre in the northern Negev region, which consists mainly of villages and small towns. The main street has been widened and many more apartments have been built in three, four and five-storey buildings.

Cold-hearted Asher became a successful lawyer who, not surprisingly, specializes in crime. He has made a lot of money by representing high-level criminals, not only from the Negev region but also from Tel Aviv.

Little Sonny became a sophisticated criminal, who adopted the sartorial style of Martin Scorsese's New York gangsters. He was known for sporting a black hat reminiscent of those worn by members of the Sicilian Mafia, as well as a well-groomed moustache, and a long fat cigar that was permanently attached to his mouth as if it were part of his face.

Manny the Whiny grew into a handsome man who charmed everyone. The girls of Netivot swooned if he threw a smile in their direction, and at the grocery store, he was offered unlimited credit, even though he only worked part-time at Biton's hair salon. He never stopped his childhood habit of complaining.

Lazy Moshiko struggled to maintain a stable job. His habitual tardiness and lack of initiative were the key causes. However, when he unintentionally discovered his artistic aptitude, life had prepared a small surprise for him. He relocated to Tel Aviv and found employment at the renowned Gordon Gallery, which provided him with a good monthly salary in exchange for his regular attendance at work, rather than just showing up when he felt like it.

Victor the contractor eventually found a wife. Her name was Sarina and together they brought three children to the world. Tragically, one was born with cerebral palsy and one was born blind. After consultations with top doctors who came from Tel Aviv, it turned out that Sarina had inherited unhealthy genes from her ancestors. Victor started consuming an excessive amount of alcohol and developed serious depression. Over the years, the inevitable happened. He lost all his fortune from gambling in a makeshift neighbourhood club in Netivot that offered card games, mostly poker.

Sima's father, Mr Mulol, who smoked like a train locomotive, died of lung cancer at the age of 55. His wife Sulika finally stopped yelling at people; age seeming to take its toll on her vitriol.

Hot-tempered Marko formed a band that still performs at weddings and bar mitzvahs.

As a hungry, poverty-stricken, and frightened child in war, I never imagined that I would survive my harsh upbringing. I didn't believe that I would have a future. I was sure I would be a criminal. The daily danger of getting caught in the web of a criminal gang that I hung around with and used to commit thefts with. The petty thefts in the market with my school friends, and the constant temptations that were too much for my empty pockets. I never dreamt of being accepted into a commando unit in the best army in the world, serving in it for twenty-eight years, and participating in the most dangerous and challenging operations that the average person does not get to experience.

As a child who could hardly concentrate on his studies at school due to the anxieties of existence, I never foresaw that I would get to study at university and excel in completing two academic degrees, this is in addition to my success in becoming an influential journalist and a lecturer. 'You must write a book and share your story with the world. It can truly be an inspiration to others,' an audience member at one of my lectures told me after hearing me speak.

I was born into war. I grew up in wars shelters and bombs. Fears and nightmares were my childhood companions. Even when playing in the playground, I could not really enjoy the games because we kept expecting to hear the feared siren that would take us to the shelter for a few hours, and sometimes for a few nights. Anxiety and fear surrounded me throughout my childhood and youth.

At the age of eighteen, I joined the army. I decided to serve in a combat unit to serve my beloved country. But to be honest, it was more the hunger to take revenge on the enemy that had destroyed my childhood. I learned that serving in a commando unit allows very close contact with the enemy. Thus, on 5 May 1975, after passing many tests and difficult challenges, I was accepted and joined the commando unit. I served three years, during which time I saw death more often than the breakfasts I ate. Years in which we did the impossible, performing feats that are only seen in James Bond movies. I then served another twenty-eight years in the Army Reserve Service, where I was involved in many dangerous activities in pursuit of wanted terrorists and in daring raids into Lebanon. However, as I got older, I hated war. I realized that war is a stupid invention of mankind. War is a primitive act. A failure of the use of brainpower. I experienced death, blood, and fear. I saw burning bodies. I could not eat meat for many years. The smell of a barbecue reminded me of burnt bodies. I lost seventeen friends and five members of my family on the battlefields. And I tell you there are no winners in wars. In war, there is only grief. In spite of the appreciation and the number of medals I received during my combat service, I hated war.

I felt I had been forced into taking part in a war I did not choose and did not want to be part of. Feelings of repulsion flooded over me whenever I remembered the horrific and irrational sights of a killing field, where civilized people were shooting at each other. The rationale of war appeared to me absurd, inconceivable, and primitive. When eradicating a terrorist, these feelings vanished, but after a few days, a wave of disgusting scenes would swim in front of your eyes, as if teasing your consciousness and letting the depths of your mind transcend the emotion. Once, I came across an army friend shooting an already dead terrorist over and over again, as though the body lying motionless still presented a threat. I was very angry with my comrade as I felt he was displaying symptoms of a warped mentality. But then, it became clear to me the unifying reality in which we were all existing. My friend's unnecessary shooting at the dead terrorist was not intended to kill, it was an act of revenge. In the moments before we eliminated the terrorist, he had fired a round of bullets from his Kalashnikov at my friend who had not previously spotted him. In firing at his already dead adversary, my friend was allowing himself to feel he had honoured the principle of being the first and quicker in killing whoever tried to kill you. The war for survival. We all felt like animals in the jungle, adopting the jungle imperative where only the stronger and faster will prevail. Animals, but with the ability to speak and think strategically. I hated being in that jungle.

It would only be natural to kill someone who came to kill me, but the more I saw of the enemy with whom I came into combat contact, the more my hatred for him diminished. The closer I was, sometimes at zero range where I could see the colour of the enemy's eyes, I would feel a pang of compassion for him; I saw in front of me a living human being even though I could end his life.

My finger would freeze on the trigger. Such situations put me in danger of death many times during an assault or a chase through Gaza. In some of these incidents, my underlying human feelings would not automatically activate my defensive combatant need to kill. This moral dilemma wounded my soul and left scars on it, scars that will probably never heal, as long as my memory is still able to function. Recollections keep taunting me with the names and faces of my dead friends, in particular one of our commanders who literary sacrificed his life to save us during one of the battles in the blazing fields of Lebanon. He was just one of our bold and inspirational commanders, who led us in battles during which I saw the impossible become possible, and certain death turned to survival.

I have been in situations where I realized how powerful the personal skills of the warrior were, more so than the weapon he held in his hand;

personal skills and qualities that may well have helped me survive the terrifying inferno of war.

The thirst to survive exists in every living soul. While animals act on instinct, humans have a significant advantage over animals in that they can use innate skills, logic, and intrinsic intelligence, rather than acting solely on instinct. I am not a genius, nor am I regarded as a man with a particularly high IQ. My drive for survival served as a compass and helped me get through my inferno, simply because I had no other place to think of living except the country where I was born. I was educated about the more than two thousand years of Jewish persecution throughout my youth. I was led by the idea that as a Jew, I could only experience freedom in Israel, a sovereign state where I could feel safe.

I have been punished twice. Once for being Jewish and once for being Israeli. I am hated in the world. I have been persecuted for more than two thousand years even though I am one of 'The Chosen Nation', who is supposed to be loved and protected by God, the Almighty who promised me the land of milk and honey. I hated that God who failed to protect me. I hated the righteous priests and rabbis who invented God just to control people and provide them with an illusionary meaning to life, 'Opium for the masses,' as a wise man once said.

Through a poignant existential experience, I gained new insights and learned ways to deal with extremely difficult situations and survive them. I was able to confront the deepest experiences of sadness and loss in the human soul, which paved the way for me to cope and survive through any horror. All of this is based on the assumption that humans have the power to deal with difficulties and tragedies beyond what they initially estimate. As the saying goes, 'You don't know how much you're capable of until you try.'

Your entire life's objectives and plans vanish the moment you have a deadly experience and are unable to perceive any hope. They become meaningless and unimportant at that point, and the only thing that matters to you is making it through those potentially fatal situations. Any thoughts of other aims or plans vanish as your mind is occupied and solely focused on ensuring your survival. Repeating a mantra to yourself that states you must survive to see your children, finish a task you started, or write a book, is the best way to survive situations of certain death, severe captivity or torture, and loss of hope. If you have something to live for, then it can help you survive any potentially fatal situation.

I was part of the best army in the world and performed things that the average person does not get to do in his lifetime. I felt like a hero when I subdued the enemy in face-to-face combat in bunkers and trenches. My own years of combat service have garnered praise and admiration and undoubtedly helped me to gain self-confidence and a strong personality. However, it left me with a bitter taste in my mouth and with a scar on my soul. I experienced horrific sights that will never leave my memory. The feeling of superiority and omnipotence dissipated whenever the horrific memories of scorched bodies reappeared in my mind, and of homeless refugees fleeing into the unknown with bags on their backs.

I hated the damn war. I hated being a commando combat.